D1187689

War

# Studies in International and Comparative Politics

PETER H. MERKL, SERIES EDITOR

# War

## •A Historical, Political, and Social Study•

L. L. FARRAR, JR., EDITOR

SALVE REGINA COLLEGE LIBRARY
OCHRE POINT AVENUE
NEWPORT, RHODE ISLAND 02840

Santa Barbara, California
Oxford, England

Copyright © 1978 by ABC–Clio, Inc.

**Library of Congress Cataloging in Publication Data**
Main entry under title:

War.

  (Studies in international and comparative politics; 9)
    Includes bibliographical references and index.
      1. War.  2. Sociology, Military.  3. Violence.
      I. Farrar, Lancelot l. II. Series.
      U21.2.W36    301.6'334   77-16620
      ISBN 0-87436-221-0

All rights reserved including the right to reproduce in whole or part without the written permission of the publisher.

*301, 6334*

*W 21*

*6/889*

American Bibliographical Center–Clio Press, Inc.
2040 Alameda Padre Serra
Santa Barbara, California 93103

European Bibliographical Center–Clio Press, Ltd.
Woodside House, Hinksey Hill
Oxford OX1 5BE, England

Manufactured in the United States of America

To our children and students
in the hope for a future without war

# Acknowledgments

It is great pleasure to record a number of debts. The Graduate School Research Fund of the University of Washington generously provided financial support during the project's initial stage. The History Department of Boston College made available its copying facilities. The authors stoically bore editorial hectoring and responded graciously to suggestions. Peter H. Merkl, editor of the series in which this volume appears, contributed mightily to the book's organizational coherence. Lloyd W. Garrison, Editor/Publisher of Clio Books, encouraged the project and helped make the text more felicitous and accessible. The credit for transforming an idea into reality is shared by all those institutions and individuals.

The author, editor, and publisher acknowledge with thanks the permissions of publishers and individuals to quote copyrighted works as indicated:

Basic Books for excerpts from Chapter XXV, "Why War? (1932)," *Collected Papers,* Volume 5, by Sigmund Freud, Edited by James Strachey, published by Basic Books, Inc., by arrangement with The Hogarth Press Ltd. and The Institute of Psycho-Analysis, London.

Chatto & Windus, Ltd. for "Anthem for Doomed Youth," and "Dulce et Decorum Est" *The Poems of Wilfred Owen.* Copyright Chatto & Windus, Ltd. 1946, 1963. Reprinted by Permission of New Directions Publishing Corporation.

Otto Nathan, Trustee, The Estate of Albert Einstein, for permission to quote from the book, "Einstein on Peace."

■

# Contents

■

**Part V: The Law, Morality, and Emotions of War**

# Preface

It is difficult to contest the immediacy and importance of war in the contemporary world. History suggests that the destructiveness of war is likely to increase: the approximately sixty million deaths caused by war between 1920 and 1945 may occur in minutes because of the potential of atomic weapons. The possibility of such large-scale violence seems to have become an integral part of our consciousness.

Although the problem demands our attention, the complexity of war, the inadequacy of resources, and the pressure of time certainly militate against our understanding it. Even if war is eventually understood, it may still not be limited or prevented. Despite the minimal prospects for success, the problem's seriousness requires an attempt. This book seeks to make a contribution to such an effort.

The volume demonstrates a variety of possible approaches, indicates linkages among them, and provides some data for evaluating them. It thereby suggests that the most fruitful means of understanding war may be a combination of interdisciplinary and comparative methods.

Since war is complex, it seems obvious that a variety of approaches is appropriate. Many studies of war are, however, narrowly focused and sometimes simplistic. As appealing as they may be in dispensing with the problem of shifting the burden of responsibility for war, such explanations are of limited use and may even discourage serious thought about war. The present volume assumes that a complex problem requires a comprehensive response and illustrates the variety of possible approaches. ∎

This diversity is represented in a number of ways. One measure is the thirty essays, twenty-six essayists, and eleven disciplines from which the authors are drawn. Although the essayists express their individual interests and cannot be expected to speak for their disciplines, they nonetheless reflect some disciplinary concerns and methods. The choice of essay topics includes a broad range in time, development, and location. Further, the several sections reflect theoretical, case study, and moral approaches, and illustrate differences of purpose. The essays of the first four sections are generally concerned with understanding; those of the last section emphasize empathy. The theoretical essays in Section I are the most abstract, while those in Sections II through IV describe war in practice. Finally, the essays are distinguished by their primary concerns: Section I focuses on causes, Sections II through IV generally on the consequences of war, and Section V on responses to it.

These distinctions are not incidental and reflect different assumptions about the comprehensibility of war. The essays in Section I assume that the general phenomenon of *war* is potentially comprehensible; those in Sections II through V suggest that one can perhaps understand individual *wars* but probably not *war* in general. These attitudes are a function of disciplinary distinctions: all but one of the eight essayists of Section I are social scientists; all but six of the eighteen essayists of Sections II through V are historians or humanists.

Such differences of approach may lead to the dead end of methodological dispute, claims of single roads to the total truth, confusion of purposes, and intellectual isolationism. These pitfalls are difficult to avoid and require considerable toleration and communication if they are to be overcome. The risk is, however, worthwhile.

What seem old, even hackneyed or sterile questions to one individual or discipline may prove stimulating to another. The unsatisfactory answers of the past may have been partially conditioned by the formulation of the questions. As a historian once observed, we need new questions rather than new answers to old questions. New questions are essential if we are to test and possibly reshape established theories of war. No final answer is offered here; perhaps there is none. The essential point is, instead, posing questions which will avoid individual or disciplinary myopia and encourage intellectual cross-pollination. Further, each perspective provides a potentially useful point of view, a portion of reality, a frame in the motion picture of a changing phenomenon, an intellectual triangulation on war.

Finally, it is desirable to seek an antidote to cultural and temporal bias. Most phenomena are perceived in terms of one's own society and time: war here and now seems to be war everywhere and always.

Although the cultural and temporal link can but perhaps should not be entirely severed, an awareness of war in other cultures and epochs can sensitize the observer to such distortions.

The essays vary in their focus upon the individual, individual-group, or group. Evolution suggests that individuals may have qualities which virtually program them for aggressiveness. Freudian theories likewise imply that individuals have drives which must be released, frequently in violence. Other essays focus on the juncture between individual and group, where violence can be caused by frustration, threats to self-esteem, or social demands on individuals, particularly males. Still other essays concentrate on the group and indicate that violence is accommodated and reinforced by social patterns, associated with certain groups such as the military, a function of socioeconomic class structure, a result of Great Power behavior, or indeed a conglomerate of such elements.

In some instances, it is argued that human aggressiveness is virtually innate and that society is practically inconceivable without war; elsewhere, violence is attributed to immediate, avoidable circumstances. The degree of determinism is not intrinsic to any particular disciplinary approach. The choice may be affected by personal experience or inclination. It may also be influenced by history. If a society has known security and peace (as, for instance, the United States and Europe during much of the nineteenth century) or has gained through war (as, for instance, the United States until the Vietnam War), it may assume a less deterministic position and regard war as controllable or even avoidable. Conversely, if a society has experienced considerable violence or setbacks in war, it may be inclined to regard war as normal, unavoidable, and uncontrollable, i.e., more deterministically. Like war itself, theories of war may be conditioned by historical circumstances.

The quantity and diversity of the views offered in this volume can suggest three quite different conclusions to the reader. One is subjectivity: these explanations may seem little more than sophisticated personal opinions and demonstrate that establishing "the truth" in any objective way is impossible. An alternative is exclusivity: it can be argued that only one of these theories can be "true" and the others are therefore "false." A third possibility is inclusivity: some or all of these theories may be regarded as partly "true" in that they reflect a segment of the problem and wholly "true" only when taken together. Since "truth" is difficult to demonstrate, the choice ultimately depends on personal inclination, i.e., which approach makes most sense of the phenomenon of war to the reader.

The process of understanding a complex problem such as war is gradual and arduous at best. Development of a satisfactory partial theory is difficult and a comprehensive explanation may prove impossible. General theory characterizes the advanced stage of a discipline's development. Since the study of war is in its infancy and depends on other branches of knowledge still in their initial stages (such as psychology, sociology, anthropology, and economics), it should not be surprising that theories about war are primitive. Major efforts should consequently be concentrated at the primary level of collecting data and at the secondary level of developing comparative approaches. The comparative method involves posing questions which may suggest useful categories and thereby reveal significant patterns.

In demonstrating that quite different methods and topics contain common features, the following essays indicate that a comparative approach is feasible and perhaps necessary. Disparate theories can be grouped into general approaches, distinct disciplines share common interests, and divergent societies are susceptible to similar questions. Doubtless, the number and specificity of these questions can be increased, the categories refined, and a better "accounting system" developed. It is nonetheless possible to make some comparative statements even at the present level of scholarship and thereby to encourage further work in this direction.

Such comparative statements can be made as answers to a number of general questions. The most fundamental is the problem of causality: why war? A related issue is the notion of control: can war be limited or even prevented? Another has to do with society: how do a society's structure and conflicts affect one another? To what extent do historical, national, and cultural differences influence the character of war? Technology is another element in the equation: how are war and technology related? Finally, there is the problem of evaluation: is war entirely destructive and dysfunctional (as usually assumed) or does it perform necessary and desirable functions?

The authors' answers are generally tentative, narrowly focused, and sometimes mutually contradictory. More important than the answers, however, is their encouragement to focus on the problem. If this volume stimulates creative thinking about war, its authors will be well rewarded.

L. L. Farrar, jr.

War

# Thinking about War

## Jon M. Bridgman

War is a complex phenomenon involving several important subordinate problems. It must be placed in a social context and its relationships to other human institutions and events ascertained. If the study of war is to be approached systematically, and the phenomenon understood, at least a working definition is required. *The Encyclopedia of the Social Sciences* and dictionaries define war in terms of actual or threatened violence of some scale and duration, and as a form of activity between politically organized bodies. These commonsense definitions, which both reflect the way war is normally understood and differentiate it from other human activities, involve at least three problems which need closer examination: duration, scale, and continuity.

All definitions of war suggest that violence lasts over a period of time. Although generally applicable, this aspect may sometimes prove misleading. Some events are called wars but are not violent. The Prussians and Austrians engaged in the so-called War of the Bavarian Succession in 1778–1779—the conflict appeared to be a war, since troops appeared in uniform, the drums rolled, and men marched. But the armies never fought and no one was killed; instead, the troops spent their time digging potatoes (and it was thus called the potato war).

Hobbes, the seventeenth-century British political philosopher, suggested that wars are analogous to storms during which the sky is cloudy for several days but rain falls briefly. The rain represents

■

battles and actual violence; the storm, war and the strong potential for violence.

Recognition of the need for more precise definition is important, since such events as the Cold War are otherwise anomalous. This consideration should not be used to subsume virtually all events under the heading of war, thus arguing that human history is equivalent to war. The distinction between war and peace is still useful, but it must account for potential as well as actual violence.

Reflection on war also involves the problem of scale. Virtually all definitions state that war is large-scale violence. The question then becomes, How large? Murders, riots, gang fights, feuds, and prison uprisings are generally excluded; revolts, rebellions, and civil wars are difficult to categorize.

Lewis F. Richardson, an English statistician, meteorologist, and Quaker, provided one solution to this problem. He was horrified by World War I and sought to comprehend war. Richardson found fairly good records kept for the most deadly events (wars) and for the least (murders); but the data on those in between (riots, revolts, etc.) were less well recorded presumably because those violent events were too small to be regarded as wars but too large to be termed murders. He then devised a logarithmic scale of "deadly quarrels" from one to seven, scale seven involving 3 to 33 million deaths; scale six, 300,000 to 3 million deaths, etc.[1] Richardson's fundamental assumption is that all violence is similar in motive and different only in scale. Riots and wars are essentially larger murders; to understand war, one must understand the general phenomenon of violence. Richardson consequently suggests that war is best defined as violence above an agreed-upon level.

All definitions of war assume a continuity from primitive to modern war. Despite differences in weapons, tactics and strategy, magnitude, participants, location, results, etc., there is a common core which allows the phenomenon to be considered in the abstract. This assumption is basic to this discussion and necessary to any categorization of wars on the basis of scale, consideration of the social context of wars, and explanations of causality.

Wars are studied for a variety of reasons. Probably the oldest and most common motive has been to understand how they could be won. Thus military schools and institutions study previous wars to find general rules which may ensure success in future wars. This approach produced two schools of thought: the geometricians and the psychologists. According to the geometricians, battles are won by the placement and movement of troops and they advocate three basic tactics. First is double envelopment, which requires turning the

---

1. See Richardson, *Statistics of Deadly Quarrels* (Pittsburgh: Boxwood Press, 1960).

flanks and encircling the enemy (the best example is the ancient Battle of Cannae). Second is oblique attack, wherein the attacker concentrates on a narrow point of an enemy front, overcomes it, and gradually rolls up the line (Frederick the Great was the most notable exponent of this tactic.) Third is breakin-breakout, which advocates punching a hole in the enemy line and spreading out behind it (Montgomery used this tactic at the Battle of El Alamein).

The psychologists, however, argue that success in war depends less upon such mechanistic concerns than upon subtle human considerations. Battles are won and lost in the minds of commanders, as one gains psychological dominance over the other. Clausewitz was the most famous exponent of this view, but Bobby Fischer's approach to his chess opponents exemplifies it even better. The key to success in battle is found in the personalities of the commanders.

Whatever that key, the aspect of continuity is of compelling interest to students of war. For instance, during the nineteenth and twentieth century, the German General Staff habitually studied ancient battles in great detail and was most fascinated with the Battle of Cannae because it produced total rather than partial victory. Cannae was thus virtually replicated at the Battle of Tannenberg (August 1914) in terms of movements, results, and scale. Despite two and a half millennia of technological and other developments, the essence of battle was not significantly altered.

The continuity of warfare was reflected in many of the battles of World War II and the Korean War; even the guerrilla tactics used in Vietnam have considerable precedent. But the atomic bomb—the potential for total annihilation of an entire population or indeed all humanity—has none. Since atomic war is beyond human experience, indeed beyond Richardson's scale, it constitutes a break in the continuity of future wars with past wars.

■

An understanding of war requires comprehension of the circumstances in which it occurs. Although it is clear that wars do not take place in a vacuum, the relationship between war and society is less clear. The operative questions therefore become, How much does a society affect the wars in which it is involved? And, conversely, how much do wars influence the societies in which they occur?

The view that war affects society seems fairly widely accepted but there is considerable dispute on whether the effects are good or bad. It has been argued that war is a vehicle of progress and the cause of all that is good in civilization. The finer human instincts, e.g., self-sacrifice and heroism, and social energy are activated by war. A nineteenth-century German sociologist put the view well: "War is an ordeal instituted by God, who places the nations in the balance. Its red hammer is the welder of men in cohesive states and nowhere but in such states can human nature adequately develop. The only alternative to war is degradation." A Frenchman writing at the same time said: "War is a condition of progress. It is the cut-whip which prevents countries from going to sleep." Lest Americans feel unrepresented, they should recall that General Patton regarded war as "the highest achievement of civilization."

Others reject this view and assert that war hinders progress and is the result of a residue of barbarism beneath the veneer of civilization. War persists because humans were predatory hunters for millions of years and were farmers for only a few thousand years. Human hunting instincts thus emerge in the form of violence. Some people conclude that war is undesirable but unavoidable because of human nature. Others argue that war can be eradicated; one of the more interesting ideas was contributed by the American philosopher William James. His famous essay, "The Moral Equivalent of War," argued that merely condemning war is an unpromising way to avoid it. He believed that the attractions of war must be acknowledged if it is to be understood and thereby eradicated and that a substitute (a "moral equivalent") must be found, to energize societies and inspire individuals as war does but without its violence. James's general insight is potentially useful but his specific suggestion, the formation of a super peace corps, may be less so. Above all, James recognized that wars influence society.

There is considerable disagreement over how much society affects war. The question is whether the shape of a society—i.e., its political organization, technology, social structure, even perhaps its art, religion, and intellectual life—determines the way wars are fought in terms of military organization and tactics and strategy. Most observers seemingly agree that the social and political structure determines the military organization and that technology affects the conduct of war. The economy is likewise a determinant. John Stuart Mill and other nineteenth-century liberals believed that war was caused by trade barriers; a free-trade society would have no wars because nations would specialize, become interdependent, and be unable to fight a modern war. Marx took the opposite view: war and trade barriers are the inevitable result of capitalistic competition for resources and markets. Both views nonetheless adopt the basic premise that the economy of a society affects, indeed causes, its wars.

It is also argued, however, that society does not determine the cause or conduct of war. Wars occur in both primitive and civilized societies and the conduct of war is often similar despite political, social, economic, and other variations. As a consequence, there is little correlation between the way a society is structured and the way its military forces are organized.

According to another argument, the differences among civilized societies may or may not significantly influence the way wars are fought, but some degree of civilization is probably necessary to war. Some observers suggest that the violence engaged in by primitive societies is not really war because such violence is limited in scope and duration. Extensive, long-term fighting occurs when a society produces a surplus of material and services sufficient to support significant conflict—war in this sense is a luxury. Since primitive societies produce barely enough to survive, they cannot afford the luxury. War is therefore possible only in civilized societies which enjoy a surplus, have an agricultural base, sophisticated political organizations, social structures, economic systems, cities, etc. Thus the level of cultural development determines whether, though not necessarily how, a society conducts war.

■

The problem of causation is simply a question of why wars occur. The answer to that question is typically subsumed under four explicanda, in descending generality: Darwinian, Original Sin, Marxist, and Great Man.

The Darwinists argue that all life is struggle, and that in each generation of any biological species, those who survive are more adapted to their environment, and are stronger or more vicious than those who die. Thus war and conflict arise from the functional biological relationship among humans and are an element of human nature. Too many humans are born into a world with insufficient food; war is the unavoidable consequence. The Darwinian argument, applied to particular forms of territorial defense by humans and animals, is appealing because it is simple and universally applicable.

The Original Sin argument dismisses theories about animal behavior as irrelevant and suggests that violence is a problem unique to humans, virtually the only species which habitually kills its own kind in large numbers. The most common cause of death in primitive society was seemingly violent: most Neolithic and Paleolithic skulls were apparently smashed by a large, blunt instrument. This evidence of human violence is explained in terms of man's ejection from an ideal state (the Garden of Eden) into a violent world. Thus wars will cease only when men return to their original condition. This return will result from individual actions affecting group behavior (e.g., pacifism, turning the other cheek); from group actions (e.g., the establishment of utopian communities); or from God's intervention. In the interim, human nature renders wars unavoidable.

The next level of explanation, the Marxist, argues that human institutions rather than individual human nature are the cause of violence. Marxist theory asserts that history is a record of the strong exploiting the weak; that political, social, and economic structures are merely a vehicle of that exploitation. In this context, forced labor is a form of covert violence which leads to overt violence, i.e., riots, rebellions, and civil wars. International wars thus are conflicts between the exploiters in different societies who seek to extend their domination. War is not an aberration or a mistake but rather a normal, indeed necessary, result of conflicting interests. The Marxist suggests that an end to war requires a fundamental change in human institutions (not human nature), to stop exploitation.

According to the Great Man theory, wars are not caused by biological nature, by human institutions, or by ordinary human beings who are occasionally violent but not warlike and do not even want wars. Rather, wars are caused by a narrow segment of humanity —leaders who seek to become "world historical personalities" or "great men" by conquering and by winning wars. Whether these tendencies result from individual personality traits or are fostered by a national leader's situation or role, the theory holds that wars are caused by the decisions of a few, aggressive individuals who force those decisions upon essentially passive and pacific peoples. It has been proposed that this tendency can be curbed by giving world leaders passivity pills or by establishing leader-selection processes which would elevate nonaggressive personalities and reward nonaggression.

The appeal of these four explanations varies; individuals' responses are influenced by intellectual predispositions conditioned primarily by academic discipline. The response to these theories is best represented by the opposing attitudes of historians and social scientists.

Historians generally tend to reject these theoretical explanations and they contend that the outbreak of war is an immensely complex event involving large numbers of often confused, ill-informed, and frequently frightened men making decisions the implications of which they seldom fathom. Consequently, historians reject unitary explanations as simplistic and useless in understanding the cause or consequence of specific wars. They sometimes contend that those who do not know history are most likely to find theoretical explanations appealing. At best, historians believe, these theories provide a list of necessary but not sufficient conditions for war. Without a potential for violence, there would clearly be no war. But, since the historian is usually anxious to explain specific wars, general theories are of little assistance.

Social scientists—political scientists, economists, sociologists, psychologists, and anthropologists—are inclined to favor theoretical explanations. They believe that historians tend to see so much detail that they cannot perceive uniformities or make general statements. Social scientists contend that uniformities are usually accepted in science—despite the problem of dealing with diversity—and should be accepted in the study of human behavior. There are similarities to be found in studying human phenomena like revolutions, governments, social classes, and wars. Furthermore, explanatory statements are not only possible but necessary, since, without them, little is really understood about human behavior.

Although any coherent explanation must start from one of these extremes, most students of war adopt an intermediate point of view.

The appeal of a theoretical explanation is also affected by prevailing social attitudes toward war. Responses to war vary from opposition to apathy to enthusiasm—usually relative to experience and emotion rather than intellectual considerations. This phenomenon occurred in the United States during the Vietnam War. People were apathetic during the early 1960s, opposition to the war peaked in the late 1960s, and we tend toward apathy again in the 1970s. Similar changes are evidenced in previous eras. There was a wave of pacifism in Europe and the United States in the 1930s, especially among college students. French students contended that if the German soldiers invaded again, they should be given free railroad tickets to Paris because war was "ridiculous." The Oxford Union voted against fighting "for king and country." When war came in 1939, the same students took up the cause against Hitler as a crusade against evil.

Thus how war is perceived will affect how it is explained at a particular time. When war is considered bad, pointless, and foolish, one explanation may be more appealing than when war is viewed as desirable and necessary. In this sense, explanations of war, like wars themselves, are influenced by historical circumstances. A more than superficial or cursory understanding of war will necessarily take these problems into consideration. Questions of definition, of social context, and theories of causation must be dealt with both to make any explanation comprehensible and to locate it in what will presumably be a continuing debate on war.

# PART *I*

# Theoretical Approaches

# Introduction

The essays in this section reflect an interest in theoretical approaches to war and violence. While not denying the uniqueness of individual instances, they seek broader patterns. They assume that beneath the surface of diversity exists a unity which is potentially susceptible to theoretical formulation. This constitutes the basic assumption of the social sciences; all but one (Legters) of the authors included in this section are social scientists.

Within this framework of shared assumptions, distinctions in approach and focus nonetheless exist. The essays vary in level of analysis from highly abstract to relatively specific, as is roughly reflected by their order in this section. They also vary in disciplinary focus. Roy L. Prosterman, interested in the general field of conflict studies, evaluates a range of theories and argues for social causation and the possibility of preventing violence. John Alcock offers a biological explanation and suggests that the theory of natural selection is essential to an understanding of human aggression. Simon Ottenberg outlines anthropological theories of war; he warns against the danger of cultural biases in studying the phenomenon. Pierre L. Van den Berghe suggests a sociological approach focusing particularly on the comparison of military structures in different societies. George Modelski, a political scientist, discusses war in terms of Great Power behavior. Ezra Stotland provides a psychological dimension by relating violence to an individual's sense of competence and self-esteem. Lynne B. Iglitzin considers, in sociopsychological terms, the associa-

■

tion of violence with masculinity as fostered by social pressures in the forms of sex, sports, and war. Lyman H. Legters introduces the economic element in his analysis of Marx's views of war.

Several themes run through these essays. The theories can be grouped under the general rubrics of intrinsic (biological and psychological) and conditioned (social, sociopsychological, and socioeconomic) impulses. The essays demonstrate the comparability of societies at quite different stages of development. They also indicate that violence is both reflected in and affected by the social structure. Although these theories can be seen as distinct and even contradictory if pushed to the extreme, they share basically similar assumptions.

# The Study of
# Lethal Human Conflict

## Roy L. Prosterman

Conflict studies comprise a new academic discipline. It is interdisciplinary, drawing upon traditional areas, as are the other new fields of environment, population, and urban studies. It nonetheless has begun to develop a coherence and method of its own, illustrated in this essay.

Lethal conflict is defined as all actions by which one human being intentionally kills another. They range from the smallest conflicts—murder—up to riots and small civil disturbances; through strikes, larger civil disturbances in the form of insurgencies and civil wars of various kinds; then wars between recognizably separate states or entities; and finally, of course, the largest phenomena, exemplified so far only by World War I and World War II, instances of what some have called total war.

The most thorough accounting of lethal conflict is provided by Lewis F. Richardson in *Statistics of Deadly Quarrels.* He found that the total number of deaths directly attributable to lethal conflict between 1820 and 1945 was approximately 59 million, 36 million of which occurred during the two world wars alone; other group conflicts—civil wars, riots, wars between states—had taken an additional 14 million lives; and murder, just under 10 million lives. During that century and a quarter, lethal conflict was not among the ten main causes of death. Even if deaths indirectly attributable to war are included, increasing the death toll by perhaps as much as 50 percent, lethal conflict is barely tenth. However, these results are reassuring

■

in only a limited sense—like saying that few people died of air pollution before 1930. The technology of lethal conflict has changed dramatically in the last quarter-century through the creation of thermonuclear as well as virulent biological weapons and other methods of mass destruction. Indeed, since we now have the capability of destroying by sudden violence *all* life on earth, we must "think about the unthinkable" if we are to make any effort to avoid it.

■

Prevention of conflict necessitates understanding. Possible explanations must therefore be examined and evaluated. We must begin, however, by dispensing with theories which complicate rather than facilitate a solution.

So-called social Darwinism argued that human society was governed by a "law of the jungle" or "law of fang and claw"—not very different from what Thomas Hobbes in *Leviathan* called the "war of all against all" in the "natural state." Freud embroidered upon this view and posited as the basis for human aggression an inherent death instinct which accumulated and periodically exploded. In *Totem and Taboo,* Freud describes the primal family: the sons, having reached adulthood, clubbed their father to death and then shared their sisters and mother among themselves; eventually a falling-out occurred and the sons began killing each other.

It cannot be emphasized too strongly that this is pure fiction with *no discernible relationship* to what we now know about the sources of human aggression. According to the findings of paleontologists and anthropologists, early man was basically peaceful. In French cave paintings, undoubtedly the work of hundreds of separate artists depicting the important events in their lives over tens of thousands of years, representations of men fighting other men date from some time after 10,000 B.C. Tools were used for hundreds of thousands of years in hunting animals but *not* to kill humans.

Unfortunately, the opposite and incorrect Darwinian and Freudian assumptions are widely disseminated. But neither the comic-strip image of Og clubbing Gog and dragging Una off by the hair nor, for instance, William Golding's *Lord of the Flies*—the tale of young boys who turn to mutual slaughter and cannibalism when stranded on an island—bears any relationship to the scientific findings of psychology. Moreover, ethologists find that intraspecific aggression (an animal of a particular species killing another member of its own species) is virtually unknown. It is therefore not particularly surprising that early man, likewise, rarely killed his fellows.

The behavior of contemporary "primitive peoples" reinforces the archaeological evidence and closely reflects what is assumed to be the life pattern of prehistoric man. They lived in small, mobile groups, obtained their food by hunting and gathering rather than fixed agriculture, and lacked a strict social or political hierarchy. As Margaret Mead has said, war was "invented" as a cultural institution to deal with certain situations. The social Darwinism and the Freudian assertion that the "war of all against all" is the natural and prehistoric state of humankind is wholly inconsistent with the mass of scientific evidence. Indeed, theirs is worse than no explanation at all, since it substitutes fantasy for evidence and encourages misleading conclusions about the inevitability of lethal conflict.

We must therefore seek explanations which accord more closely with the evidence. One category of theory focuses on innate or genetic determinants. Sometimes called the "hydraulic-accumulator" model, it suggests that aggression accumulates physiologically until it has to be discharged. Physiologists, however, are unable to locate an accumulation-discharge mechanism. In addition, cultures differ widely in the amount of lethal conflict which occurs. Episodes of violence—such as war—years or whole generations apart are incompatible with the notion of a regular discharge process within the individuals of a society. Perhaps the most telling evidence against the hydraulic-accumulator view of aggression is the fact that the vast majority of human beings in any society never kill another human being.

A second group of explanations relates possibly innate determinants to specific environmental settings. One such model is "attack/self-defense," according to which certain genetic factors cause people to defend themselves when attacked, i.e., when the environment provides a stimulus. This covers, at best, relatively few situations, and even in these offers an incomplete explanation, since it does not indicate why the *attack* occurs.

Another model could be called "affirmative-propensity"; it assumes that basic needs—such as food—demand aggression if they are not fulfilled. Again, evidence opens this theory to question. There are societies in which people will starve to death without even attempting to steal food from a cart standing next to them.

Still another, the "status-seeking" model, proceeds from the notion that particular genetic factors may impel certain people to become the "alpha male" or leader. These individuals strive for status, might continue that striving as leaders, and then seek to preserve their position through war. This is a significant phenomenon in a genetic and a cultural sense, since people do become leaders—largely through personal striving—and then make crucial decisions about large-scale conflict. The model also raises important and interesting questions about the possible confusion between the rhetoric and the actual motivations of leaders. This theory, however, may ultimately tell why the call to arms is made but not why the populace responds. It is therefore at best a partial explanation for only one aspect of lethal conflict.

A third type of explanation focuses on universal environmental constants. One example is the Oedipus complex, which suggests that the growing male child wishes to kill his father and marry his mother. There is little evidence of this mechanism's operating lethally in the sense of actual efforts to destroy fathers.

Anthony Storrs in *Human Aggression* offers a more modern psychoanalytic example, an "infantile-dependency" model. Humans develop more slowly from birth to puberty than other species; the chimpanzee, for instance, requires about seven years to mature, while humans need thirteen or more. During this period—particularly in modern societies—the infant, subjected to many restrictions, is constantly frustrated. The resulting submerged sense of rage causes the adult to strike out and kill other humans. This provocative hypothesis, however, does not explain why only a few adults resort to such violence.

A variant of environmental explanations relates to *specific* individuals or cultures. These range from brain damage, which may in rare cases cause lethal activity, to the commonly used "frustration-aggression" model, which suggests that aggression arises out of frustration produced by particular events.

A famous study, for example, showed that over a long period of time lynchings of blacks in the South increased as the price of cotton fell. When the poor white sharecropper found that he could not make ends meet, he presumably became frustrated, went more frequently to Klan meetings, and eventually participated in lynchings. According to the study, he attacked blacks rather than the landlords, moneylenders, and merchants—the real cause of his difficulties—because the latter were too threatening. Yet, when a "focusing" revolutionary ideology and widespread frustration exist, people have in fact turned their rage on landlords and moneylenders. A central element in the civil conflagrations in Mexico, China, Russia, Spain, and Vietnam, which each took over a million lives, was the uprising of landless peasants. Frustration-aggression theory can sometimes provide a useful explanatory tool.

The "stress" model suggests that environmental features such as crowding, noise, or overstimulation might in some cases directly foster lethal behavior. (Alternatively, overpopulation may operate indirectly, creating pressures on land and water resources which cause intense frustration.) The "boredom" model can be seen as environmental *under*stimulation, i.e., stress in reverse. In a brilliant and insightful piece, Arthur Miller suggested that the slum youngster's need to feel he is alive and really exists often motivates him to join in violent "games," even in lethal acts, which become "his trip to the zoo."

A particular society's attitudes and mores are another specific feature of the environment that can encourage aggressiveness. Ideologies—whether medieval Christianity or modern communism —have fostered and indeed justified lethal behavior; immitation— real-life models rather than mental constructs—is another significant cause. People kill people more easily when they have observed models of such aggressiveness, especially in their early lives. This may help explain the different rate of lethal aggression among various groups within a society. For instance, American blacks commit murder approximately fifteen times as frequently as do American whites (about nine times out of ten, the murder victim of the black who kills is another black person). Clearly, this behavior is not biologically determined, since the murder rate in numerous African societies is less than one per 100,000, i.e., roughly one-fiftieth the American black murder rate and less than one-third the American white murder rate. The explanation must consequently be social. Most American blacks are exposed much more than most American whites to intense frustrations, which lead directly to violence and create models for later imitation. The impact of TV violence, still a subject of hot dispute, may also be considerable for both blacks and whites. Of potentially great importance for subsequent imitation is the behavior of parents, above all those who batter their children; there is some evidence that a very high proportion of murderers were severely beaten as children.

■

Most of the above explantions—except perhaps "ideology"—assume that the person who kills another feels a sense of anger or rage. A considerable body of testimony and evidence indicates that this is *not* so in most wars or large-group conflicts. Perhaps one of the most promising explanations for group violence is the "command-and-obedience" model, best analyzed by Stanley Milgram in a famous experiment at Yale. Subjects were commanded to administer "extremely dangerous" electrical shocks to another individual in what they were told was a learning experiment. Despite the other individual's shouting and apparent pain, more than three out of five of the subjects obeyed the scientist's command to continue the shocks. In fact, the shocks and cries of pain were not real but the subjects believed they were. These results came as a surprise to researchers. Psychiatrists had estimated that only one person in a thousand would be fully "obedient"; in fact, six hundred times as many actually obeyed. Milgram's experiment has since been repeated in Germany,

Italy, Australia, and South Africa, where the levels of obedience proved even *higher* than in the American case. Women have been found to be as obedient as men.[1]

Milgram's results suggest that people placed in a command-and-obedience structure—such as in military combat—kill each other not because they have a sense of rage against the enemy but rather because they are "following orders" or "doing their job," a conclusion borne out by interviews of combat veterans and by other evidence on combat behavior. Extensive interviews of World War II front-line infantrymen indicated that only about 15 percent ever fired their rifles, whereas those who worked on crew-served weapons (machine guns, artillery, airplanes, etc.) performed at virtually a 100 percent rate. Milgram, too, found that when a group collaborated to administer the "shock," full obedience was over 90 percent. Apparently the critical element is the immediate proximity of a commander, and a very important secondary element is the mutual example and dispersion of "responsibility" provided by a group.

From the above discussion it is possible to draw some tentative conclusions. The most persuasive explanation of large-scale, organized lethal behavior—particularly in its most threatening form, twentieth-century total war—seems to involve a combination of two or more separate mechanisms. One element apparently is status-seeking leaders who may be driven by severe personal frustration, or by a desire to protect their own status, or by a perception of what they believe is required of them by the ideology of their societies, or perhaps by all three. The other element appears to be the command-and-obedience structure characteristic of modern, organized societies and frequently supported by an ideology justifying or indeed requiring violence. Together, the frustrated, status-protecting, ideology-affirming leaders, and the obedient, ideology-accepting followers, make war.

■

The ultimate purpose of understanding lethal conflict is to prevent it. Conflict resolution is presently where the medical profession was in the early nineteenth century, i.e., before the discovery of germs, vaccines, or chloroform but beyond patient-bleeding by barbers. Conflict studies is beginning to develop a methodology which, it is hoped, will produce results comparable to those of medicine: indeed, it *must* do so if human life is to continue. Several different approaches are discussed below.

---

1. For further details on Milgram's experiment, see my *Surviving to 3000: An Introduction to the Study of Lethal Conflict* (Belmont, Ca.: Duxbury Press, 1972), pp. 85ff.

The "control" paradigm describes the whole range of techniques by which one or several countries—whether through a "Pax Americana," a "Pax Russo-Americana," or a U.N. "peace keeping" force—may *compel* people to stop fighting. Externally, it uses the apparatus of large armies and military technology; internally, it takes the form of police forces and prisons. Although some "control" is undoubtedly necessary until we find something better, "fighting fire with fire" seems the most dangerous and least satisfactory long-term solution to any kind of lethal conflict. In effect, it implies suppression of the outward manifestations of lethal conflict, without touching the underlying causes.

The "agreement" paradigm suggests treaties or similar mutual understandings as a method for reducing or eliminating causes of potential conflict, such as oil prices or nuclear arms. This approach involves the corollary of maintaining such agreements through satisfactory monitoring procedures, especially in the area of disarmament.

The "initiatives" paradigm implies a variety of unilateral measures to encourage more peaceable behavior—a unilateral reduction of arms, for example, might persuade an opponent that he is less threatened, and strengthen his own "doves," and might thereby encourage a similar response. Ideal initiatives of this type would involve little risk for the originating party and thus avoid domestic political opposition (e.g., starting with a one-year moratorium on building *new* submarines, rather than trying to get political consensus on unilateral scrapping of *all* submarines). If favorable response does in fact result, a formal agreement can embody the new situation.

The "amelioration" paradigm involves reduction of causes of potential internal conflict such as starvation, poverty, and resource shortages. For example, genuinely adequate foreign-aid programs at perhaps three times the current, shamefully inadequate level could help underdeveloped societies solve their problems of sharecropping and food production. Land reform and rural development, in turn, have usually created the social and economic conditions in which smaller family size becomes desirable to farmers. Explosive frustrations might thereby be reduced and civil war avoided.

Utopian paradigms envisage conditions conducive to material and psychological satisfaction for all humans. One approach might be choosing leaders who are unlikely to opt for war and rewarding those who behave peacefully—such as by renown traditionally reserved by historians for successful warriors.

If the discipline of conflict studies is given a fraction of the support—in terms of human enthusiasm and material resources—

that medicine enjoyed as it began its sustained growth in the nine-teenth century, our current primitive perception of the paradigms for conflict resolution and prevention may develop rapidly enough to see the planet through another millennium—to 3000 and perhaps beyond.

# Evolution and Human Violence

## John Alcock

A grasp of evolutionary theory and especially its key concept, natural selection, is crucial to understanding human behavior. This theory has nonetheless been ignored or misunderstood by the overwhelming majority of mankind, including almost all academic social scientists and humanists. There is probably a complex set of reasons why this is so.

First, there is a tendency for the academic disciplines to become isolated entities with their own special assumptions and language. Social scientists and humanists perhaps feel that evolution is the property of biologists and that they have enough to worry about without trying to assimilate what seems to be an esoteric concept.

Second, and more important, is the pervasive belief that biology simply does not apply to any of the significant aspects of human behavior. Even people who accept the idea that humans are an animal species with an evolutionary past often say that evolution deals only with fossils, anatomy, and structural traits, not with behavior. It is commonly claimed that humans learn everything from their environment; the history and genes of the species can therefore safely be ignored. This essay argues that these ideas are incorrect and seeks to demonstrate that evolution has a great deal to do with the behavior of all animals, including humans. Students of evolution are interested in answering the question, How does the history of an animal species account for its special structural, physiological, biochemical, and behavioral characteristics? The solution to this histori-

■

cal problem is founded upon the concept of natural selection. Charles Darwin recognized that changes would inevitably take place within populations of animals simply because some members of the population reproduced more successfully than others. Those individuals that have offspring which survive and reproduce obviously contribute more to future generations than those which fail to reproduce.

To take a simple example, imagine a population of six aardvarks. Three have very sticky tongues and can trap termites more readily than the other three, which are endowed with somewhat less sticky tongues. Because they are better food gatherers, the three sticky-tongued aardvarks tend to survive longer and reproduce more than their fellows. Thus the genes that promote the development of highly sticky tongues will logically become more common in the next generation. If this process continues, the population will eventually be composed entirely of extraordinarily sticky-tongued aardvarks.

Thus the concept of natural selection is beautifully simple. Some individuals happen, for whatever reason, to have traits which help them have more surviving offspring than other members of their species. The hereditary basis of the adaptations that confer relative reproductive success will become more common as the result of reproductive competition between the members of a population; those traits that do not promote the production of offspring will be eliminated as their bearers become less and less common. This is natural selection, fundamentally a reproductive phenomenon which affects the transmission of genes to subsequent generations.

The idea of natural selection is tremendously powerful and useful. It makes biology a reasonably coherent and unified discipline. Every biologist agrees that no matter what he or she chooses to study —genetics (the aardvark's genes), physiology or biochemistry (the aardvark's sticky tongue), or ecology (the aardvark's relation to termites in its environment)—evolution applies because it helps explain why the animal has the genes, the physiology, the biochemistry, and the ecological relations that it does. A biologist knows that trying to understand anything about an animal without knowing something about natural selection is like trying to understand where cars come from without the vaguest idea that General Motors, Ford, and Chrysler exist.

■

An animal's behavior determines its relative reproductive success in a population, that is, how well it copes with its environment in its efforts to convert resources into offspring. All aspects of behavior are therefore subject to selection, which acts to perpetuate those behavioral characteristics that enhance an individual's chances to pass its genes on to future generations. The entire focus of natural selection is on behavior. Evolution will favor individuals that carry the genetic foundations for adaptive responses to their environment.

This relationship between genes and behavior is a major sticking point for many humanists. They feel that, although some insect behaviors might be genetically influenced, human behavior is exempt because of the strong role cultural environment and upbringing appear to play in the development of human behavior. This view stems from their incorrect distinction between innate behavior which is "genetic" and learned behavior which is "environmental." In reality all behavior is the product of an interaction between genes and environment.

Development occurs because an individual possesses a set of inherited genetic instructions that structure the use of environmentally supplied building blocks. The genes by themselves are simply fragments of DNA molecules. Without the environment, genetic information would remain unused and the egg would remain a single cell; without genetic instructions, there could be no development either. Only through the complex interplay of genetic rules for the growth and specialization of cells and the environment is the creation of a behaving animal possible. Instincts are not "genetic"; learned behaviors are not "environmental." Each type of behavior depends on neural systems which are the product of the developmental process, the interaction of genes and environment.

Two examples from human behavior illustrate this point. One could reasonably be called innate. When a human infant is several weeks old, smiling can be triggered by showing the baby a two-dimensional mask with two black dots for eyes. Three-dimensional masks, complete models of a human face, even the mother's face, are no better at causing the infant to smile than this simple stimulus. The fact that a complete smile can be produced at an early age in response to a specific stimulus suggests that the behavior is innate. The action probably depends on neural circuits within the baby's brain which are highly sensitive to particular visual events (the appearance of two, not one, contrasting dots on a face-sized background). This physiological mechanism then orders a set of facial muscles to contract in such a way that the baby "smiles" when it detects the two contrasting dots. Without both genes and environment, i.e., the developmental process, there would be no baby with special neural mechanisms to smile at certain visual stimuli.

A second example concerns the acquisition of language. Nearly every human being picks up information from the environment that is used to modify the sounds he or she produces in ways that help the person communicate. This incredibly complicated task, perhaps impossible for even the most advanced computers, is easy for a three-year-old human. The child learns language without formal instruction or with little conscious effort on the part of its parents. This could not happen had not the operation of natural selection on human populations favored those individuals who happened to have the kind of neural "wiring" which made it possible for them to learn to speak easily and skillfully. But human learning mechanisms are selective and limited. For instance, most people have a terrible time learning the principles of physics. Yet a neutral observer from another planet would find it difficult to understand how humans can comprehend complex streams of spoken words more easily than they can a few elementary physics equations. This explanation is simple: humans have long been selected for their language ability but only recently for skills in physics.

■

The moral thus far is that differences in reproductive success can, over time, shape the behavioral abilities of animals and provide some creatures, ourselves included, with certain innate behaviors and specific learning abilities. There is no reason to assume that aggressive behavior is exempt from natural selection. The widespread aggressive activities of many animal species suggest that such capabilities are useful to individuals in the competition to reproduce. A certain amount of aggressiveness in the struggle to acquire limited resources —food, space, mates, and so on—can influence a creature's reproductive output. Thus some aggressive traits, tendencies, or predispositions become a norm within a population as their genetic foundation becomes widespread.

It is not surprising that most threatening or violent disputes between people revolve around contested "ownership." Many murders in our culture and in a variety of "primitive" cultures involve confrontations over property or wives, both valuable but limited resources. The fact that such individual-versus-individual aggression is sometimes socially disruptive and is often judged morally reprehensible by groups within a culture is largely irrelevant from an evolutionary perspective. The capacity to get angry in situations in which one is losing something has almost certainly contributed to the reproductive success of human beings throughout the course of human evolution.

■

Warfare probably is due to different causes, which are nonetheless determined by selection. This common human activity has biological foundations rooted in many thousand years of selection for specific

abilities that facilitate war-making. The human attributes that under-
lie organized group violence probably have relatively little to do
with the capacity to get angry at someone. Instead, paradoxically,
warfare depends on the cooperative, group-bonding, authority-
accepting aspects of human nature. Consequently, it is likely that
group aggression has very different motivational bases than individual-versus-individual fighting, although the two may overlap in some
situations.

The capacity for cooperation among humans is extraordinary.
Most students of human evolution argue that this ability is closely
related to two aspects of human history as a species. First, early man
lived in small bands in which individual survival and reproductive
success were intimately tied to the group's survival and productivity.
Second, the development of big-game hunting by groups of men
working as a unit with weapons to capture large and often dangerous
animals was a crucial adaptation in human evolution, Both factors
place a selective premium on individuals who (1) feel a strong sense
of membership and loyalty to their group and possess the capacity to
form affectional ties with other persons within the band; (2) are
highly sensitive to the feelings of other group members so as to
anticipate their actions; and (3) are likely to accept what they perceive as legitimate authority.

The strong sense of identification with a specific group (and a
corresponding sense of nonidentity with other human bands) has
expressed itself in the widespread tendency of tribes to call themselves "*the* human beings" in contradistinction to neighboring
groups. Anthropologists have been impressed because all cultures
possess elaborate systems of kinship, which serve to define groups
and bond people together; even tribes with almost no material possessions have kinship rules, some of which are extraordinarily complex and difficult to define. Social psychologists have also investigated
the human predisposition toward groupness. Muzafer and Carolyn
Sherif divided a boys' camp into two groups, the Bull Dogs and the
Red Devils, separating budding friendships in the process. By encouraging competition between the two "clans," they found that in
short order former friends became enemies, while members of the
same team soon developed intensely loyal friendships. By the end of
the summer the situation had become nearly uncontrollable—open
warfare between the two groups involved night raids, violence at
meals, and verbal assaults at all times. Only by inviting an external
"enemy" into the camp (a ball club from a neighboring town) were
the camp managers able to mute the extreme hostility between the
Bull Dogs and the Red Devils.

Humans are also exceedingly sensitive to the feelings and attitudes of other people, a trait perhaps epitomized by the modern
obsession with opinion polls in Western cultures. Social psychologists

have completed some illuminating experiments on this point. For example, in one of a series of tests conducted in recent years by Bibb Latane, smoke was pumped through a vent into a room where the subject and a "companion" were taking a test. Because the latter remained impassive, the subject failed to take action for a much longer time than did individuals who were tested singly. In another "disaster" prepared by Latane, a secretary invited the subject and the "companion" into a room and then went into an adjoining office where she turned on a tape which made it seem that she climbed onto a chair, fell heavily, moaned and cried for help. Only a few of those tested (7 percent) went to her assistance when the companion was unresponsive, whereas most of those tested alone tried to help. Latane interviewed individuals in the test group and found their failure to react did not stem from indifference; quite the contrary, those tested felt considerable stress. They wanted to report the "fire" or help the secretary but did not because the companion behaved as if nothing was the matter. The subjects tried to respond in a manner consistent with their perception of the companion's attitude.

Finally, human beings are profoundly receptive to authority. Stanley Milgram has explored this phenomenon in his famous shock experiments. The subjects, adult men with solid reputations in their community, were told to give an unseen "learner" a shock each time the learner made a mistake in a memory exam. Since the learner's errors were frequent, the subjects were obliged to obey or disobey the instruction to increase the voltage with each mistake until it reached dangerously high shock levels. The learner at first protested (on tape), then moaned, and finally became silent when the shocks became lethal. The subjects often asked to stop the experiment, but a substantial majority of those tested nonetheless administered apparently fatal shocks when told by the experimenter to continue.

These experiments often paint a grim picture of human behavior. The underlying attributes which they illustrate have nonetheless contributed to reproductive success in the past and probably do so today. Individuals who evidence these characteristics—identification with a group, sensitivity to the desires of their fellows, and responsiveness to the direction provided by their leaders—are likely to form cohesive cooperative units capable of accomplishing goals advantageous to all group members. It is important to realize that natural selection favors fundamentally selfish behavior in the sense of encouraging people to maximize their reproductive output. Indeed, this is the logical and inevitable outcome of natural selection. Thus we need not expect cooperative behavior to extend to members of *other* groups because the individual does not depend on outsiders for his welfare. In fact, they may represent an obstacle. It is highly possible that warfare was one of the key factors which favored a high degree of group harmony and cohesiveness among early humans. On one hand, pressures exerted by hostile bands favored members of groups that could cooperate effectively in defense of their resources. On the other hand, well-organized, well-led attacking bands enjoyed rich booty (captured women, food, and territory) when they could defeat and destroy other groups at little risk to themselves.

It is clear that modern war-making is promoted by the very characteristics that make group cooperation possible. An examination of the history of the Vietnam War reveals these factors at work. First, a sense of group identity was involved. "We" Americans (the Bull Dogs) confronted "them," the Communists (the Red Devils)— we were the human beings, they were not quite human, since they are unlike us in appearance, in their "Oriental disregard for life," and in their treatment of prisoners (for many Americans, My Lai was forgivable and forgettable; the torture of a captive pilot was not). Second, our sensitivity to the attitudes of others was a factor. The public was told by various presidents that most Americans supported official government policy and the message and the effect were clear. Most people do not like to feel that they are swimming against the tide, isolated from the majority, or causing a public scene. Third, a great many American citizens accepted the simple proposition that if their leader, The President, was for it, they should support him without question. His authority helped many comply as the voltage was increased against Vietnamese, Cambodians, and Laotians.

It should be stressed that these traits are generally adaptive. In the past and probably in the present, they have helped individuals maximize their reproductive contribution to the next generation. They are also the foundation of many commendable human activities such as group efforts to eradicate disease, build attractive communities, solve scientific problems, improve standards of living, and so on. But they simultaneously encourage groups to feel hostile toward other groups.

■

Human evolutionary history and natural selection suggest an explanation of the human proclivity for warfare. Fundamental reproductive selfishness, a high degree of sociality, and a strongly developed capacity for cooperation are at once the product of evolution and the preconditions for war. Individuals who would alter the violent behavior of groups must first understand why they behave as they do. Humans must recognize that they all belong to one group, that each person's welfare depends in some measure on the welfare of all other people. Only then can the characteristics which contribute to war-making find constructive, rather than destructive, expression.

# Anthropological Interpretations of War

## Simon Ottenberg

A useful starting point for an anthropological discussion of war is the definition offered by Margaret Mead.[1] She states that war requires an organization for killing, willingness to die on the part of its members, social approval within the societies concerned, and agreement that it is a legitimate—not necessarily desirable—way of solving problems.

Mead rejects the argument that war is caused by genetic factors; there is no innate drive for territory or property. Biological differences among individuals doubtless exist but do not account for violence. She views war as a social invention, developed at different times and places in prehistory to deal with certain situations.

Resolving or avoiding conflict consequently means finding ways to alter learned behavior. Some of her suggestions are neither unusual nor helpful—she urges agreements not to fight but does not tell how they should be reached. Potentially more fruitful, however, is her observation that warfare serves functions which must be performed in other ways if we are to avoid conflict. War effectively diverts internal aggressions; we must either find a substitute which does not threaten others or reduce internal pressures. An example of such a solution is found on a remote Pacific island, where a small

---

1. Margaret Mead, "Alternatives to War," in Morton Fried, Marvin Harris, and Robert Murphy, eds., *War: The Anthropology of Armed Conflict and Aggression* (Garden City, N.Y.: Natural History Press, 1968), pp. 215–28.

■

group of persons conduct war neither among themselves nor against their distant neighbors. Instead they turn their anxieties and aggressions against spirits they perceive as hostile. This effective substitute for warfare relieves hostility while uniting the society.[2]

■

Warfare and conquest have existed from very early times. Archaeological evidence indicates, for example, that hunting and gathering peoples moved against one another and against agricultural peoples, that agricultural societies attacked each other and pastoral societies. The gradual evolution of large, traditional kingdoms—such as those of the Inca and the Maya, as well as those in ancient Ghana and Mali —was at least partially due to conquest and absorption. Further, migration of traditional peoples often provoked violence, as in the movement of American Indians from Asia to the North American continent, black Africans from the northern forest to South Africa, and Mongolian and Turkic peoples in Asia. There is little truth in the vision of a "noble savage" who was inherently peaceful but corrupted by civilization. Equally incorrect and dangerous is the stereotype of traditional peoples as more cruel and barbaric than modern man; they were less savage and destructive because they lacked the technology to kill large numbers at great distances. There are a few peoples who do not wage war—small groups of hunting and gathering peoples in Africa, the Toda of southern India, some Pacific island peoples, and a few Eskimo groups—but they are isolated and relegated to unproductive areas. The vast majority of traditional peoples conducted war, which played an important part in the evolution of their societies.

The expansion of western Europe from the fifteenth to the nineteenth century involved some bitter fighting but usually ended with the defeat of traditional societies. Some members of the conquered societies were pleased because they either were tired of fighting or could achieve personal goals through peace, but others were unhappy, since they lost power and position. During these centuries of colonial control, traditional peoples were infrequently exposed to open warfare.

This pattern was altered abruptly in the twentieth century. Traditional peoples have been forced to accommodate modern warfare as they have other aspects of modern civilization. They were involved in the two world wars, when colonial troops were employed by the Great Powers. The struggles for independence have caused the most destructive wars fought since World War II. Because a

2. Melford Spiro, "Ghosts, Ifaluk, and Teleological Functionalism," *American Anthropologist* 54 (1952):497–503.

major part of the world's population falls into this group, war and violence often involving traditional peoples with Western countries is a major world problem.

Traditional peoples have consequently had three quite different experiences with war. After a long period of war among themselves, they were conquered and pacified by Europeans for several centuries, but are now in another period of intensive violence, sometimes in confrontation with Western and communist countries.

Until recently most anthropological research into war among traditional peoples was conducted during the period of colonial dominion. This fact influenced the results in two important ways. The imposition of peace made it necessary for anthropologists to rely on indirect evidence such as tribal lore and the memories of participants. Consequently, there are few good case studies based on direct observation of warfare.[3] Perhaps more significant, anthropologists were anxious to overcome the prejudice and ignorance prevailing in the West about traditional peoples. Many were cultural relativists who sought to demonstrate that traditional societies were as developed, organized, and viable as Western society. As a consequence, they minimized both internal and external conflicts within the societies they studied. It is hoped that both the paucity of evidence and the anthropologists' own biases will be corrected by new work being done.[4]

■

Three kinds of studies are being conducted by anthropologists—social, cross-cultural, and intracultural.

Social anthropology stresses the importance of studying the nature of social relationships, and social anthropologists view war as only one type of social relationship and conflict. It is less the termination of a social relationship than a change in form, since people continue to relate while fighting.

3. Napoleon A. Chagnon, *Yanomanö: The Fierce People* (New York: Holt, Rinehart & Winston, 1968); Ronald M. Berndt, *Excess and Restraint: Social Control Among a New Guinea Mountain People* (Chicago: University of Chicago Press, 1962); D. F. Ade Ajayi and Robert S. Smith, *Yoruba Warfare in the 19th Century* (Cambridge: Cambridge University Press, 1964); Joseph Bram, *An Analysis of Inca Militarism*, American Ethnological Society Monographs, no. 4 (New York: J. J. Augustin, 1941); Bernard Mishkin, *Rank and Warfare Among the Plains Indians*, American Ethnological Society Monographs, no. 3 (New York: J. J. Augustin, 1940); Frank R. Secoy, *Changing Military Patterns on the Great Plains*, American Ethnological Society Monographs, no. 21 (New York: J. J. Augustin, 1953); A. P. Vayda, *Maori Warfare*, Polynesian Society, Maori Monographs, no. 2 (Wellington, New Zealand: Polynesian Society, 1960).
4. See Fried, Harris, and Murphy, eds., *War: The Anthropology of Armed Conflict and Aggression*; and Paul Bohannan, ed., *Law and Warfare: Studies in the Anthropology of Conflict* (Garden City, N. Y.: Natural History Press, 1967).

An example of this approach is provided by the author's field-work among a group of Nigerian Ibo villages called Afikpo.[5] In this study of warfare, all cases of fighting within the group were collected and the social relationships among those involved, the causes of violence, and the means of resolution, if any, were ascertained. Violence fell into four types which determined the responses.

Murder within a clan does not require punishment, since it is regarded as a misfortune. Instead the group must be purified by mandatory ritual steps.

In the case of murder outside the clan but within the Afikpo group, the murderer or a member of his clan must die and the matter is thereby closed. The nature of conflict among Afikpo is illustrated by disputes over their palm groves from which are derived valuable palm oil and much-desired wine. When it is time to harvest the fruit, members of two villages may quarrel over who owns the grove. They scream and wave their machetes at each other but seldom hurt anybody seriously; their objective is to scare the other group away. The rules for this mock warfare are strict: participants are allowed to hit with the flat of the blade and even nick an opponent but killing is forbidden and necessitates revenge.

Warfare between Afikpo and the four neighboring, related Ibo groups is another type of conflict. Disputes over border farmland can cause killings and retaliatory killings, small-scale fighting back and forth which can continue for years. But sooner or later one of the other related groups invariably suggests mediation. A series of meetings follows and a resolution usually results even though the third party has no superior authority and can only offer suggestions. Such practice is common in traditional societies.

Finally, the Afikpo conduct warfare against the unrelated peoples who live across the Cross River, speak a different language, and are described as poisoners by the Afikpo. There is considerable raiding, much of it for pure excitement. Genuine wars have, however, been fought for control of movement and fishing on the river. This fighting is intermittent, long-term, and unresolved because the opponents see themselves as total strangers and no mechanism for mediation exists.

The nature of conflict and the responses to it consequently vary according to the social relationships between the opponents. At each of the social levels—family and kinship groups, village, groups of villages, and beyond—the rules of fighting and settling fights change. The social anthropologist's perspective suggests that an under-

---

5. Simon Ottenberg, *Leadership and Authority in an African Society: The Afikpo Village Group*, American Ethnological Society Monographs, no. 52 (Seattle: University of Washington Press, 1971).

standing of war requires an awareness of all social relationships in the societies concerned.[6]

■

The cross-cultural approach starts from the assumption that war can be understood by studying a number of different societies. Unfortunately, few studies of this type have been conducted.[7]

One of the most notable examples is the work of Keith F. Otterbein, who sought to correlate the characteristics and warfare of a considerable sample of traditional societies.[8] Political organization rather than economic or ecological factors is the most significant variable in Otterbein's study. He categorizes traditional societies as being either centralized or noncentralized. The former usually have strong leaders, social rankings, and some formal system of justice. The latter often do not and are composed of distinct social segments, quasi-independent or independent settlements without central authority—like the Ibo discussed above.

Political organization is related to the degree of control over war. Centralized societies generally have professional or nonprofessional military personnel over which the central government has clear and effective control; war is begun by the central authority rather than by individuals. In noncentralized traditional societies individuals can, however, start wars. For example, a few Plains Indians might get restless, raid another tribe, "count coup" (i.e., kill and take scalps), and thereby involve two tribes in war. Noncentralized groups have insufficient authority to check their members.

The conduct of war is also affected by political organization. Centralized societies tend to fight using shock (hitting) rather than less efficient missile weapons. Motives for fighting tend to be multiple in centralized societies, but single in noncentralized groups. Centralized societies tend to have higher casualties and to be more aggressive. Neither centralized organization nor military efficiency seems to preclude attack by others. This apparently indicates that carrying a "big stick" is not always a deterrent.

Otterbein concludes that political organization and war-making potential, in a process of mutual reinforcement, affect the develop-

6. E. E. Evans-Pritchard, *The Nuer* (Oxford: Clarendon Press, 1940); Max Gluckman, "The Peace in the Feud," in Max Gluckman, *Custom and Conflict in Africa* (Glencoe, Ill.: Free Press, 1955), pp. 1–26.
7. The more recent are William T. Divale, "Migration, External Warfare, and Matrilocal Residence," *Behavior Science Research* 9:2 (1974):73–134; and Stanton K. Tefft and Douglas Reinhardt, "Warfare Regulation: A Cross-Cultural Test of Hypotheses Among Tribal Peoples," *Behavior Science Research* 9:2 (1974):151–72.
8. Keith F. Otterbein, *The Evolution of War: A Cross-Cultural Study* (New Haven: HRAF Press, 1970).

ment of traditional societies. Centralized authority tends to correlate with military efficiency and professionalization. Since in a competitive situation the fittest society survives and military success determines fitness, there is a tendency among traditional societies toward centralization which produces military efficiency.

■

The intracultural approach focuses on the problem of war as a concomitant of confrontation between cultures and of rapid cultural transformation.

One such situation—perhaps the most prevalent and significant —is the collision between modern and traditional societies in the Third World. Eric R. Wolf sees the revolutions of Mexico, Russia, China, Vietnam, Algeria, and Cuba as conflicts between two fundamentally different systems, peasant society and what he calls North Atlantic capitalism.[9] In a peasant society, labor is tied to kinship and moral obligations; it can be borrowed but is seldom sold. Goods often have important social values beyond their economic price and economic activity reinforces the sense of community. Market time provides a chance to gossip. Land has high mystical significance, being involved with religious values and kinship. By contrast, the North Atlantic capitalistic system converts labor and land into commodities and economic activity becomes an end in itself, ideally without emotional overtone or significance. Wolf contends that the market economy and mentality constitute a severe threat to peasant culture.

Peasant culture is further threatened from within. It is frequently dominated by traditional elements which have usurped power—the landlord, mandarin, or tribal chief. At the same time the rapid rise of peasant populations during the last century has increased pressure on resources and traditional social structures. The peasant is consequently caught between local economic pressures and exploiters and the distant threat of modern capitalism.

The result is frequently peasant violence. By attacking his local enemy, the landlord, the peasant ignites rebellion (which Wolf defines as an attempt to change the leadership of a society) while leaving the system unchanged. This rebellion is, however, converted by intellectuals, government officials, and others into a revolution, i.e., a fundamental change in the political and social structure. The peasant thereby loses precisely the traditional society he rebelled to preserve and falls increasingly within the orbit and control of North Atlantic capitalism.

---

9. Eric R. Wolf, *Peasant Wars of the Twentieth Century* (New York: Harper & Row, 1969).

■

Each of the anthropological approaches to the study of war—the social, the cross-cultural, and the intracultural—offers a distinctive perspective on the phenomenon. Although they differ in specific method and focus, all are concerned with warfare in its broadest sense and assume that war is best examined in a multicultural context. Anthropological interpretations of war suggest that understanding can be gained only through the recognition and elimination, insofar as is possible, of cultural biases.

# Dimensions for Comparing Military Organizations

## Pierre L. Van den Berghe

War is defined in sociological terms as international conflict, that is, organized violence between groups that regard themselves as foreign, either culturally or politically or both, and thus as either *ethnic groups* or *states*. These two terms are not synonymous. Most states are not nation-states but multinational states; a large number of nations or ethnic groups are not organized in politically centralized systems. A great many traditional African societies, for example, are not politically centralized, do not have states, and yet they engage in warfare. Those societies are usually called acephalous; they are in fact polycephalous, i.e., their authority is diffuse and usually vested in the older age groups. Those societies are typically democratic (for adult men) and bellicose at the same time. War, then, can occur either between states as we conventionally define them (i.e., organizations in which political power is centralized in holders of political office) or between societies that are acephalous or stateless.

A comparison of military organizations in different societies requires the definition of important analytical dimensions. A thorough study of the problem would involve a large number of categories but the most important are ritualization, professionalization, and objectives.

One of the central questions in understanding war is the degree to which it is ritualized. Strictly speaking, there has never been a total war, in the sense that belligerents inflicted maximum destruction. During World War II, at least some rules—the Geneva Convention, for example—were observed. In the Pacific theater of operations, however, fewer rules obtained. Nonetheless, all wars are limited to some extent by ritual.

There are forms of warfare, similar to an American football game, in which the whole procedure is designed to minimize destruction and casualties. Many stateless societies are organized as perpetual war machines with universal military service for all younger men, who are expected to go on raids and military expeditions more or less continuously. There are, however, definite rules as to who may or may not be killed. In this type of highly ritualized warfare, casualties are low and the object is to capture cattle and women.

In medieval Europe, the Truce of God prohibited fighting on religious holidays, and ceremonials associated with warfare arose. The aristocrats, the specialists in violence, developed a code of chivalry which essentially ritualized warfare and minimized casualties.

■

Professionalization of warfare is another critical dimension. The operative question is the extent to which being a warrior is a specialized, full-time occupation, a part-time unspecialized occupation, or a full-time unspecialized occupation. In some societies, such as the so-called primitive societies that engage in endemic warfare, every able-bodied man is equally available for warfare, since soldiering is not an occupation which demands special training. These societies have citizen armies similar to the Western type introduced by the French Revolution. These armies are not a new phenomenon; they were used by many societies for thousands of years.

In other societies, the highly centralized states, warfare is a specialty of a small minority of the male population. One of the key dimensions Stanislav Andreski deals with in differentiating among societies is what he calls the *military participation ratio*,[1] i.e., the ratio of warriors to the total population of male adults. Andreski concludes that a high proportion of adult men engaging in warfare indicates a more democratic society. This conclusion is disturbing to many Americans because of their facile assumption that democracy makes for peace and that the more peaceful societies tend to be more democratic. It was, however, no accident that the Second Amendment to the U.S. Constitution accorded citizens the right to bear arms. In the eighteenth century, it was evident that one of the basic conditions for democracy was a widely armed citizenry. In an un-

1. See Stanislav Andreski, *Military Organization and Society* (Berkeley: University of California Press, 1968).

armed society a small group of military specialists could be used by a despotic state to oppress the masses.

In societies in which warfare is a specialty, war is either an aristocratic monopoly or a low-status, mercenary occupation. These two types occur in very different political organizations. War as an aristocratic monopoly was best typified in medieval Europe and medieval Japan, where waging war was a caste or quasi-caste occupation which was hereditary and required training for a decade or more, as well as expensive equipment. In medieval Europe, the cost and availability of horse and armor made war an aristocratic prerogative. This type of military organization was accompanied by a fairly decentralized "feudal" political system. The inalienable and hereditary share of the means of violence allowed every noble to maintain a certain degree of independence from the central authority.

Soldiering as a low-status, mercenary occupation was typical of highly centralized despotic states, e.g., most of the large-scale agrarian empires. The surest way to establish a strong central government is to transfer the means of violence from an aristocracy to persons, preferably foreigners, who have no stake or status in the society. These low-status mercenaries were used to maintain domination over the masses and the nobility, when there was a nobility. Mercenary armies became prominent in the fifteenth century. The emergence of Switzerland as a democratic state was perhaps a product of economic conditions: poverty discouraged invaders and at the same time encouraged its inhabitants to become mercenary soldiers. In the Ottoman Empire, mercenary and slave armies were prevalent. Despots exploited the power of these tools as a means of external aggression and internal repression.

■

The third major comparative dimension of military organizations is the aim of war. War objectives fell broadly into three main types: some wars are fought to gain livestock, women, slaves, or a combination of these; others are fought to gain and keep new territory; still others seek to gain, control, and exploit new territory and populations.

Raiding wars typically are highly ritualized; their object is to steal livestock and people, especially women. Capturing women is one way for an ethnic group to increase its size geometrically. The population of the Zulu kingdom in southern Africa, for example, increased from approximately 50,000 in about 1800 to something like half a million by 1828. This tenfold increase in one generation was achieved by getting women from other groups and instituting a system of polygamy like that which prevailed in most African societies. The seizure of cattle is important when the bridewealth system requires payment in head of cattle. Raiding also seeks slaves and in a few cases it is done for purposes of ritual cannibalism.

Wars of conquest that stress individual courage and acts of military expertise are often highly ritualized. In some instances (described in the Bible and elsewhere), mass slaughter was avoided by having opposing armies designate as combatants a champion or ten of their best warriors. The less ritualized wars of conquest emphasize the seizure and the exploitation of territorial resources. These wars tend to be genocidal and are typical of frontier situations. In the nineteenth century, the object of the American frontiersman was not to enslave or exploit but to exterminate the intractable Indian and expropriate his land. This type of war has also occurred in parts of South Africa and Australia, and to a lesser extent in New Zealand and Brazil as a feature of territorial expansion.

In most cases, however, wars of conquest seek to conquer territory and also to exploit populations. Genocide "pays" only when a population is too thinly spread, too refractory for servile labor, and too susceptible to diseases imported by the conquerors. The choice between territory and exploitation of population is usually determined by the conquered people's level of social organization. Agricultural populations have been almost invariably conquered and exploited, whereas nomads usually were conquered and exterminated. Agricultural populations defeated in war were in many cases part of a stratified society already exploited by an indigenous ruling class; military conquest in those cases merely substitutes one ruling class for another. Since most of the world in the last few centuries has been inhabited by agriculturalists, recent wars of conquest have usually emphasized the exploitation of population rather than the conquest of territory. As a consequence, many states in existence today are conquest empires in which one ethnic group imposed its political domination on others and exploited the conquered indigenous population. The Soviet Union, for example, is a successor state to the Czarist Russian conquest empire.

There are two basic formulas for conquering territory so as to exploit its population. One is assimilation, in which conquered populations are absorbed culturally into the dominant group and forced to use its language, customs, etc. Such assimilation is often conceived as benevolent but can be quite brutal in practice, as demonstrated by the conversion to Christianity in the Portuguese and Spanish empires and by the conversion to Islam during the eighth century in North Africa. An alternative to assimilation is what Lord Lugard, the British governor of Nigeria, called indirect rule. This ancient and probably cheapest way to organize conquered territory consists in control through an indigenous ruling class, which is deprived of real power but maintains its privileges. This method was used by the British in India and Nigeria.

Finally, it is important to distinguish between military organization and technology, two separate but related dimensions. Military technology clearly effects military organization and vice versa. For instance, the change from medieval aristocratic armies to the Renaissance mercenary armies was largely a product of the development of firearms. Firearms made armor obsolete and metallurgical technology resulted in the development of cheap and more efficient means of destruction. The aristocracy's monopoly over the tools of war was thereby shattered.

Forms of warfare are linked to social structure and particularly to military organization. As the social structure varies, so also does the nature of war. Only in a comparative approach to these variations is it possible to understand war as a broad human phenomenon rather than a narrowly defined feature of specific cultures.

# Wars and the Great Power System

## George Modelski

The conventional concept of war assumes that the basic unit is the state or nation-state. This conception obscures more than it clarifies; a more enlightening analysis might begin with the premise that war is engaged in most of all by the Great Powers.

War is obviously a sport of the Great Powers, but the implications of that observation have not been thoroughly explored. Wright surveyed the wars of the past five centuries and concluded that "clearly the Great Powers have been the most frequent fighters." France participated in 47 percent of the 2,600 most important battles involving the European states; Austria-Hungary fought in 34 percent of these battles; and Great Britain and Russia each in about 22 percent.[1] The Small-Singer listing of international wars between 1816 and 1965 is indicative of the same conclusion: the "major powers were the most war-prone . . . no major powers were able to escape this scourge . . ."; among the smaller powers, on the other hand, "more than half the nations (77 out of 144) which were at one time or another members of the system were able to escape international war entirely." Of twenty-five international wars since 1914, the

This essay is based on the author's *Principles of World Politics* (New York: Free Press, 1972), Chapter 14, and "Wars and the Great Powers," *Papers, Peace Research Society (International)* 18 (1972).
1. Quincy Wright, *A Study of War* (Chicago: University of Chicago Press, 1942), pp. 220–21.

■

Great Powers actively participated in at least nineteen.[2] A survey of all armed conflicts of some magnitude from 1945 to 1970 (see Table 3) reveals only a few incidents in which there was no military participation by the Great Powers.

In other words, empirical evidence suggests that Great Power participation in recent wars has approached a rate of 80 percent. This participation is not merely a contemporary development, nor is it peculiar to some Great Powers. Rather, it is a long-range phenomenon which must therefore be associated with the Great Power system itself. This conclusion is hardly surprising, since the Great Powers have commanded most of the world's military power in recent times. In this century the Great Powers as a group regularly accounted for between 75 and 90 percent of the total world armament expenditures and for most of the usable and mobile military force. Between 1945 and 1970, the defense expenditures of the United States and the Soviet Union alone never amounted to less than 65 percent of the world total and in 1953 reached 75 percent.[3] It is therefore to be expected that they would also be the major users of that power and that their involvement in armed conflict would be roughly proportionate to their share of world military expenditures.

If war is primarily a Great Power activity, then the basic concept of war needs to be recast. War can no longer be regarded as a form of activity normally distributed over the entire population of members of the international system. Rather it is a form of behavior peculiarly characteristic of states occupying the position of Great Powers. Hence the actors in war are the Great Powers (and those aspiring to that rank, because it is by war that such rank is established).

This proposition is of some consequence in thinking about the control of war. Altogether too much of conventional analysis proceeds from the assumption that units of war are states or nation-states and that the control of war requires the control, limitation, or even "abolition" of states. A closer analysis suggests that since Great Power dominance is a governing characteristic of the nation-state system and makes it liable to wars, the reduction of that dominance would alter this propensity. Constructive thinking about the control of war thus involves conceiving of the world as capable of being organized without the Great Power System.

---

2. Melvin Small and J. David Singer, "Patterns in International Warfare 1816–1965," *Annals of the American Academy of Political and Social Science* 391 (Spring 1970): 151–52, 149. In "Capability Distribution, Uncertainty and Major Power War 1816–1965" (in B. Russett, ed., *Peace, War, and Numbers* [Beverly Hills, Ca.: Sage, 1972], pp. 19–48), Singer, Bremer, and Stukey view the powers as comprising a separate subsystem.
3. George Modelski, *World Power Concentrations: Typology, Data, Explanatory Framework* (Morristown, N.J.: General Learning Press, 1974), p. 10.

■

In modern history the major powers have functioned as part of a well-understood European system of balance of power.[4] They comprised a close network, initially of the European monarchies of the first rank and, more recently, of the governments of the great national states. At first their cohesion rested largely on family solidarity but diplomacy, as the web of official representation among sovereigns, soon assumed major functions of communication and evaluation. Diplomacy remains a major element of the global political network which constitutes the Great Power system. This has also been the system which, if the world is ruled at all, has come nearest to doing just that.

The relationship between war as principally and primarily a Great Power activity and the Great Power system is circular. Not only does war occur because there are Great Powers (Great Powers "cause" war) but, as important, the Great Power system exists because there is war (war "causes" the Great Powers). War justifies and legitimizes the international status system at the summit of which are the Great Powers; that status system in turn validates war as the means of its preservation. It is not status inconsistency which explains war but rather the strains which a particular status system, one based upon war-making achievement, imposes upon the world at large. Global war may therefore be seen as a disorder, consequent upon the Great Power political system.

World diplomacy itself is, in the main, the instrument of the Great Power system; Great Power capitals are its principal nodes and Great Power diplomatic services its mainstays and workhorses (employing about one-quarter of the world's diplomats). This diplomacy is geared to processing only a limited range of information and functions poorly as an information collector on global problems; it is also weak in judgmental matters and too loosely structured to achieve compliance with global norms. Diplomacy, furthermore, is not a truly autonomous global network but is "fused" strongly with national networks. Hence disorders generated in national networks easily translate into global malfunctions and vice versa. But diplomacy is no more than an instrument. More fundamentally, therefore, war-proneness may be associated with structural deficiencies of the

---

4. As an explicit political institution, the Great Power system dates only from 1815, but the earlier rise of the major military states coincided with the growth of the European system. The rules of the system were made explicit at the Congress of Vienna and have since been adhered to with a good degree of consistency. The prominent features of the institution are summit meetings, major peace settlements, and the governing arrangements of international organizations.

Great Powers as a system of global authority. Several such deficiencies may be mentioned: (1) crisis orientation, hence an inbuilt tendency to resort to short-term solutions and the "need" for crises as opportunities for exercising authority; (2) intermittency or lack of continuity in the exercise of global functions (in part the result of crisis orientation); (3) nonrepresentativeness, hence an inability to relate its functioning to all the interests that need to be taken into consideration; (4) lack of resources for dealing with problems susceptible to other than military solutions.

The Great Powers form an exceedingly "simple" structure wherein the bulk of world authority is concentrated in a very few exceedingly powerful organizations. A complex society, on the other hand, requires a greater number and variety of global organizations in judicious combination with an intricate web of autonomous social networks. The Great Power system obstructs the growth of new global networks and organizations; so world society is deficient in such global structures. War itself is a destroyer of networks for the benefit of organizations and the organizations benefiting most from it are those of the Great Power system.

Power concentration may therefore be seen as the fundamental reason why a system based on Great Powers cannot remain stable; instability, in turn, is likely to take the form of war. That is not to say that the consequences of this system are all negative; the Great Powers give the world a framework of minimum order, especially at times of war-induced chaos. But they fall short of the requirements for a modern system of world politics.

■

Global war,[5] the principal disturbance of the Great Power system, might be defined as an armed conflict concerning the constitution, that is, the identity, the structure, and arrangements of order and justice, of the global political system. Both the motives of the participants and the effects of the process define the conflict as global.

Global war might also be expected to occur with particular intensity within, and in relation to, global networks. In this sense, too, it might be considered a disturbance of these networks. Indeed, a global war need not be regarded as one into which the entire world is equally drawn. Rather it might concern only those directly involved in various global networks. Important global wars, such as those of the English and the Dutch against Spain during the sixteenth and seventeenth centuries, occurred primarily on the world's oceans and concerned the control of sea lanes; in the short run, directly

---

5. The concept of global war is a development of a paradigm of global (or "geocentric") politics.

affected only a small part of the world's peoples; and had limited effect on territorial arrangements anywhere.[6] No world war has been fought uniformly over the whole of the globe and over all networks. Wars of global significance involve large resources and tend to "fuse" other networks and commonly spread beyond their "proper" limits. For the future it might, however, be important to remember that a global war could conceivably destroy the Great Powers without necessarily affecting the rest of the world.

If a conflict can be defined as global when its primary location is a global network, the temporal domain of global wars obviously begins with the establishment of a worldwide political system. This was brought into being as the result of the Age of European Discoveries in the fifteenth and sixteenth centuries. The Spanish conquests in the Americas and Portuguese penetration of the Indian Ocean inaugurated an age of sea power, and global wars have since been linked with oceanic ventures. Only since the mid-twentieth century has air and missile technology altered this perspective and thereby changed the character of global warfare.

Table 1, a tentative list of wars that qualify as global, deserves close study because it presents a large portion of the entire empirical domain of a crucial political phenomenon. This relatively short list might well be more important than longer lists of less homogeneous events. It is a way of dealing with the problem of the uniqueness of the great wars of the twentieth century which cannot be dismissed as statistical "outliers" or exceptions in an otherwise normal distribution of wars in the nineteenth and twentieth centuries.

The criterion for inclusion in this list is significance for the constitution of the global system. Conceptually this makes global war a subset of a more inclusive set of global political conflicts, in addition to being a subset of the larger set of wars of all kinds. In practical terms, however, the difficulty of choosing satisfactory empirical indicators is considerable. Since conflicts as a rule have far-reaching repercussions, the criteria for determining the globality of a conflict or war are rather soft. Global conflict concerns the distribution of world authority and who gets what and how in the global system; it involves disputes over the resolution of global problems such as authority, access to wealth, control of trade, or political status.

A global war would be labeled as such if hostilities occur over wide areas or intercontinental distances; if they concern military forces; and if they are network phenomena, implicating and involving a substantial part of global networks. Global wars are not necessarily the largest wars but they might be.

---

6. Wright, *A Study of War*, p. 223, also observes that the major battles of the European state system have tended to concentrate in highway areas between regions otherwise separated by natural barriers—Flanders, the Po valley, and Egypt.

Empirically global wars might be identified by an analysis of the peace settlements which followed them. They could be regarded as global if they disposed of global matters, e.g., if they involved territorial settlements on at least two continents, settled matters of universal significance (for instance, the legality of the slave trade), or founded or altered global political institutions (such as the League of Nations). Wars can be classified as global if the participants include all of the Great Powers, for it is reasonable to suppose that such wars would raise basic constitutional issues. Most of the wars in Table 1 belong in this latter category.

TABLE 1
GLOBAL WARS

| Dates | War | Major Participants | Outcome |
| --- | --- | --- | --- |
| 1566–1569 | Wars of Dutch Independence | Netherlands, Spain, Portugal | Spanish-Hapsburg world position checked; Asian spice trade seized by Dutch |
| 1585–1604 | War of the Armada | Spain, England, France | Spanish monopoly of the New World challenged |
| 1652–1655 1665–1667 1672–1674 | Anglo-Dutch wars | England, Netherlands | Dutch world position challenged |
| 1683–1714 | Wars of Louis XIV | France, Austria, Spain, Netherlands, Portugal, England | Louis's attack on the Netherlands fails; England assumes world position; Spanish succession regulated |
| 1756–1763 | Seven Years' War | France, Britain, Austria, Prussia, Russia, Spain | France loses colonial empire in India and America |
| 1775–1783 | American Revolution | Britain, France, Spain, Netherlands, United States | Britain checked |
| 1792–1815 | Revolutionary and Napoleonic wars | France, Austria, Prussia, Britain, Russia, Spain, United States | Britain's global role reaffirmed; diplomatic system regulated |
| 1853–1855 | Crimean War | Britain, France, Russia | Russia checked in Near East |
| 1914–1918 | World War I | Britain, Germany, Russia, France, Japan, United States | German challenge fails; League of Nations founded |
| 1939–1945 | World War II | Britain, Germany, France, U.S.S.R., Japan, United States | United States succeeds to Britain's role; United Nations founded |

Global wars presuppose a global political system. The construction of such a system was set in motion by Spanish conquests in the Americas and by Portuguese successes in establishing naval control in the Indian Ocean. These campaigns (1509–1512) laid the foundations for a global system comprised of a network of maritime communications. The nodal points of this network were numerous Portuguese and Spanish forts linked by regular ship convoys. The system became further integrated between 1580 and 1640, when Spain and Portugal were united under one ruling house. Yet the establishment of this global framework did little to disturb the empires of Asia.

Within a century the claim of the Catholic monarchies to world rule was decisively challenged, most effectively by Protestant rebels in the Netherlands and by English maritime enterprise. "Since the Iberian possessions were scattered around the world," remarks a recent historian of the Portuguese empire referring to the war with the Dutch, "the ensuing struggle was waged on four continents and on seven seas; and this seventeenth century contest deserves to be called the First World War rather than the holocaust of 1914–18 which is commonly awarded that dubious honour."[7] The Dutch and the English East Indies companies broke the Portuguese trade monopoly from the East and the Dutch West Indies Company challenged Spanish and Portuguese possessions in the Western Hemisphere. Spain and Portugal retained most of their territorial holdings but lost their claims to all unsettled portions of the New World. Above all, the vitality of their communications system was lost and it was eventually replaced by superior Dutch, English, and French efforts. Amsterdam was the economic capital of the world in the seventeenth century but by the early eighteenth century the hub of the new global network moved to London. By that time the Netherlands and Portugal were dependent on Britain, which thus indirectly inherited the bulk of the Iberian world empire. When the French colonial empire was dismantled after the Seven Years' War and Spanish rule in Latin America ended following the Napoleonic wars, Britain was without a rival in most of the world during the nineteenth century.

All this time Europe was the core of the new global system but in a wider perspective its affairs held no more than regional significance. Europe might well have been dominated by one great conqueror who would have introduced the question of arranging world authority. But that eventuality was avoided through a series of balance of power wars and the purely intra-European conflicts were allowed to run their course. All global wars since Louis XIV have

7. C. R. Boxer, *The Portuguese Seaborne Empire 1450–1825* (New York: Knopf, 1969), p. 106.

either consolidated or threatened the world structure established following the defeat of the Iberian empires. The only exception in the course of three centuries was the American Revolution, which severed parts of North America from the London network. Even this setback was remedied when the United States rejoined that system of authority in the two world wars of the twentieth century.

Modern global wars have progressively introduced more severe disturbances of the political and social constitution which has held the international system together for the past three centuries. This constitution nourished and advanced the commercial and industrial revolutions, withstood severe challenges, and now takes the form of a nation-state system governed by a Great Power network. It has, however, proved resistant to change and generated increasingly severe strains, of which the two world wars of the twentieth century are the most obvious examples.

■

Global wars have been characteristically severe involving approximately two-thirds of all the battles fought during the past four centuries by European states (see Table 1). The first peak of severity was associated with the establishment of the system of major military states in the seventeenth and eighteenth centuries. The two great wars of the twentieth century greatly exceeded those levels and compiled new records of intensity and increased numbers of casualties. The number of war dead, the number of important battles fought, and Sorokin's index of war intensity, suggest that the severity of major contemporary conflict has reached unprecedented levels.[8]

Lewis Richardson has shown that for the entire period 1820–1945, the two world wars have caused by far the most significant loss

TABLE 2

CONFLICT FATALITIES 1820–1945

| Conflict Magnitude[a] | Total number of deaths (millions) | Percentage |
|---|---|---|
| $7 \pm \frac{1}{2}$ (two world wars) | 36 | 61 |
| $6 \pm \frac{1}{2} - 1 \pm \frac{1}{2}$ | 13.75 | 23 |
| $0 + \frac{1}{2}$ (murders) | 9.7 | 16 |
| | 59 | |

[a] The logarithm to the base of ten of the number of people who died because of the conflict. Magnitude $0 + \frac{1}{2}$ involves one to three deaths.
SOURCE: Adapted from Lewis Richardson, *Statistics of Deadly Quarrels* (Pittsburgh: Boxwood Press, 1960), p. 153.

8. Wright, *A Study of War,* pp. 651, 655, 656.

of life due to "deadly quarrels." Richardson's data suggest a scale for evaluating the importance of global wars relative to other wars and social conflicts. The two world wars clearly emerge as *sui generis,* and therefore need to be compared primarily with other past and hypothetical global wars, rather than with recent national and subnational conflicts.

If the magnitude of war measured in terms of fatal casualties is an adequate indicator of social cost, then Richardson also provides a scale of priorities for research on conflicts. The global war is the most critical type of conflict and it therefore deserves the highest research priority since it could result in annihilation if the trend toward increasing severity continues. Murder and related forms of personal and local conflict, for which remedies are commonly assumed to be personal counseling, police work, and community development are next in importance.[9] The in-between forms of armed conflict—including national, civil, international, and subnational conflicts—appear to assume lesser priority and deserve possibly only residual attention. Many of them are, in fact, no more than spillovers from the Great Power conflict system.

The disproportionate distribution of social costs among these several types of conflict may also indicate flaws in world organization. At the risk of overgeneralizing, it might be argued that the world functions worst at the global level, better but less than adequately at local levels, and best at an intermediate level of national organization. Alternatively, it may be said that the national level of organization displaces violence at the global and local levels. In view of the risks inherent in global conflict and the disorganization of personal identity inherent in local disorder, such a tendency bodes ill for world stability.

■

Table 3 presents a list of all known armed conflicts in the years 1946–1970 of magnitude 3 and above (that is, of more than approximately 1,000 conflict-related deaths), involving at least two relatively organized parties. It excludes spontaneous riots and anomic violence (for lack of organization), mass purges and governmental terror (one-sided organization) and natural disasters.

9. Murder might be regarded as a disorder of certain personal networks, particularly ". . . those that include intimate, close, frequent contacts. Close friends and relatives alone account for more than half of those that involve male offenders and much more than half of those that involve female offenders." Marvin Wolfgang, "Crime: Homicide," *International Encyclopedia of Social Sciences,* 3:492. A subculture of violence has been suggested as an explanation for homicide frequency. War might be a result of another possibly related subculture of violence.

## TABLE 3
## WARS 1946–1970

| Dates | National Wars | Magni-tude | Great Powers | U.N. |
|---|---|---|---|---|
| | | | Participation | |
| 1946–1949 | Greek Civil War | 5 | X | X |
| 1946 | Bolivia | 3 | | |
| 1946–1949 | Chinese Civil War | 6 | X | |
| 1947–1948 | Kashmir | 3 | X | |
| 1947 | Paraguay | 3 | | |
| 1948–1949 | Israel I | 4 | X | X |
| 1948–1952 | Philippines (Huks) | 3 | X | |
| 1948–1964 | Colombia | 6 | | |
| 1950–1953 | Korea | 6 | X | X |
| 1952 | Bolivia | 3 | | |
| 1954–1958 | China (Quemoy) | 3 | X | |
| 1956 | Sinai and Suez | 3 | X | X |
| 1956–1959 | Cuba (Castro) | 3 | | |
| 1956 | Hungary | 4 | X | |
| 1957–1961 | Indonesia | 4 | X | |
| 1958 | Lebanon Civil War | 3 | X | X |
| 1959–1962 | Laos | 4 | X | X |
| 1960–1965 | Congo | 5 | X | X |
| 1961–1962 | Nepal Civil War | 3 | | |
| 1961 | Cuba (Bay of Pigs) | 3 | X | |
| 1961 | Tunis | 3 | X | |
| 1961– | Vietnam | 6 | X | |
| 1962–1970 | Yemen Civil War | 5 | X | X |
| 1962 | Burundi | 3 | | |
| 1962 | India-China Border | 4 | X | |
| 1962– | Guatemala | 4 | X | |
| 1963– | Guinea-Bissau | 4 | X | |
| 1963–1964 | Cyprus | 3 | X | X |
| 1964–1967 | Malaysian confrontation | 3 | X | |
| 1964– | Laos | 5 | X | |
| 1964 | Zanzibar | 3 | | |
| 1965 | Dominican Republic | 4 | X | |
| 1965 | India-Pakistan | 4 | | |
| 1965 | Burundi | 4 | X | |
| 1965–1966 | Indonesia | 5 | | |
| 1967– | Philippines | 3 | X | |
| 1967– | Thailand | 3 | X | |
| 1967 | Israel (Six Days) | 4 | X | X |
| 1969 | El Salvador-Honduras | | | |
| 1969 | China-USSR Border | 3 | X | |
| 1969–1970 | Suez fighting | 4 | X | |
| 1970– | Cambodia | 4 | X | |
| 1970 | Jordan | 4 | | |

| Dates | Subnational and Local Wars | Magni-tude | Participation Great Powers | U.N. |
|-------|----------------------------|------------|---------------------------|------|
| 1945–1949 | Indonesia | 4 | X | X |
| 1945–1954 | Indochina | 5 | X | |
| 1947 | Taiwan | | | |
| 1947 | Hyderabad | 3 | | |
| 1947 | Madagascar | 3 | X | |
| 1947–1952 | Malayan emergency | 3 | X | |
| 1948– | Burma | 4 | | |
| 1952 | Tunis | 3 | X | |
| 1952–1954 | Kenya (Mau Mau) | 4 | X | |
| 1954–1962 | Algeria | 5 | X | |
| 1954–1964 | Nagas | 3 | X | |
| 1956–1961 | Cameroons | 3 | X | |
| 1956–1959 | Cyprus | 3 | X | |
| 1959 | Ruanda-Urundi | 5 | | |
| 1959 | Tibet | 4 | X | |
| 1961–1970 | Kurds | 4 | | |
| 1962– | Angola | 4 | | |
| 1963–1967 | Aden | 3 | X | |
| 1963– | Sudan | 4 | X | |
| 1965 | Mozambique | 3 | | |
| 1965– | Eritrea | 3 | X | |
| 1967– | Chad | 3 | X | |
| 1967–1970 | Biafra | 5 | X | |

These conflicts, however, are not global wars. Of the sixty-six conflicts shown, only four come close to the conventional concept of war between two equally recognized sovereign states: the India-Pakistan war of 1965, the El Salvador-Honduras war (of all things!), and China's border clashes with India and the Soviet Union. More often than not, conflict is associated with conditions of cloudy legitimacy, absence of firm jurisdictions and withheld or incomplete recognition, even lack of clear political identity. The four Middle Eastern wars involving Israel, the Malaysian confrontation, the Hungarian revolt, even Korea and Vietnam are marginal and uncertain cases. They involved governments of various degrees of recognition and standing but it is not helpful to assimilate these clashes into the nineteenth-century concept of war. The decline in classical forms of war can be explained in terms of declining legitimacy (illegality under the United Nations Charter); a declining use of the earlier formalities of war (declarations of war, peace treaties, neutrality proclamations); and global politics in which war has important consequences for the role, status, and contemporary relevance of national military forces.

It may therefore be more useful to consider the concepts of

national and subnational wars. National wars are armed conflicts involving the constitution of a national political system. Such conflicts are confined to the network they concern and minimal harm to surrounding societies results. Civil wars such as the Greek conflict at the end of World War II and the Dominican turmoil are clear examples of national wars. Conflicts between divided states such as Korea and Vietnam, the conflict between India and Pakistan stemming from the Partition of 1947, and the Middle Eastern wars fit this classification since they concern the establishment, identity, and political functions of individual national states. Two-thirds of the armed conflicts since 1945 can be categorized as national wars.

Subnational and local armed conflicts arise when subsections of larger political structures find parts of their constitution unsatisfactory. Subnational conflicts which involve war usually concern a degree of autonomy which demands independence or "separatism," that is, the separation of a partial network from its links with a national network. The twenty-three wars classified as subnational include fourteen colonial wars which almost without exception ended in national independence due to a value system in world politics which discouraged the continuance of colonial empires. At least seven others were wars of separatism involving local autonomy in recently established nation-states (including Burma, Tibet, Kurdistan, Biafra, Southern Sudan, Nagaland). In a basic sense, subnational wars are also disturbances of the nation-state system which concern only a localized portion of national arenas and seek to alter the constitutional position of only a part of the society.

National and subnational wars frequently involve the Great Powers and other forms of international authority. The Great Powers have militarily participated, i.e., provided combat troops or military advisors, air, naval, and logistic support, arms and technical aid) in forty-eight of sixty-six wars, that is, in about two-thirds of the cases. In eleven cases there has been a substantial United Nations commitment on the ground, including peace keeping and observer missions. If symbolic involvement were considered, the proportions would be even higher for both types of action. There is, however, no cause to believe that Great Power intervention for the period 1945–1970 was at a higher level than in the preceding quarter-century.[10] It is therefore apparent that the Great Power system, on account of its "fused" character, may be causing disturbances not only at the global but also at the national and subnational levels.

---

10. According to Richardson's data (*Statistics of Deadly Quarrels,* Chapter 2), of the 22 armed conflicts of magnitudes 4, 5, 6, and 7 begun between 1919 and 1944, 16 attracted and involved the Great Powers, as compared with 27 out of 36 conflicts (over the same range of magnitude) in the more recent period.

■

War has been, and still is, preeminently a Great Power activity and hence a product of Great Power dominance in global wars and in the majority of national and subnational armed conflicts of the past few decades. It follows that the limitation of war will require control of Great Power activity and the construction of alternative political managements.

Global war constitutes a separate class of armed conflict that demands both empirical and theoretical investigation when viewed as a species of conflict about global political issues. The real question is how to avoid global conflict and how to pursue its fundamental issues in another manner or medium. The Great Powers play a crucial, though not exclusive, part in the arenas in which global issues are fought and their responsibility for the strategic nuclear forces gives them the capacity to fight global war. A revised concept of war might produce a differentiation of world military forces that would confine the use of strategic forces to global conflicts and keep them functionally separate from national-level military establishments.

National wars are numerically significant but they are qualitatively a less important factor in world conflict. They indicate a malfunction of the nation-state system, especially in the Third World, but existing states are more than strong enough to cope with them. Great Power involvement in national wars may be a form of malfunction of the global system; hence limitation of national wars also requires control of Great Power activity.

Local war has been a form of separatist activity resulting in national independence from colonial rule in an appreciable number of cases. It has, however, failed in attempts to shake even newly established nation-states. Its relative frequency suggests the need to recognize more widely the importance of local autonomy and the negative consequences of monopolizing power at the national level.

Through a process of disaggregation, several types of war have been identified and related to a separate arena of political conflict. The control and limitation of each type of conflict depends on the nature of the arena in question and on the degree to which these action settings can be separated. Great Power dominance unfortunately acts to fuse these arenas. Reduction of conflict consequently requires limitation of Great Power dominance and, ideally, dismantling the Great Power system.

# Self-Esteem, Competence, and Violence: Psychological Aspects of the Kent State Killings

## Ezra Stotland

This paper is an attempt to explain some of the psychological forces which led Ohio State National Guardsmen to fire at students and kill four of them at Kent State University on May 4, 1970. The objective is not to fix moral or legal blame—however important that is—but to provide a basis for preventing the recurrence of such tragedies.

On Friday afternoon, May 1, 1970, there was a peaceful protest at Kent State against the just-announced invasion of Cambodia.[1] Later that evening, students in taverns near campus started chanting antiwar slogans and then, apparently without police interference, began throwing beer bottles, lit a bonfire, and broke windows. After an hour or two, the police closed the taverns and fired tear gas; a state of emergency and a curfew were declared.

The next day, the mayor of Kent asked Governor Rhodes to send the National Guard to Kent, partly because it was rumored that

The author is indebted to Professor Jerry Lewis of Kent State University and to James Martinez of Evergreen State College for their invaluable help.

1. The analysis is based on the following reports: Joe Eszterhas and Michael D. Roberts, *Thirteen Seconds: Confrontation at Kent State* (New York: Dodd, Mead, 1970); James A. Michener, *Kent State: What Happened and Why* (Greenwich, Conn.: Fawcett, 1971); President's Commission on Campus Unrest, *Report* [Scranton Commission Report] (Washington, D.C., 1970); I. F. Stone, *The Killings at Kent State: How Murder Went Unreported* (New York: New York Review, 1970); Peter Davies, *Truth About Kent State* (New York: Farrar, Straus & Giroux, 1973). There is substantial agreement among these sources about the main outlines of what happened, and this analysis is based primarily on those areas of agreement. The Stone volume contains the FBI report.

■

further violence was planned by students. A mob of students meanwhile set fire to the ROTC building and hampered firemen in their efforts to put it out. When Guardsmen arrived that evening, they cleared the campus but could not save the ROTC building.

On Sunday, Guardsmen were posted all over campus. The governor made a statement attacking student and nonstudent agitators as being responsible for the violence. That evening, another group of demonstrators staged a sit-down on a street adjoining the campus but were dispersed by Guardsmen with tear gas after a series of "negotiations."

An antiwar rally was scheduled for Monday at noon in the center of campus. Despite university and Guard attempts to forbid the rally, the students assembled. They were apparently motivated by a number of considerations, including opposition to the war and to the presence of the Guard, defiance, and curiosity; some were just walking between buildings or on lunch break. The students responded to orders to disperse by throwing a few stones and many insults.

The National Guardsmen, having hurled tear gas canisters at the students to no avail, formed a skirmish line and began to advance across campus toward the students, who fell back and to the sides. The Guard advanced up a knoll and, after seeing that the students had retreated but not dispersed, proceeded down the far side into the middle of a football practice field with high cyclone fences on two sides. The students shouted and occasionally threw rocks and the Guard's tear gas canisters back at the Guardsmen. The Guardsmen remained on the practice field for several minutes, and a few momentarily assumed a crouched firing position, aiming at the students.

The Guardsmen then formed another skirmish line and retreated up the knoll. Just before they reached the crest, about twenty-eight of the seventy-six men turned and fired back toward the students. Four students were killed and nine wounded. The Guard then returned to the base of operations.

■

These events can be explained in a variety of ways. The approach suggested here is psychological and starts from the assumption that a person's self-esteem is closely connected with his sense of competence in dealing with his fellow human beings and his environment so as to attain his goals. This sense of competence is affected by various direct and vicarious experiences. It is dependent in part on the individual's perception of his own abilities. It is also influenced, however, by others' evaluations of him; praise and blame, even from strangers, have their effects.

Threats to the sense of competence and thus self-esteem can take many forms, from actual failure and membership in a failing group to genuine or even imagined insults. An individual confronted with such threats can react positively by ignoring inaccurate criticism or by improving his competence. He may, however, respond negatively, even violently.

Several considerations seemingly encourage a resort to violence. A person may have learned by observing others that violence is sometimes effective in attaining his goals, especially if he is a member of certain subgroups in American society, including the military. Violent actions, when successful, often have immediate results and thereby quickly restore a sense of competence. Violence is admired under certain circumstances and even legitimized, consequently any sense of shame is mitigated. Inflicting violence reduces the perceived competence of others so that the violent person feels more competent in comparison. It is assumed that the threats—insults, missiles, or whatever—will cease if violence is used.

■

A central consideration in applying this theory to the events at Kent State must be the degree to which being violent affected the Guardsmen's sense of competence and self-esteem. Effective violence is clearly a requirement for members of a military organization; such skills as marksmanship were emphasized in training. The Ohio National Guard had an outstanding military history and had been in a partial state of combat readiness. In addition, its long record of involvement in civil disturbances legitimized the use of violence against civilians. Despite federal directives to the contrary, the Ohio Guard leaders explicitly sanctioned the use of weapons against civilians in certain circumstances and against the students at Kent State in particular. This order was supported by the governor's strong statement denouncing some of the students and by the general antagonism which the people of Kent and of Ohio in general appeared to feel toward the students.

The obvious threat to their self-esteem may also have influenced the Guardsmen's behavior. The Guard perceived the students to be strong, and that view implied that the Guardsmen had relatively less power and therefore threatened their competence. This perception was probably reinforced because the Guardsmen were well aware that the SDS and other student activities at Kent State had been effective in disrupting campuses by bombing, and committing other acts of violence.

Student power was also demonstrated during the "riot" Friday night in which students stoned police cars, forced parked cars to move, blocked off a street, started a bonfire, and broke windows—with little police interference. It was rumored on Friday night and Saturday that the SDS leaders intended to burn the ROTC building and when they succeeded on Saturday night the burning verified the student strength—neither the campus police nor the fire department could cope with them. On Sunday the governor publicly called the students "the strongest, well-trained group that has ever assembled in America."

Guard impotence seemed evident on Sunday evening, when about seven hundred students defied the curfew, sat down on the street between the campus and town, and ignored Guard and police orders to leave. A self-appointed student leader "negotiated" with the Guard for an hour and a half—another indication of student power. The students were finally driven back to the campus and the Guardsmen remained, insecure in a dark, unfamiliar, and unfriendly area.

On Monday morning, students defied an order prohibiting the rally and insulted the officer ordering them to disperse while the Guardsmen watched. The Guard fired tear gas at the students but a shifting wind blew it back and students hurled some of the canisters at them. The Guard advanced, against the crowd as it appeared to grow larger and its insults louder. The students stoned the Guard in the football practice field but no Guardsman was hurt. The inability to disperse the students undoubtedly affected the Guardsmen's sense of competence and that feeling was reinforced by the barrage of taunts and insults particularly since the Guardsmen wore uncomfortable gas masks, which reduced peripheral vision and made communication difficult. In addition, the Guard was affected by several days with little sleep on a campus which was "enemy territory."

■

This theory suggests that the behavior of the Guardsmen can be explained by a reduced self esteem and sense of competence resulting from their perception of aggressive student power, their own ineptness and physical limitations. They responded violently because effective violence was directly related to their self-esteem as soldiers and because attacks against civilian dissidents had been legitimized. Violence restored their sense of competence and self-esteem.

The events at Kent State suggest several corrective actions to prevent future tragedies of this kind. Guardsmen should be armed with non-lethal weapons which are unloaded until absolutely necessary and then only on order. Leaders should instill better discipline so that Guardsmen will not fire unless ordered. Guardsmen should be trained to feel competent when showing restraint and coolness under stress. Their leaders should neither encourage a hostile view of civilians nor exaggerate civilian power. Leaders should develop alternative ways to control confrontations so that they do not have to rely on tear gas, bayonets, rifle butts, and bullets. Riot control requires cool, confident, and well-trained troops with a secure sense of self esteem. Then it may be possible to avoid a resort to violence and future tragedies like that at Kent State.

# War, Sex, Sports, and Masculinity

## Lynne B. Iglitzin

Despite the vaunted myth that we are a peace-loving country which has historically settled its disputes by conciliation and compromise, American history is full of wars, violence, and bloodshed. Historian Tristram Coffin has effectively described the devastating results of this paradox:

> The American missionary spirit is not exclusively peaceful. There is no evidence that we are peace-loving or ever have been. We have taken what we wanted by force if need be, sometimes muttering a proper prayer over the vanquished. . . . Through it all we have maintained a righteous air, contending that we have committed mayhem and felony with the purest motives. This is the result of our Puritan inheritance, which requires proof that God is on our side in every expedition and sanguinary action.[1]

The ideal of masculinity is interrelated with the qualities which make the good soldier: aggressiveness, obedience, and the capacity to be violent when necessary. Unquestionably, most people have the capacity for aggressive reaction when frustrated. But in America, it has been *men* who have fought in wars, *men* who have committed the great majority of violent crimes, and *men* who have made up the political elite whose decisions involved the use of violent force in domestic and foreign confrontations.

In our society, as in almost every patriarchal society, militarism and violence have been identified with manliness. Boys learn lessons

---

1. Tristram Coffin, *The Passion of the Hawks* (New York: Macmillan, 1964), pp. 2–3.

■

of violence early through a variety of socializing agents in our society. The most important of these has been the glorification of war, through war heroes and war games. Violence is inculcated into boys by sexual norms and violent sports which equate virility with aggressiveness. Although war, sex, and sports are interrelated in their effect on masculinity, each has a unique influence on our culture.

■

War has been the ultimate testing-ground for manhood in our country. In contrast to females, males have always been more subject to societal pressure to participate in war. The hero in Stephen Crane's famous Civil War novel, *The Red Badge of Courage*, is worried about how he will perform on the battlefield. He is terrified that, when the first cannonball comes, he will turn and run, an act he considers weak and feminine. The first time, he actually *does* flee, but so does most of his division. He goes through a terrible process of soul-searching, deeply concerned that he is not a true man. When he gets a second chance, he not only stays and fights but leads the charge. He is euphoric when he realizes he has met his test and thereby proved himself a man:

> So it was all over at last! The supreme trial had been passed. The real, formidable difficulties of war had been vanquished. He went into an ecstasy of self-satisfaction. He had the most delightful sensations of his life. Standing as if apart from himself, he viewed that last scene. He perceived that the man who had fought thus was magnificent.
> He felt that he was a fine fellow. He saw himself even with those ideals which he considered as far beyond him. He smiled in deep gratification.[2]

Spending time in the army or in military school has generally been regarded as a good, toughening experience for young men, despite the traditional American suspicion toward military men in positions of political power. In 1895 a measure proposed in Congress to establish a bureau of military education which would carry out uniform military drills in all public schools received support from *Harper's Weekly:*

> The military instinct is innate in the American boy. All that is wanted is that it should be properly fostered. . . . If such exercises were carried out . . . in a month the slouchy lad would have all the warp and wobble taken out of him. More, however, than the finer bearing of the boy, he would be taught obedience, respect, and thus a high sense of patriotism would be the resultant . . . the early lesson of the soldier would then become an integral part of the boy's life, and he would not be likely to outgrow it.

Although the bill did not pass in Congress, this editorial reflected and continues to reflect the views of many Americans on the merits of a military upbringing for boys.

---

2. Stephen Crane, *The Red Badge of Courage* (New York: Bantam, 1964), p. 51.

War has generally been glorified for its encouragement of manly virtues. During the pre–World War I era, statesmen from Otto von Bismarck to Theodore Roosevelt, philosophers Georges Sorel and Herbert Spencer, writers Rudyard Kipling and Jack London celebrated war and warriors while deprecating peace and passivity. Theodore Roosevelt said: "The nation that has trained itself to a cancer of unwarlike and isolated ease is bound in the end to go down before other nations which have not lost the manly and adventurous virtues."[3] More recently, President Nixon's view of America's role in the world clearly illustrates the masculine fear of being thought a sissy (i.e., feminine). After the invasion of Cambodia in 1970, Nixon went on television to reassure the American people that we would not become "a pitiful, helpless giant . . . a second-rate power."

The ready availability of firearms has also helped inculcate violence and warlike values in men. Masculinity is closely associated with the power to defend oneself, with a weapon if necessary. Guns have always been easily available and widely used by soldiers and policemen and by many others as well. Firearms have been an important part of American life: the armed citizen-soldier was our first line of defense; the "Kentucky long rifle" opened the frontier; the Winchester repeater "won the West," and the Colt revolver "made men equal."[4] The frontier has disappeared but the frontier tradition remains. The use of violent weapons is almost entirely related to men, just as it is mostly males, between the ages of fifteen and twenty-four, poor and nonwhite, who commit violent crimes.[5]

What makes men turn so often to crimes of violence and the use of guns and knives? Perhaps many men in our culture feel insecure in their manhood, and continually use the slightest pretext to prove it. In *Soul on Ice*, Eldridge Cleaver describes what happens when society builds in institutional blocks which prevent black men from achieving manhood and self-respect in the eyes of their women:

> In back rooms, in dark stinking corners of the ghettos, self-conscious black men curse their own cowardice and stare at their rifles and pistols and shotguns laid out on tables before them, trembling as they wish for a manly impulse to course through their bodies and send them screaming mad into the streets shooting from the hip. Black women look at their men as if they are bugs . . .[6]

---

3. As quoted in Theodore Roszak, "The Hard and the Soft: The Force of Feminism in Modern Times," in Roszak and Roszak, *Masculine/Feminine* (New York: Harper, 1969), pp. 122–25.
4. *Firearms and Violence in American Life*, Staff Report to the National Commission on the Causes and Prevention of Violence (Washington, D.C.: U.S. Government Printing Office, n.d.), 7:1.
5. *To Establish Justice, To Insure Domestic Tranquility*, Final Report of the National Commission on the Causes and Prevention of Violence (Washington, D.C.: U.S. Government Printing Office, December 1969), pp. 21–22.
6. Eldridge Cleaver, *Soul on Ice* (New York: Dell, 1968), p. 84.

No wonder such men might feel emasculated and see in the gun an extension of sexual prowess. There seems to be the conviction that, through some real or imagined shortcoming of their own, they have fallen short of the American culture's standard of manliness.

The spirit of militarism appears to be increasing in American life, bringing with it unrest and disorder. During the 1960s, there was a sharp rise in violent domestic turmoil, in response to the unpopular Vietnam War. Dissent, protest, and the use of increasingly militant tactics met harsh police and military response. As a result, the American public has grown accustomed to war and violence, to uniforms, to guns. More and more people have become conditioned to think of violence as the appropriate way to settle both foreign *and* domestic conflict.

Ex-Marine Corps Commander David Shoup charges that World War II produced "a nation of veterans," thoroughly inculcated with the manly, i.e., military, virtues of strength, toughness, patriotism, and courage in the face of danger.[7] Shoup argues that a powerful complex of defense industries and military service organizations have helped strengthen the military view of the world as divided into friends and enemies, still carrying on the Cold War mentality of the "Free" versus the Communist world. To the degree that this view does indeed permeate American political culture, young men will be the most directly affected.

■

War is related to the masculine mystique through its association with sex. In feudal times, the institution of chivalry encouraged men to prove their love of women on the battlefield. Men fought duels to preserve the honor of women or settle disputes over women and thereby demonstrated masculine prowess. Countries fight duels to preserve national honor or settle disputes—the principle is the same.

The forcible sexual violation of women has historically been the companion of warfare. Battle commanders have often rationalized rape by arguing that soldiers need a release from tension. Journalist Seymour Hirsch relates a 1966 incident of American GIs who took turns raping a Vietnamese girl in an "outing" planned by their sergeant. Those who refused were called "chicken!" or "queer!"—epithets clearly intended to question their masculinity.[8] Rape stories abound in connection with the infamous My Lai massacre. Reports of GIs in Vietnam raping women before killing them and of whole

7. General David M. Shoup, "The New American Militarism," *Atlantic Monthly* (April 1969):51.
8. As quoted in Lucy Komisar, "Violence and the Masculine Mystique," *Washington Monthly* 2:2 (April 1970).

platoons raping women after burning their huts have been cited by journalists and helicopter pilots.

We need not be surprised at this identification of sex and violence on the battlefield, for a distinct American tradition links the two. Mickey Spillane, Henry Miller, and Norman Mailer all glorify sexual violence. Their male characters are hard, raw, and unyielding in the act of sex and dominate submissive and pliant women. Mailer vividly spells out close connections between sex and violence in war but also the almost orgiastic excitement battle provides for some men:

> All the deep, dark urges of man, the sacrifices on the hilltops, the churning lusts of night and sleep, weren't all of them contained in the shattering, screaming burst of a shell? The phallus-like shell that rides through a shining vagina of steel. The curve of sexual excitement and discharge, which is, after all, the physical core of life.[9]

■

Violence is likewise associated with games and sports in American culture. Games such as cowboys and Indians and the toys which accompany them foster a sense of elation in besting and overpowering others. Parents who tell their sons to fight "like a man," who scold them for acting "like a sissy" in schoolyard confrontations, who taunt boys who cry when hurt helps socialize boys in a culture which equates masculinity with toughness and aggressiveness. Hard-nosed gym teachers consider it their task to use physical and psychological tests designed to instill "acceptable" masculine behavior into nine-year-olds.

So-called contact sports—football, lacrosse, rugby, boxing, wrestling, and ice hockey—are essentially controlled violence. Apologists argue that these games teach serious, no-nonsense, play-by-the-rules violence which mirrors the ethics of the rest of society. These games are regulated by strict rules as to how violence can be carried out. As long as these rules are observed, one can push on toward the goal, no matter how many are bruised and battered along the way. The most popular sports encourage the view that life is basically an irreconcilable struggle in which winning becomes equated with domination. As one college football coach commented, a tie is like kissing one's sister. Another sports personality observed that winning was not just best—it was everything.

Violence is specifically encouraged by coaches. Football players are admonished to drive through their opponents and are rewarded with points for putting opposing players on the ground. Many foot-

9. Norman Mailer, *The Armies of the Night* (New York: New American Library, 1968), p. 228.

ball players claim that the game is bloody only because the crowd wants it that way. If a few bodies are not carried off the field, the crowd is not happy and does not think it has seen a good game or gotten its money's worth. These sports teach the young men who play them that violence is acceptable on the playing field as long as the rules are observed.

It is not surprising that some men occasionally become confused. Soldiers periodically "go berserk" after returning from war and go on shooting rampages. But the same thing may happen to athletes. An ex-college football player recently went to prison for kicking a man to death after an argument in a parking lot, the second such incident in which he had been involved. For this one man, the playing field and the city street became confused, with tragic consequences for all concerned.

■

The question remains whether it is possible to erase or diminish the tendency to equate war and violence with masculinity. To the degree that violence is made to seem desirable to humans and particularly to men, we ought to be able to reduce the resort to violence by modifying our criteria for masculine behavior. This is not to assert that all human violence is caused by social demands. Humans like other animals probably have an innate capacity for aggression when frustrated or threatened. Since it is difficult and perhaps impossible to alter possibly genetic traits, it is necessary to alter social norms in order to discourage rather than validate or even stimulate violence. We should reexamine our definitions of "masculine" and "feminine" and question those traditional standards which require men to be aggressive and violent if they are to be thought of as "men among men." We must encourage new values emphasizing the importance of love, tenderness, compassion, and gentleness and recognize these characteristics as human and not exclusively feminine traits. Manly courage could then become associated with an ability to assert "humanity" rather than the old, stereotyped "masculinity." Both men and women secure in their own identities, would not need to play aggressive and submissive roles, but could strive for human relationships based on mutual respect and equality.

Such a goal can probably not be easily or fully achieved. Nonetheless we must attempt to modify the violence we encourage through media, sports, literature, and sexual mores. War games for children, violence-filled cartoons and television programs, sadistic "comic" books can all be eliminated without loss. Contact sports, such as football and ice hockey, can be regulated to reduce their violence. Similar modifications have occurred historically without diminishing spectator pleasure. Boxing in early England was a bloody, bare-handed sport which continued until one opponent was virtually demolished; increasingly rigid regulations over the years have made the sport less violent and thus more humane. In Portugal the bull is not killed nor are as many matadors gored because the bull's horns are blunted. The violence is reduced, but the excitement remains just as high.

The educational effort entailed in reorienting our sexual lives to reduce their aggressive component will be most difficult. Some people will undoutedly bemoan any diminishment of excitement of the sexual act. A recent "sophisticated" sex manual (*The Joy of Sex* by Alex Comfort) includes detailed instructions for whips, tying up one's partner, and beatings ("but not brutality"). Such an extension of masculinity-cum-aggressiveness is hardly an improvement. Rather, we should strive to replace pain and aggressiveness with pleasure and gentleness as the basis of human relations. Perhaps someday men and women will assert not their respective masculinity and femininity but their common humanity.

# Marxism and War

## Lyman H. Legters

In a consideration of Marx's fundamental attitude toward war, there are four sources of possible misunderstanding. Each of these must be examined to avoid the conclusion that all things done in Marx's name are by definition a part of his teaching or even compatible with it.

The first source of possible misapprehension has less to do with anything said or done by Marx or his followers than with our own tendency to apply anachronistic standards. The issue here is the sheer horror of modern warfare as we have come to know it in tandem with the matter-of-fact way in which Marx, Engels, Lenin, and others usually dealt with the phenomenon of war. Marx lived through the period regulated diplomatically by the unusually successful post-Napoleonic settlement concluded at the Congress of Vienna. He was witness to numerous military conflicts among European countries; by twentieth-century standards, however, these conflicts would for the most part count as minor skirmishes. Marx's experience embraced only three significant wars, the Crimean, the American Civil War, and the Franco-Prussian conflict that triggered the Paris Commune. He was eyewitness to none of these. Because of his intense concern with shifting relationships among the European states, he followed them closely and carefully analyzed their implications for the working-class movement and for the prospect of revolution. Marx knew the history of warfare, and especially the violence of the French Revolution. Yet none of this prepared him to foresee

■

the capacity of twentieth-century military technology for wholesale destruction.

Although Marx projected laws or tendencies of social development into the future, he is no more accountable than his contemporaries for anticipating subsequent developments. It may help to recall that Khrushchev was considered by some of his confreres to have taken an untenable *Marxist* position in his doctrine of coexistence, which was essentially a recognition of the infinite destructive capability of modern warfare. Despite Marx's rather acute perceptions of likely future developments, he could no more forecast the nature of nuclear warfare than he could predict the details of the multinational corporation.

The second consideration in assessing Marx's attitude toward war involves the intellectual division of labor obtaining between Marx and Engels. It was doubtless inevitable in this striking intellectual partnership, in which Engels always acknowledged the senior status of Marx with neither rancor nor self-abnegation, that they should develop specializations. Given the prodigious amount of work the two accomplished, the range could not have been as great if they had not deferred to each other in their respective strengths. Engels became the expert on military affairs and historical periods and topics that Marx never managed to pursue. Thus, when Marx was writing regularly for the *New York Tribune* and certain papers in Europe, he commented frequently on the progress of the American Civil War. He felt comfortable in dealing with the respective merits of the two opposed causes and especially in assessing the worth of British working-class affinity for the Northern side. But in military issues, such as the ineptitude of Northern military leadership in the early phases of the war, he turned to Engels for suitable commentary. In terms of the military aspects of European conflicts, Marx followed Engels's perception of the strategic implication of French and Austrian interventions in Italy, thus opening one of his notable disagreements with Lassalle.

It is therefore natural that when questions are raised about the Marxian attitude toward war, attention should immediately turn to the military expert of the pair. To say that this reaction is potentially misleading is not to say that Engels's observations diverge from Marx's. The deceptive quality arises rather from a situation roughly analogous to Marx's complaint about the classical economists, that they assumed as a given the very capitalist system the development of which they should have been explaining. Engels's military expertise was useful in dealing with the actualities of armed conflict once unleashed. But it was Marx's understanding of modern wars as manifestations of the endemic conflicts of capitalism that was fundamental. In other words, the Marxian view of war springs not from the study of military history but from the theoretical construct designed

to explain the economic, social, and political world in which the two
men lived.

The other two sources of potential misunderstanding involve
later generations of Marxists, some of whom were pacificists, while
others advocated certain types of wars, e.g., wars of national liberation. These postures may be consistent with Marxism, or at least with
certain phases of political strategy undertaken in the spirit of Marx's
program, but it does not follow that they serve adequately as summa-
tions of final Marxian wisdom on the question of war. Indeed, it must
be obvious that pacifism and belligerency cannot be equally valid
indices of Marx's position. As tactical approaches to particular circumstances, on the other hand, both can be legitimate derivatives
from his teaching about war. The confusion stems from mistaking a
political line or policy of a given moment for the basic theoretical
position.

In the United States, Marxism first impinged significantly on our
consciousness as the claim to legitimacy of a revolutionary movement and, soon thereafter, of an avowedly revolutionary regime in
Russia. American opponents and proponents of that revolution and
of subsequent events were alike in that they knew Lenin before they
knew Marx. They may be forgiven for confounding particular manifestation with theoretical underpinning and for thinking that Soviet
practice would provide the definitive test of Marxism. But we can
now recognize that they accepted all too uncritically the claim of the
regime to speak for Marx, if for no other reason than that some of the
most strenuous critiques of Soviet practice arise from those who
know Marx's work intimately and take it seriously.

The antiwar aspect of the Marxian tradition rests on the assumption, voiced in *The Communist Manifesto,* that if capitalists can organize themselves across national boundaries to promote their
common interests, so can the working class. Proletarian spokesmen,
Marx and Engels prominent among them, argued that national conscription of the working class to fight capitalist wars was precisely
such an issue, one that united the working class internationally
against the national states. In the name of the First International,
Marx celebrated the fraternal impulse that led French workers, in a
communication to German workers, to disavow the aggression they
attributed to their government. At the annual congresses of the Second International, immense amounts of time were spent discussing
the means whereby an internationally united working class might
hinder the outbreak of war. And, in an era closer to our own, Moscow's program of rivalry and coexistence with the capitalist world
has featured repeated appeals to pacifist sentiment, seeking to foster
an international peace movement tied to international communism
and opposed to allegedly aggressive imperialism.

Whatever the gradations of opportunism reflected in these

successive stages, several factors have been variously combined: the desire to gather potential adherents on the strength of the most obvious appeal in order to complete their conversion to the proletarian cause; the urge to mobilize all available segments of public opinion behind a proletarian goal not limited to that class; and the desire to identify the proletariat or international communism as peace-loving, its enemies by implication as warmongers.

It is neither surprising nor necessarily a proof of gullibility that international socialism has attracted a generous assemblage of pacifists. The First International could entertain relations with a bourgeois organization devoted to the prevention of war. Many of the fissures of the Second International were papered over because of the common desire to prevent the outbreak of a war that threatened increasingly as the nineteenth gave way to the twentieth century. Lenin's effort to revive the International in a revolutionary form during World War I was ornamented, not to say hindered, by the strong infusion of pacifists who shared his exile in Switzerland.

But neither the appeals to pacifism, whether genuine or calculated, nor the sporadic successes of one version or another of the united front in attracting pacifists demonstrate any Marxian proclivity for pacifism. Although Marx was plainly opposed to national wars, regarding them as belonging among the outmoded characteristics of a dying capitalism, he did not object to the class warfare that signaled a proletarian determination to attain power. Both the doctrine of class struggle and the assumption that violent upheaval would probably have to accompany the effort to wrest power from the bourgeois ruling class have been proof among his followers against the lure of pacifism as an overriding commitment.

Neither, however, does Marxism glorify war and violence. From the mindless assumption that all revolutionaries prefer violent methods, to the factual observation that communist movements and regimes have at least taken advantage of and at most fomented international conflict, there is no evidence that war is an essential ingredient of Marxist theory.

Marx could celebrate the cause of Polish independence and the insurrections that he saw as potentially eroding the dread power of Czarist Russia. He could hope for an Irish uprising against Europe's preeminent capitalist power. He could seemingly underplay the massacre that ended the Paris Commune for the sake of erecting a monument to proletarian self-governance (though he had counseled against the working-class initiative in the first place). And he could view the bloodletting of the American Civil War as accompanying the victory of a comparatively progressive socioeconomic order over an archaic one. But this was the same Marx who waged unremitting struggle against anarchists who preached the cleansing value of destruction without having a positive program to replace what was to be destroyed. He likewise opposed the nationalistic particularisms that promised violence without advancing the cause of proletarian revolution.

In short, Marx was not for or against war; he saw the wars of his time as fruitful or regressive, like other human events, measured always according to his estimate of what would advance the revolutionary cause. Wars in the bourgeois era were, for Marx, essentially outgrowths of the tensions and conflicts within capitalism. A transformation of the capitalist system would eliminate war, he believed, as a by-product of human emancipation, not as an indication that peace, at whatever price, was the highest good.

It has become difficult to tell whether the advocacy of wars of national liberation is intended as a direct application of Marxian teaching or as a tactical maneuver of Soviet foreign policy. Conceivably it could be both. But the suspicion persists that intensification of the problem of uneven revolutionary development, feared by Marx as an obstacle to any orchestration of revolution on a global scale, has wrought a change that may be all but fatal to his teaching about an international proletarian cause. Socialism in one country (or in a few) has siphoned off the universal appeal of human emancipation in favor of claiming legitimacy through Marx. In this sense, the aggressiveness that has sometimes characterized the policies of socialist regimes (Leninist, Stalinist, or Maoist), and has done so much to identify Marxism with belligerency, seems to have more in common with conventional diplomacy than it does with a revolutionary message echoing out of the last century. It certainly falls short of proving a fondness for violence and war at the root of Marxian theory.

In this attempt to correct or offset possible misperceptions of Marx's view of war, there are clear indications of what his view actually was. In the world that Marx acutely observed and assiduously studied, he took war to be a manifestation of tensions and contradictions intrinsic to the system. A particular war could be more or less advantageous in advancing the revolutionary cause. But no act of will and no reform of the system would eliminate war. The prevailing order itself had to be overturned before the causes of war could be erased. Working-class organizations should oppose wars of the bourgeois powers, but more for the sake of solidifying their own international bonds than out of any expectation of efficacy. It is impossible to know what Marx would have said of the unexampled conflagrations of the twentieth century. One can be certain, however, that the objective of eliminating war would have remained subsidiary to the overriding demands of his quest for unconditional human freedom in a transformed and reconstituted social order.

PART *II*

# War in Preindustrial Societies

# Introduction

The essays in the following three sections are case studies focusing on particular societies. They contrast in general with the essays of the previous section in their concern for the results rather than the causes of war. In addition, the approach to the problem of war is based on somewhat different assumptions. While they pose significant questions with broad implications, these essays examine specific cases and imply that useful statements can be made about war in specific historical instances but probably not about war in general; they are consequently inclined to formulate the problem as *wars* rather than *war*. This tendency may reflect academic discipline: in contrast to the previous section, which numbered only one historian (Legters) among eight social scientists, the following three sections include only three nonhistorians (Townsend, Stern, and Thornton) among twelve historians. In a very general sense, these three sections reverse the approach of the previous section. Instead of seeking to demonstrate a theory by particular examples, they focus on particular cases from which they draw limited conclusions.

The essays in Section II are linked by a concern for preindustrial societies and are arranged in roughly chronological order. Carol G. Thomas concludes that warfare was crucial to the social and political development of ancient Greece and also affected the relationships of Greek political entities with one another and with non-Greek societies. Frank F. Conlon contends that the reputation for nonviolence misrepresents Indian history, which was in fact characterized by

■

repeated warfare and pervasive militarism. Peter F. Sugar argues that war and the military's position profoundly shaped Ottoman civilization. Jon M. Bridgman suggests that the evolution of early modern western Europe was closely related to developments in warfare.

Although these essays pose specific questions in examining particular societies, they share general interests and some patterns emerge both from their questions and from their conclusions. All approach war as part of a general social problem and suggest that war and the society in which it occurs are interdependent. Thus war affects a society's political, religious, and moral institutions, which in turn determine the nature of war. Violence is also linked to the periods of continuity and change in a society's evolution. Taken together, these essays suggest that war should be studied in a comprehensive, interdisciplinary fashion.

# War in Ancient Greece

## Carol G. Thomas

Greek history in the strict sense dates from roughly 2000 B.C., or the Middle Bronze Age, when small nomadic groups of Greek-speaking peoples entered the mainland, where their superior military tactics and equipment—in particular the horse and chariot—allowed them to dominate the larger and culturally more advanced resident population. The newcomers established, during the four centuries of the Middle Bronze Age, a settled mode of existence and consolidated their power. Archaeological evidence indicates that military strength remained the foundation of civilization in the Late Bronze Age (1600–1150 B.C.), when individual kingdoms began to emerge. One of the most important centers was Mycenae (hence the term "Mycenaean Age" for this period), a citadel surrounded by walls of massive rocks. From these strongholds, the Mycenaeans, a military aristocracy, ruled the immediate region.

The military superiority of the Mycenaeans affected their role in the larger Mediterranean world. These Greeks were known by such powerful peoples as the Egyptians and Hittites as both traders and military adventurers. While details of the ten-year siege of Troy celebrated by Homer cannot be accepted as fact, archaeologists have demonstrated the existence of a site called Troy and its destruction at the end of the Bronze Age. Furthermore, a century of exploration has shown that people living at this site in the northwest corner of modern Turkey were in contact with the Mycenaean Greeks throughout much of the Late Bronze Age. The actuality of a Trojan

■

War is consequently enhanced and seems to be reinforced by the quantity of military artifacts that survive from the Mycenaean citadels. In fact, some of the most impressive remains are carefully worked weapons and it has been suggested that the Mycenaeans served as middlemen in the manufacture of military equipment, importing unworked metals and exporting finished products.

A proclivity for warfare among the independent kingdoms during the Late Bronze Age helps to explain the destruction of the Mycenaean civilization. In approximately 1480 B.C., certain of the Mycenaean Greeks were powerful enough to take Knossos, the political and economic center of Minoan Crete. Thereafter, Mycenaean Greeks supplanted the Minoans in trade with Egypt, the Levant, and the Aegean region. Since most Mycenaean kingdoms probably did not share the conquered Minoan wealth, it is possible that it was Mycenaeans who attacked their kinsmen at Knossos and destroyed it around 1400 B.C. Thebes, center of a mainland kingdom, rose to a similar position of economic prosperity but was attacked and destroyed suddenly ca. 1300 B.C. As there is no evidence of foreign invasions, the cause was probably other Mycenaean Greeks. Thebes, in turn, was succeeded by Mycenaean Pylos, which was destroyed ca. 1230 B.C., apparently by other Greeks. The specific cause of the collapse of Mycenaean civilization is unknown; it may have been brought about by foreign invaders, perhaps by climatic change, plague, or famine. It is fairly clear, however, that the pattern of recurrent internecine warfare was a contributing factor.

■

During the Dark Age, a span of some four centuries (1150–750 B.C.), the Mycenaean heritage was reshaped into the basis for Classical Greek civilization. Warfare was a major ingredient in this process, particularly in the invasions during the twelfth and eleventh centuries by new groups of Greek speaking peoples.

The Dorians, one group of newcomers who would play a vital role throughout the remainder of ancient Greek history, seem to have moved into Greece from the northwest and settled in the area of the Peloponnese. They were probably tribal and nomadic like the first Greeks and they may have established themselves in a similar fashion, by military superiority. This conclusion is suggested by the history of Sparta, one of the regions settled by the Dorian Greeks. To meet their needs for additional land and resources, the Spartans expanded across most of the southern third of the Peloponnese, enslaving much of the resident population. These serfs worked the land for Spartan citizens, who devoted themselves to the business of war and became a military aristocracy which equated citizenship with soldiering. Although Sparta was extreme among Greek states in this regard—the rigorous training of a Spartan youth began at birth and ended only with his death—Athens too recognized the importance of war. During the Classical period, the only public officials not subject to the limitations on the number of times a citizen could hold office were those concerned with military affairs.

Warfare was critical not only during the conflict between newcomers and remnants of the Mycenaean population but also in the subsequent development of *poleis* (city-states). While the first two centuries of the Dark Age were dark in the sense of being bleak, the period from roughly 950 B.C. witnessed a cessation of outside invasion and a gradual settling down into territories with boundaries more or less fixed by geographic conditions. The emerging states claimed autonomy in every sphere of life and developed a philosophy that made perpetual conflict a factor in the lives of all citizens. Apparently central to the city-states' formation was the rule that a group of people maintained as much territory as it could physically preserve. The *Odyssey* reveals this state of affairs in no uncertain terms: it was extremely difficult for someone even as clever as Odysseus to preserve the integrity of his state against both pretenders to power from within and threats from without.

The city-states developed under the leadership of kings who resembled chieftains more than constitutional monarchs. The leaders had to be wise and strong, able and willing to make decisions for their people and to fight in order to preserve the communal territory. At the end of the Dark Age, when this type of military leadership was no longer necessary, kings began to be supplanted by aristocracies.

■

Near the beginning of the Classical period (750–323 B.C.), a major alteration in tactics and strategy occurred. The previous heroic manner of fighting involving single hand-to-hand combat between the leaders of society gave way to the hoplite phalanx, a unit of heavily armored soldiers in formation. It appears that the city-state Argos used the hoplite phalanx first on the Greek mainland. Other *poleis* had to adopt that style of fighting in order to stand their ground against Argos. As these states called upon larger segments of their populations for military service, internal repercussions followed. Hoplites who fought and risked death recognized their own importance to the state and claimed a voice in decision-making. Thus, over a century or so, the so-called hoplite revolution led to a wider sharing of power among those men who fought for their *poleis.*

Among the city-states generally, location determined relationships: neighbors tended to be enemies, but neighbors' enemies were frequently friends. This situation allowed foreign states such as Persia and Macedon to play city-states off against each other and thereby establish first a foothold and then, in the case of Philip II of Macedon, control over the Greeks.

Warfare was particularly important during the Golden Age (500–400 B.C.). As a result of the unexpected victory over the Persians (479 B.C.), the Greek states and especially Athens went on to develop a magnificent culture, one of the bases of Western civilization. The Peloponnesian War began a train of events which were to spell the end of Greek independence in the ancient world. Although Sparta and her allies were nominally victorious in 404 B.C., Greek society had been severely weakened by a generation of constant warfare.

The true winner was Philip II, a barbarian chieftain from the north who ruled by effective leadership in war and by his own cunning, much like the kings of the Dark Age. From approximately 360 B.C., Philip consolidated his kingdom and began to interfere in the activities of Greeks, who continued to fight one another in large measure because none was able to achieve a decisive victory. In such military stalemates, the practice was to call in a strong outside power; Philip was summoned and, on several occasions, decided the outcome of war and then did not leave. The *poleis* recognized by 339 B.C. what was occurring and prepared for battle with the Macedonians but it was too late. At Chaeronea in 338 B.C. the Greek citizen militias were defeated by the standing army of Philip II.

The work of his father paved the way for Alexander the Great, whose meteoric career was in all respects that of a military man. To be recognized as king of the Macedonians, a man had to be acclaimed by the assembly (in essence, the army); to retain the kingship, a man had to be successful in the field. Alexander's empire was the largest that the world had ever known. One can only ponder how the mutiny of his soldiers at Beas may have altered the course of world history.

Alexander died in 323 B.C.; his successors were unable to maintain the integrity of his empire. During the Hellenistic Age (323–30 B.C.), the three kingdoms ruled by Macedonians and Greeks in Egypt, Asia, and Macedon continued the constant warfare that had marked earlier Greek history. The end result would be reminiscent of fourth-century Greece: while the Hellenistic monarchs fought one another, the Romans consolidated their control of Italy and by 200 B.C. Rome was a recognized power in the entire Mediterranean. During the second and first centuries B.C., Rome—sometimes invited, other times uninvited—helped to decide the affairs of the eastern Mediterranean. By 133 B.C. the pattern was clear: one of the Hellenistic rulers willed his kingdom to Rome. In 30 B.C., after Augustus Caesar defeated Mark Antony and Cleopatra at Actium, the last independent Greek kingdom in the east was incorporated into the Roman Empire.

Warfare was not the only influence in the development of ancient Greek society; no period of history can be understood adequately through a monocausal explanation. The requirements of war not only influenced the formation and development of Greek political and social entities but affected the relationships of Greek political bodies with one another and with non-Greek societies.

# War in Ancient India

## Frank F. Conlon

The concept of India as a land of peace and nonviolence probably is derived from modern impressions, notably Mahatma Gandhi's interpretation of Indian tradition and Jawaharlal Nehru's advocacy of peaceful means to resolve world conflict. The ideas and practices of these men seem to mesh with India's traditional ideals of asceticism and meditation to achieve ultimate salvation. India has, however, produced men who sought worldly power and wealth. Indeed, Indian history is punctuated by repeated warfare, and a form of militarism was a hallmark of early Indian society. These factors significantly affected ancient Indian social, religious, political, and cultural patterns and the institution of kingship, in particular the specific rights and duties of secular rulers as validated by Indian social and religious values.

Ancient India's political and military history, virtually unknown to most foreigners, is a long and cluttered chronicle of thousands of petty rulers, chiefs and kings, whose sovereignty extended no farther than one day's ride from their capitals. Political unity in the form of an extensive imperial structure was infrequent. Culture was the basis for unity in early India and embodied concepts of sovereignty and statecraft. Yet multicentered political and military power encouraged a continuous supply of warriors who fostered frequent, though not intense, warfare.

In the Vedic period (ca. 1500–900 B.C.), men who could lead in warfare were chosen as king (*rājā*): "those who have no king cannot

■

fight." Subsequently the ideal of a warrior-leader was elaborated to incorporate the ideal of a powerful figure who would patronize and support religious observances, thus guaranteeing the preservation of righteousness in the land.

The Indo-European or Indo-Aryan peoples who migrated into South Asia after 1500 B.C. initiated a military and cultural conquest of northern India. The continuing spread of their distinctive religion, social order, and political forms has been a major historical factor in India into the twentieth century. This "Aryanization" process was intimately connected with the development of what became known as Hinduism. The Aryan culture, dominant in India until the arrival of Islamic rule between the eighth and thirteenth centuries A.D., amply supported a militarism which conceived of war as the "sport of kings" rather than merely a violent means of resolving conflict.

This conception of kingship existed in conjunction with a predominantly rural social and economic order. Many foreign observers from classical antiquity to the present assumed that the peasants were untouched by warfare and were inherently peaceful, living according to principles of consensus, undisturbed by outside influences in their "little republics." Mahatma Gandhi said that India's future society should be reconstructed on this decentralized agrarian consensus model. War, however, intruded on village life. Furthermore, the apparent consensus was often imposed by powerful men in the community. Consensus and nonconflict were largely unfulfilled ideals.

■

The system of social stratification known to the West as caste had specific implications for warfare. In the caste system, each person is born into a particular group within which he or she will have all important social relations, living life according to predetermined rules and duties. There were literally thousands of castes spread in different parts of India, all generally ranked according to a fourfold system known as *varna*. The Aryan priesthood or *brahmans* created the *varna* system to classify the standing of all people within the society. Since the word signifies "color," it has been thought related to racial distinctions between Aryan and non-Aryan people; there were also ritual colors involved in sacrifices. Further, the boundaries between *varnas* appear to have been somewhat fluid.

Each *varna* had designated duties and a ritual standing. The *brahman* performed the priestly function; the second rank, only slightly less exalted, the warrior or *kshatriya*, had the protective functions, governing and fighting. The two others, the *vaishya* who were to produce wealth and the *shudra* who were to serve the other three, are not relevant here, since we are most concerned with the *kshatriya varna.* Today not all *brahmans* are priests and not all *kshatriyas* are warriors, but in Indian tradition they were. Each *kshatriya* ought to be a king or at least competent to carry out royal functions if need or opportunity arose.

Early Indian society believed that strong kings were vital, since they could maintain order, not merely day-to-day law and order, but also the earthly side of the cosmic order. There was a pronounced dread of anarchy in early Indian thought and kings were expected to prevent it. The epic poem, the *Mahabharata,* said: "A man should choose first his king, then his wife, and only then amass wealth; for without a king in the world where would wife and property be?" One might also ask where *brahmans* would be without kings. Through their rituals and their theory of *varna,* India's religious specialists erected an elaborate rationale for kingship and martial behavior. The roots may be found in the earliest Aryan religious lore, which portrayed the gods as military heroes. Indra, a most influential early deity, was seen as a hotheaded, hard-drinking chieftain who led the ever-victorious Aryans against their foes.

After Aryan dominance was established in north India (ca. 1000 B.C.), the predominant religous trend was toward elaboration of ritual sacrifice, including some ceremonies connected with kingship. One of the best-known was the *ashvamedha* or royal horse sacrifice. Priests consecrated a horse from the royal stable; thereafter it wandered with the royal herd accompanied by a band of selected warriors often led by the king's son and heir. If the horse went into a neighboring kingdom, the ruler was obliged to pay homage or do battle. After a year, the horse and troop returned to the king's capital, where the horse was sacrificed and the greatness of the king and fertility of his lands ensured.

The horses could be kept from wandering into territory where it might be impolitic to do battle. The eventual battles appear to have been more akin to European chivalric conflict than all-out war; defeated kings paid homage and remained as rulers. The entire ceremony reflected the symbiotic relationship between priests and kings in early India. Priests could confer cosmic legitimacy upon rulers who in turn could demonstrate their excellence by liberally rewarding the priests.

The religious sanction for pursuing the duties of the warrior is also found in major sacred literature. In the *Bhagavad Gita* or Song of the Lord, passed down as a portion of the larger *Mahabharata* epic, the setting is martial and the ethical lesson supports the ideal of the *kshatriya varna.* The poem is a dialogue between the warrior Arjuna and his chariot driver who turns out to be the Lord Krishna himself. When Arjuna recognizes some of his relatives and old teach-

ers on the opposing side in an impending battle, he is horrified and
announces that he has no taste for blood: "I foresee no welfare having
slain my kinfolk in battle . . . I wish no victory, Krishna, nor kingdom
nor joys." Though he really is worried only about killing his own
family, any person who is ordered to fight and kill faces this dilemma.
Krishna's reply precedes a larger teaching on the importance of
being devoted to Krishna, but its thrust is significant: "yield not to
unmanliness." He elaborately justifies Arjuna's entering the battle
because it is Arjuna's duty, his *dharma,* as a warrior. If he is true to
his duty, he will commit no sin. Krishna explains that the underlying
monistic unity of the cosmos makes all reality but one unity of illusion; he who thinks that he slays and he who thinks himself slain are
both deceived. Krishna thus sanctions the warrior's entering into
battle and "doing his duty"—there is no better act for a warrior than
to fight and it is better to be a dead lion than a live dog.

The religious support for royal power emphasized the king's role
as upholder of *dharma* and defender of the faith. The king also
wielded secular power. Besides the ritualized conflicts of the *ashvamedha,* there was a more intense and destructive aspect of war as
an element of state policy. One well-known text of political theory
provides a useful corrective to the image of otherworldly and nonviolent India.

The *Arthasastra* or Science of Gain (of power) is attributed to
Kautilya, a *brahman* minister to the first ruler of the Mauryan empire of northern India in the third century B.C. It is often compared
to Machiavelli's *The Prince* in its rational catalogue of the means by
which royal power might be maximized. Interstate relations were
seen as a set of six options—only one was true peace; the others were
war, waiting for the enemy to strike the first blow, attacking first,
alliance with your enemy's enemies, and the "double policy" of alliance or peace with one enemy while continuing war against another.
There were four ways of winning wars: persuasion through concilia-
tory speech, bribes, sowing dissension, and, when all else failed, battle. A dialogue between Kautilya and a young prince, his student,
emphasized worldly concern. A conqueror should know his own and
his enemy's strengths and strike only if he has the advantage. The
student contended that enthusiasm is better than power and power
better than intrigue. That youthful idealism was quickly squelched.
Kautilya assured him that skill in intrigue is bettter than prowess in
battle and enthusiasm is of little help. If battle appeared unpromising, a king should conduct a "treacherous fight" employing spies,
harlots, bribed officials, cooks, and courtesans to undermine the
enemy. The *Arthasastra,* although perhaps atypical, probably reflects the realities of war and statecraft better than texts emphasizing
war for glory.

The idealized texts nonetheless inspired generations of Hindu warriors and their militaristic behavior. Fighting unto death in pursuit of duty constituted immediate attainment of the spiritual objective, final release from the chain of rebirth that binds us to this world. These ideals were adapted by later invaders who were assimilated into Hindu society as the Rajputs and Marathas. Their internecine warfare during the eleventh and twelfth centuries A.D. may have weakened the defense of India against the military onslaught of the Turkish muslims. The Turks subsequently conquered northern India, but the Rajputs under siege of Muslim armies refused to surrender and instead sent their wives and children to die in a funeral pyre while the warriors fought to the death in a final sortie.

Two themes consequently run through the history of Indian warfare: pragmatism which sometimes approached cynicism and idealism which led to mass suicide. These tendencies are combined in the career and policies of the third Mauryan emperor, Asoka (ca. 273–232 B.C.). Asoka's grandfather is said to have fought Alexander the Great before launching India's first empire, the state supposed to have been organized along the lines of Kautilya's *Arthasastra.* Asoka pushed his frontiers to their natural limits and sent an expedition to chastise the warlike tribes in the jungled fastness of Kalinga (modern-day Orissa). After this conquest, Asoka appears to have had a change of heart and in a series of edicts, which survive in rock inscriptions throughout northern India, Asoka proclaimed that he would hereafter conquer and govern only by "righteousness," inspired by the Buddhist *dhamma* or *dharma.* He made nonviolence his state policy; modern India honors his legacy in its official symbol, the lion-headed capital of an edict column. Some people dismiss Asoka as an idealistic dreamer, and others regard him either as a cynic who renounced war after he had become all-conquering or as a hypocrite who threatened to punish those who did not choose to live by righteousness. Asoka's work proved ephemeral: he was succeeded by weak kings who failed to understand the merits of his policy. Nonetheless his contribution and its implications for warfare and statecraft remain intriguing. He was one of the most attractive figures in the ancient world and few Indian kings endeavored so mightily to spare their subjects the horrors of war.

■

Although military technology is one of the most adaptable elements of human material culture, the organization of the Indian army appears to have changed little from the time of Alexander the Great in the fourth century B.C. until the Turkish victories in the thirteenth century A.D. The *Arthasastra* gives elaborate instructions on how an army should organize camp and march, but it is difficult to ascertain how well they were carried out. The four basic units of organization —elephants, cavalry, chariots, and infantry—remained fairly constant and were accompanied by an unofficial fifth unit composed of camp followers. It has been reckoned that for every soldier there must have been six or seven servants plus assorted wives, courtesans, gamblers, pimps, prostitutes, artisans, mechanics, drovers, and all of their respective establishments. Thus a substantial army probably traveled perhaps eight miles a day at best.

The employment of war elephants had distinct tactical advantages. Elephants towered over troops engaged in battle and kept the king visible—an important consideration in the fortunes of war when the king and state were virtually one. They provided mounts for archers, and they evoked terror. The tactics of elephant warfare so impressed the Hellenistic rulers of the ancient Middle East that the beasts were introduced into the arsenals of the Mediterranean world. Gifts of elephants were a factor in the diplomacy of the stronger Indian rulers in their relations with external powers. But the Turks proved the mobility of light cavalry, and the introduction of gunpowder and artillery created a new problem. Explosions caused elephants to move suddenly, often into the foot soldiers closely ranked behind them.

Military conservatism did not end with the Muslim conquest. Indeed, subsequent medieval Muslim empires ultimately foundered upon their evolution of similarly ponderous Indian-style armies.

■

The assumption that warfare, restricted to a few combatants fulfilling caste duties and fighting gentlemanly duels, had a limited impact on Indian society is an enduring myth. The romantic British officer Charles Metcalfe, who wrote of "little republics," imagined that the peasants plowed or harvested their crops while armies fought in adjoining fields. This vision, however, bears no relation to the dynamics of a massive army with hordes of noncombatants and camp followers moving across the countryside at the rate of eight miles a day. A military expedition can be compared to a slightly inefficient plague of locusts cutting a swath from which an agrarian economy might not recover for several seasons. A vivid description of an army breaking camp is provided by the seventh-century A.D. court poet Bana, who concludes that the event resembled "the dooms-day ocean gone abroad to swallow the world at a gulp, a hell formed to embower great serpents," that "the whole world was swallowed up in dust."[1] Unfortunately the dust was often dampened by the freely flowing

1. *The Harsa-carita of Bana,* trans. E. B. Cowell and F. W. Thomas (London: 1897).

blood of generations of Indian warriors. Perhaps the ultimate judgment on war was uttered early in Indian history by the Buddha
himself when he intervened to halt a battle: "Victory breeds hatred,
for the conquered sleep in sorrow/Above victory or defeat, the calm
man dwells in peace."

Several views of warfare in ancient Indian society have persisted
which emphasize a vision of a country that was largely peaceful save
for limited, chivalric conflicts fought among kings as much for religious merit as for political and material gain. Certainly power was
more often divided than united in early Indian history, but warfare
constituted one means by which a ruler could validate his social and
religious standing according to the values of brahmanical religion.
However, it is clear that there was a gap between ideals and realities,
that warfare and militarism were an integral component of ancient
Indian society.

# A Near-Perfect
# Military Society:
# The Ottoman Empire

## Peter F. Sugar

The Ottoman Empire is the best example of a military society; it was not, however, totally under military control. "Men of the sword" had to share power with "men of the pen"—the lawyers, teachers, and clergy—and with "the palace"—a variety of people from members of the ruler's family to gardeners, from the grand-vizier to harem eunuchs. The influence of the military was nonetheless pervasive and profound. Soldiers were prominent in the administrative branches normally considered part of the civil service. They were teachers in the sultan's palace school, which trained most of the leading statesmen and administrators during the empire's heyday. The military judges of the highest rank were among the most important and influential members of the judiciary. Military considerations dominated the economic-fiscal organizations and policies of the state. Ottoman society was based mainly on military considerations and soldiers both dominated all aspects of society and represented its social elite.

Military rule has characterized most of Ottoman and Turkish history. Only during a short period—from 1826, when Sultan Mahmud II (1808–1839) destroyed the janissary corps, to roughly 1877, when Sultan 'Abd-al Hamīd II (1876–1909) suspended the constitution he had granted the previous year—did civilians play a leading role in the Ottoman Empire. Thereafter, both conservatives and reformers, in order to realize their respective goals, relied once again on the armed forces. From the Young Turkish Revolution in 1908 to

■

the present, i.e., during the last decades of the empire and the entire history of the Turkish Republic, military men have ruled the country for all but ten years, from 1950 to 1960, when the republic had a president, Celâl Bayar, who was not a former general. Most of the mistakes made by Turkey's leaders, including Mustafa Kemal Atatürk, were committed because military thinking outweighed economic and other considerations. In spite of its civilian government and parliament, Turkey is currently ruled by and in many respects for the military. Given that the Ottoman legacy is far from dormant and given the role of the army in contemporary Turkey—regrettable as that role may be—the country might well plunge into utter chaos should something drastic happen to its armed forces.

An important distinction must be made between what has been called a military society and a militaristic society. A militaristic society greatly values its armed forces, spends a large percentage of its budget on them, gives much weight to the demands and advice of its soldiers in policy decisions, and grants the military corresponding privileges and prestige. A militaristic society values certain virtues, such as bravery, discipline, and comradeship, and it often is bellicose or appears to be aggressive, and is frequently expansionistic. In spite of these basic characteristics, a militaristic society neither subordinates its entire existence to nor shapes its social structure in accordance with purely military considerations and exigencies. Even in those societies that are militaristic and totalitarian, the army still serves the state.

A military society has all the features of a militaristic society and also bases its social structure, economy, policy, and the justification for its existence on military values and characteristics. A military society exists to support the military and its organization conforms to that of a large army. The Ottoman Empire, a military society, declined when its army failed and disappeared when its army disintegrated.

■

Osman (1300–1324)—'Uthman in Arabic, which is the derivative of Ottoman and Osman—lived on the income from a *timar* (military fief) near the small town of Sögüt in northeastern Asia Minor. Osman, a Turk and a *ghāzi* warrior, was a subject of the Sultan of Konya, one of the many Saljūq princes who ruled in Anatolia. He founded the Ottoman Empire and was the first of ten great sultans who ruled consecutively until the death of Sulaymān in 1566. These statements identifying Osman have profound implications.

The Turks came from Central Asia (where they were converted to Islam) into what is today Iraq as mercenary bodyguards for the caliphs. Soldiers before and after their move south, they became known by the names of the men they followed. References to the Saljūq and Ottoman Turk have no specific ethnic meaning; the terms denote Turkish followers of the Saljūq and Ottoman families. The Saljūqs became commanders of the caliphs' guards and eventually attained sufficient power to expand their limited role by putting their relatives in command of cities and forts in various regions of the state.

It was customary for a new commander to exile his predecessor, even if they were relatives. Asia Minor was a convenient place of exile for generals and armies of questionable loyalty: it became a sort of frontier or no-man's-land on the border of the Arab and Byzantine empires after the Battle of Manzikert in 1071. Two centuries of constant large-scale and guerrilla-type warfare ruined the cities and economies of Asia Minor and produced a new type of man, the *akritoi* on the Byzantine and the *ghāzi* on the Muslim side. They fought each other for the glory of God and the true faith; their economy and daily life resembled the American frontiersmen; they developed the *futūwah,* a code of honor and behavior which, in Western terms, was a combination of chivalric regulations, a highwayman's ethic, and a syncretic religion. On both sides of the fluid border, these bandits of God created a military society in which loyalties constantly shifted as able leaders emerged and disappeared.

By 1300 the Saljūqs established several principalities (states) in Anatolia populated mainly by *ghāzi*-s and *akritoi.* Leaders had to find a way to keep their soldiers happy, loyal and willing to fight. Muslim leaders also needed soldiers to fulfill their religious obligation to extend the realm of Islam. State and prince consequently had to support themselves and the Muslims, the only segment of the population that mattered. The Saljūqs were therefore forced to develop the *timar* system. It recognized the interdependence of state and soldiers, and became the basis for maintaining loyalty, and for economic activity, security, and military action.

The number of soldiers grew because tradition and financial reward made soldiering the preferred occupation of most Muslim males. The state had to expand correspondingly to find more land for more *timar*-s. That was very difficult when a given state or a potential leader's domain bordered on those of other Muslim states or leaders; Muslims were forbidden to fight each other. This consideration made Sögüt's location important: it bordered on what was left of the Anatolian provinces of the Christian Byzantine Empire. Osman not only had the ability and personality to lead the *ghāzi*-s but also could offer them legal even canonical war. That the legal aspect was more important than the canonical and that employment was what the *ghāzi*-s really needed is proved by the legend according to which Osman rallied his followers in a crucial battle with the original battle cry: *timar isteyen bana* (all those who want a *timar* follow me). Trying to change his status from holder of a small *timar* to independent prince, Osman needed soldiers and knew what they needed. He utilized the precedent at hand in the Saljūq states and established the Ottoman Empire.

The *timar* system is almost always equated with western European feudalism, with which it had one basic feature in common—the exchange of land-derived income for military obligations. The feudal system, however, was basically a contractual, religiously sanctioned arrangement for assigning hereditary fiefs. The *timarli* (holder of the *timar*) had no contract with his overlord and their relationship was based purely on personal loyalty without religious connotation. Only the income was granted to the *timarli;* the land remained in the possession of the ruler, and even this income reverted to the sultan once the *timarli* died. Sons had to win their own grants, although they were given preference in the reassignment of their fathers' holdings if the merits of all claimants were equal. As a rule, young men were, however, first assigned smaller holdings and had to prove themselves in battle,

The smallest *timar* yielded an income of 3,000 aspers and obligated the man who received it to present himself as a fully armed cavalryman for each military campaign. The largest *timar* paid 20,000 aspers and obligated the beneficiary to come to the army's assembly point with three fully armed cavalrymen besides himself, that is, with one horseman for every 5,000 aspers. Those with holdings yielding between 20,000 and 100,000 aspers (*za'im*-s) had to field one mounted soldier for every 5,000 aspers. Only a provincial governor or a member of the imperial family was assigned a larger revenue and then from lands lying outside the province under his jurisdiction.

These figures can be considered from the point of view of the central budget to indicate how much the Ottoman state spent on its armed forces. The most reliable estimate of the state's income under Suleiman the Magnificent (1520–1566) is 15 million ducats per year, a considerable amount in the sixteenth century. Of this amount only 2 millions finally wound up in the sultan's treasury, leaving a yearly expenditure of 13 millions. During Suleiman's reign, the *timar* system raised 130,000 cavalrymen, the equivalent of state-assigned incomes of 650 million aspers. If this amount is divided by 60 to get the ducat equivalent, 10.8 million ducats or roughly 83 percent of all expenditures were used to support the feudal cavalry alone. But the sultan also had to pay the expenses of four squadrons of professional mercenary cavalry, the *sipahi*-s of the court (roughly 11,500 men; approximately 3,500 aspers per *sipahi*), and those of his janissaries (about 25,000 men; 2,500 aspers per janissary)—another 1.7 million ducats. Although this amount increases the total of military costs to 96 percent of total expenditures, it does not include the monies spent on the schooling and training of the mercenaries or those which went to the artillery and the manufacture of their equipment. Adding these amounts would indicate that *all* state expenditures were employed to maintain the army. All other expenditures had therefore to come out of the sultan's treasury. It is thus clear why a reversal of fortunes brought on total bankruptcy as quickly as it did.

The military establishment weakened the economy in other respects as well. Besides the already mentioned 130,000 cavalrymen, soldiering attracted numerous other elements whose absence from their places of residence also meant a decline in production and, consequently, taxable income. Best-known were the *akinci*-s, a scouting force which later grew considerably and in the nineteenth century perpetrated the "atrocities" which gave the Ottomans such a bad reputation in Europe. The *akinci*-s, not part of the regular army, had to find their own sustenance in the country they traversed and thereby ruined its productivity and taxability, and fought for booty and tax exemptions. They were recruited from the tenants of the feudatories, whose lands yielded correspondingly less. While the *akinci*-s were Turkish and nominally Muslims, a considerable number of others who were not also earned tax exemptions and various other privileges in exchange for service. These people of the European provinces of the empire performed many tasks mainly connected with the army's supply train. These auxiliaries were closely tied to the military by profession, social status, activities, privileges, etc., and represented a drain on the productive forces of the economy on which the entire military establishment rested.

Ottoman society was a military society not only in the economic and social senses but also in its administrative organization. The sultan was head of the government and commander-in-chief of the army. The first ten, from Osman to Suleiman, regularly campaigned with their forces. By Suleiman's time, the grand-vizier was both a capable soldier and chief of the civil administration. His "cabinet," the *Erkani Devlet* (Pillars of State), included the three chief military judges (quadi-askerler), the commanders of the Asian and European armies (*beylerbeyler*), the three chief financial officers (*defterdarlar*), the commander of the janissaries (*janissary agva*), the commander of the navy (*kapudan pasha*), and the man authorized to affix the ruler's signature to documents (*nishanci*). The number three in the case of the military judges and financial officers represents the three major divisions of the empire for which they were responsible—Anatolia, Europe, Asia-Africa. On this twelve-man council, eight represented the military.

In the provinces, the entire administrative organization, except for tax collection, the duty of the local *defterdar*-s, was in the hands of the military. The *timarli*-s and *za'im*-s were the local administrators, and their holdings were grouped into *sancak*-s (first roughly the equivalent of provinces, later of counties) administered by the officers who commanded the feudatories on active duty. These *sancak bey*-s were subordinate to the two *beylerbey*-s.

The military also dominated the legal profession. The *qaḍi-asker*-s were also responsible for all courts and law enforcement in their respective provinces. They appointed all judges and served as the empire's supreme court, with their powers limited only by appellate functions vested in the grand-vizier and finally the sultan. Even after Selim I (1512–1520) created a new office, that of *Shaykh al-Islam*, supposed to control the entire theological and judiciary structure, the *qaḍi-asker*-s' power remained virtually unchanged because the duties of the holder of the new office were mainly ecclesiastical.

Civilians performed only ecclesiastical and educational functions (with the exception of the schools which produced all the administrators) and were tax collectors. Only the last was of real importance but its fruits quickly found their way into the pockets of the military. The taxpayers were, of course, also civilians, but they could not match the military in status, importance, and influence, or attain sufficient power to sustain the state economically or culturally once the military began to falter. These taxable producers, Muslims and non-Muslims alike, were starved for capital, enjoyed no real support from the state, and—with the exception of the imperial palace and the establishments of leading notables—had really no market in which to make their fortunes. Although they lived in the empire, they were not participants in Ottoman society.

The professional Ottomans, the military, judiciary, theologians, and others who served the House of Osman and were loyal only to it, had no national identities—the word Turk among them had the meaning of country bumpkin. Ottoman society was based on traditions which went back to Central Asia, the Caliphate, and the Saljūq states, reinforced by the requirements and limits imposed by Islam and the *ghāzi* tradition. It consequently became inflexible, a military, command-oriented society with no alternative if the commander proved incompetent or if the military became unable to function properly.

For slightly over two hundred and fifty years the Ottomans were lucky: ten able and competent rulers succeeded each other without interruption and the army was ably led and had opportunities for action. But then their luck turned. After Suleiman's death, the House of Osman only occasionally produced an able ruler and the army lost the ability to function as it had previously. State and society collapsed with amazing speed, although appearances were maintained successfully for a while longer.

■

It is not easy to determine which, if any, of the many ills that befell
the Ottoman Empire was the basic cause of its deterioration and
ultimate dissolution. It appears, however, that the gradual corruption of the armed forces are foremost. In a military society everything can be checked except the undermining of the armed forces.

The armed forces consisted of feudatory and mercenary units by
the time of Suleiman. Both the mercenary cavalry (the *sipahi*-s of
the court) and the janissary corps were composed of slaves, the human booty of victorious wars. The ruler thus had an armed force
which did not depend on the *timar* system and was therefore not
part of the regular army. The sultan could use this force at his discre-
tion, an advantage in view of the growing power of certain *timarli-s*
and the consequent possibility of the development of a hereditary
aristocracy. But there were problems as well. The mercenaries broke
the homogeneity of the armed forces and required large additional
revenues but provided no new economic base. Further, the sons of
the mercenaries had to be absorbed into precisely the feudatory
group their fathers had kept in check. When it proved impossible to
find land for new *timar*-s, the mercenaries became a serious liability,
for they demanded that their sons be enrolled as janissaries. By 1660,
nearly 55,000 men drew pay as janissaries, and about the same number were officially members although they did not serve and drew
no pay. They were exempt from taxes and always supplied additional
men when the corps presented new demands to the ruler. Out of this
situation grew another which was both militarily and economically
ruinous.

Since nobody can live from tax exemptions alone, the inactive
janissaries stationed in Constantinople infiltrated various trades, such
as baking. The basis of this "alliance" was the old *ghāzi* code, the
*futūwah,* kept alive by such dervish orders as the Mevlevis and
Bektashis, which already had close ties to the janissaries. Not only did
such additional revenue losses as the tax-exempt janissary baker
thereby come into being, but every demand of the unruly soldiery
was backed by both armed and economic pressure.

The rulers attempted to solve this problem by transferring as
many janissaries as possible to the provinces for garrison duty. There,
however, they came into conflict with the feudatories, who were no
longer the old *timarli*-s or *za'im*-s but real landlords who owned
their farms and estates (*çiflik*-s) outright. As the empire grew, so did
the number of provinces and administrators—there were, for example, 290 *sancak*-s and 20 *beylerbey*-s. Most of this administrative
proliferation occurred, however, after the empire ceased to expand,
and was therefore intended to create administrative positions for
soldiers. A military society functions best when the lines of command

are clearly defined and power is highly centralized. The introduction of the *sipahi*-s of the court, janissaries, and palace school–trained slave administrators, however, created a slave mentality even among the free-born. The chain of command was thereby blurred and the situation invited chaos.

This tendency reinforced the development of the *çiflik*. Suleiman's codification of the law was an attempt to prevent abuses of the *timar* system, but roughly fifty years after his death, it was quite usual to see several men claiming the income of a *timar* without any presenting himself for military service. By the end of the sixteenth and the beginning of the seventeenth centuries, sons of *timarli*-s and of janissaries and their descendants looked for a living but no new land was available. The obvious tendency was to keep holdings acquired earlier and to transform the *timar*-s into hereditary possessions (*çiflik*-s). The weakened central authority could not prevent this. Not only did the old connection between military service and the basic economy disappear but also local power structures, often quite independent of the central authority, emerged by the end of the eighteenth century. These local lords recognized their nominal dependence on the sultan and as a rule delivered at least a portion of the taxes to him. In other areas, the owners of *çiflik*-s delivered taxes and developed a relationship with the people working their lands which, while often unsatisfactory to the cultivators, was at least known and stable.

This already unhealthy stability was upset by the irregularly paid janissaries stationed in the provinces. They displaced and often killed the landowners, upset the existing social and economic relationships, and appropriated the produce of the land. This eliminated a considerable percentage of the state's income, diminished production in general, and finally led to revolt. The Serb uprising of 1804, which finally brought about the independence of Serbia, started as a peasant uprising directed against the misrule of the janissaries and aimed at the restoration of the sultan's legitimate rule in the *pashalik* of Belgrade. In this manner the decline of miltary organization and discipline went hand in hand with economic bankruptcy and started the process which finally resulted in the disappearance of the Ottoman Empire.

These problems might have been dealt with if the empire had had able rulers. The development of a Byzantine-style court and the growing isolation of the ruler from society contributed to the sultan's reduced authority. The decline in personal abilities of sultans after Suleiman was a factor. In a nonmilitary society all these disadvantages would, however, have been less important than they were in the Ottoman Empire. There are numerous weak rulers in history whose reigns prospered due to the action of able ministers. In the

Ottoman Empire not even the string of able grand-viziers in the seventeenth century stemmed the downward trend. No military society can function properly unless it obeys a chief, and the sultan, leader of the faithful and commander of both his *ghāzi*-feudatory army that owed him its living and the slave-mercenary soldiers who owed their very life to him, was irreplaceable. When central power declined, Ottoman society remained a military society without a commander, run by people whose command-oriented mentality could not function properly when orders were either not given or not enforced. Seen in this light, the behavior of provincial governors and the transformation of *timar*-s into hereditary holdings were at once individual cupidity and an attempt to establish a local socioeconomic order which the central-imperial government was unable to provide.

Had the empire continued to expand, the military would have been happily occupied. Expansion would have kept the state treasury in balance by supplying revenue over and above the tax income which went fully to the army and would have made land available for additional *timar*-s. However, expansion in Europe was desirable but impossible, in Egypt possible but unprofitable, and in Persia possible but undesirable.

Ottoman technology and organization limited expansion. Every spring the army and its supply train had to be assembled, then had to march to the limits of the state over inadequate roads, often in bad condition due to the previous campaign, before it could begin to fight. In late autumn the fighting had to end and the long march home begun, to allow the feudatories and tax collectors to get their due from the harvest. Every mile added to the empire lengthened the road and shortened the campaign season. Victory became possible only when the enemy was very weak and permanent possession of new territory, even in case of victory, became very difficult. The end of expansion was thus caused by practical factors more than by the deterioration of the army.

A nonmilitary society might have prospered on Ottoman territory. It was large, contained fertile and rich provinces, was located in some of the economically and strategically most important lands of late medieval and early modern Europe. After all those lands supported the Roman and Byzantine empires. But all these advantages could not be exploited by a military society with its own peculiar structure and requirements. As long as these were satisfied, the state flourished and the society functioned. When the situation changed, the society faltered and could not adjust. The features which had allowed the empire to grow and function had developed in such ways as to cause its decline. What had begun as strength eventually became weakness.

■

This survey of the Ottoman experience offers some insights into the process by which societies are founded, develop, atrophy, and eventually collapse. In particular, it raises questions about military societies—above all, whether or not they are more inclined to rigidity than nonmilitary societies. These are significant issues for the modern world, which seems inclined to produce military societies under the threat of atomic war.

The passage and observance of laws is necessary to the functioning of any society and such obedience is a particular requirement of military organizations. What sets a military society like the Ottoman Empire apart from nonmilitary societies is the extension of military obedience to society at large. This practice discourages independent and original thinking, which in turn precludes innovation. It also tends to foster absolute reliance on authority; confusion results when the authority is ineffective or nonexistent.

The Ottoman experience is indicative of the general features of a military society. The strong central authority pays undue respect to military demands in formulation of national policy. The economy devotes an extremely high percentage of its surplus to nonproductive enterprises, usually related to the military; economic adjustment is consequently difficult and progress slow. Society is divided into two clearly defined groups—the dominant military and subordinate civilians. The civilian sector is politically and economically dependent on and obedient to the military. The prevailing mentality encourages conformity rather than independence. The Ottoman Empire accordingly provides a standard by which other military and nonmilitary societies may be judged.

# Gunpowder and Governmental Power: War in Early Modern Europe (1494-1825)

## Jon M. Bridgman

The age of exploration and the political, institutional, religious, and economic and financial events in Europe justify calling the period 1494–1525 "revolutionary." And the use of gunpowder was a revolutionary event, marking the first fundamental departure in the development of weapons. From Neolithic times until the end of the fifteenth century, propelled weapons depended on human or animal energy. Although certain modifications produced larger launchers and more efficient mechanical devices to store energy, the principle remained the same. But the harnessing of chemical energy in the use of quick-burning powder meant that larger objects could be hurled greater distances with increased accuracy. The art of war was transformed.

It is difficult to attribute the invention of gunpowder to a specific person, place, or time, and its development probably consisted of small, unsystematic discoveries which cumulatively produced a breakthrough. For example, it was known as early as 1100 that a rapid burn would result from mixing certain things together; at about the same time, fireworks and small rockets, perhaps invented by the Chinese, appeared in the West. Eventually it was noted that a particular mixture of charcoal, saltpeter, and sulfur produced explosions. There is unambiguous evidence that gunpowder was used in the fourteenth century to propel a stone from a primitive mortar. In most large battles in Europe during the next two centuries, similar machines were probably used, as much for prestige and morale as for

■

their actual effects. Gunpowder was virtually irrelevant to warfare during this period and war was conducted more or less as it had been during previous centuries.

Experimentation continued, however, and all manner and sizes of guns—from huge guns with six-foot bores to tiny handguns—were built to find the most effective combination. Inventors sought ways to resolve the central problem of stronger barrels which would not shatter. Early multibarreled guns were inefficient because they required excessive time to reload; they nonetheless were precursors to the modern machine gun. Experiments employed different projectiles including arrows, stones, iron, and scrap materials.

The impact of gunpowder on warfare was limited by technological problems and by rival weapons systems. During the fourteenth and fifteenth centuries, bows and arrows developed more rapidly and were preferred to guns. Armorers, anxious to compensate for improvements in the bow, produced stronger, lighter armor through advances in metallurgy, particularly the development of tougher steel. Consequently, traditional weapons and armor remained dominant.

Gunpowder, however, became important in the conduct of siege operations. Early fifteenth-century artillery lacked the mobility necessary for use in battles but it could be used when sufficient time and labor were available. The most striking and historically significant example was the successful Turkish siege of Constantinople in 1453. Gigantic guns on huge sledges were dragged into place by teams of oxen. Hundreds of men prepared the way by knocking down trees and building bridges. After weeks of labor the guns were finally in place. Monstrous hoists were constructed to lift huge stones into the guns and a small city was created to service the machines. Finally the walls of Constantinople were gradually and relentlessly battered down. The whole process required time and security to make elaborate preparations. Similar operations were conducted by the French kings during the 1450s and 1460s against castles of recalcitrant nobles and by the Spaniards in their siege of Granada during the 1480s. These isolated events were significant in the political development of Europe but they had little impact on the conduct of war.

The marginal importance of gunpowder from 1450 to 1490 was also due to limited opportunities for its application, since after a century of extensive warfare Europe had become relatively peaceful. The technology continued to develop, however, and when war recurred, it employed revolutionary techniques.

The renewal of large-scale warfare, first in Italy during 1494 and throughout western Europe during the next generation, introduced the new techniques. Artillery became technically feasible. Iron replaced brass in gun barrels to withstand explosions. Trunnions, small knobs on either side of gun barrels, were invented so guns could be supported and aimed. Gun carriages made guns more mobile. Milled powder was introduced to reduce misfiring. These new guns rendered the medieval walled city obsolete, and increased mobility made elaborate preparations and control over adjacent countrysides unnecessary.

Large guns were also used at sea and hulls were designed to accommodate them. By the beginning of the sixteenth century, warships appeared which remained as a basic prototype for three hundred years—similar to those used by Nelson at Trafalgar.

In addition, handguns became efficient during the period of 1494–1525. Steel barrels fastened to stocks were designed to absorb the shock of recoil and allow the user to hold the gun against his shoulder. The ingenious firelock, a spring-loaded trigger which drives a burning wick into the fire hole to ignite the powder, appeared and that was followed by the invention of the cartridge, with powder and ball encased in a piece of paper. Soldiers bit off the end of the cartridge, poured some of the powder into the firing pan, the rest down the barrel, rammed paper and ball into the barrel with a ramrod, and fired. Cartridge-loaded guns were an improvement, in that they could be fired more rapidly than the old guns, but they were still slower and less accurate than bows. These guns could pierce armor at 300 yards and unarmored soldiers at 400 yards; arrows were effective at half the distance. That difference gradually became significant and by 1525 most soldiers were armed with guns.

■

The introduction of relatively efficient mobile artillery and handguns revolutionized the conduct of warfare at the beginning of the sixteenth century. Guns made cavalry largely obsolete. From the Battle of Adrianople (378) until the late fifteenth century, cavalry dominated European battlefields. Cavalry units were heavily armored, carried long pikes, and simply rode over infantry. The pattern changed rapidly. In the late fifteenth century, armies were about 50 percent cavalry and by 1525, cavalry was reduced to 15 percent or less and was used for reconnaissance, or pursuit when the enemy was in retreat.

The weapons developed with little fundamental change since the Bronze Age also became obsolete. Battle-axes, bows and arrows, lances, swords, daggers—all whirling and striking weapons—were retained mostly for ceremonial uses. There was one exception: the pike (a long spear, up to fifteen feet, tipped with iron) was used by infantrymen to protect musketeers while they reloaded.

Battles no longer opened with cavalry charges. They began with artillery duels, followed by an infantry advance in which the men held their fire until the last possible moment, to inflict maximal losses on the enemy and cause his discipline to break, his lines to crumble. The cavalry was then sent in to finish the job. Battles were conducted in three stages instead of one.

Armies also changed. The semiprofessional, semiprivate, occasional armies comprised of men having feudal obligations or a desire for adventure were replaced by permanent, professional, mercenary, and king-controlled forces. The development of such standing armies was partly fostered by new technologies which required a certain expertise, especially in the artillery.

Although the fortified cities which dominated the medieval period proved to be no match for artillery during the late fifteenth century, fortifications were redesigned and remained important. During the early sixteenth century, single high walls of the traditional forts were replaced by a series of lower, even sunken, walls. They were protected by outworks and promontories to keep an enemy at maximal distance and to support firing on those forces which succeeded in breaching the walls. Long, gradually sloping, open areas masked the approaching enemy's view of objects inside the fortification until the attacking forces were in range. The increasing complexity of these edifices required military engineers; they, in turn, reinforced the necessity for standing armies. The first fortifications to appear around Italian cities by 1525 proved to be increasingly impregnable. Consequently, the siege again became a feature of warfare after a brief disappearance.

■

European political institutions were profoundly affected by military changes. The feudal nobility was dealt a severe blow. Their castles were no longer impregnable, so they became dependent on the king. The new weapons made their cavalry obsolete and they thus were of no use to the king. Their power over local inhabitants was reduced, since their role as defenders became even less credible. The gradual decline in the prestige and power of the nobles, which began in the sixteenth century, continued for several hundred years. In addition, the appearance of new weapons and infantry gave the common man an important role in warfare.

Kings alone could afford to finance the development of new technologies and armies. Taxation as a means of raising money revived methods largely unused since Roman times and kings launched an ever-accelerating process: new taxes supported new armies, new armies imposed higher taxes, and higher taxes necessitated larger armies. Kings then became the ultimate repositories of violence within their societies, and the bureaucracy—-civil mercenaries analogous to those who staffed the new armies—grew in accordance with royal power. By the beginning of the sixteenth century, the French king employed approximately 12,000 civilians.

European kings effectively conquered their own societies; the nations of Europe conquered the world. The speed and extent of the conquest is striking. The Portuguese armed a few small ships and sent them around the Cape of Good Hope to the Indian Ocean, where in a few years they deposed the Arabs, who had ruled for half a millennium. The Portuguese and Spaniards created huge empires in the Western Hemisphere. These unprecedented events were the result of technological developments.

The developing military technology had an economic impact. The manufacture of guns required iron, with a resultant revival of mining throughout much of Europe. Old mines were reopened and new mines dug. New sources of power were required to drain and ventilate mines, transport ore, and extract the metal. Animal and human power was used but the use of water power was most successful and it sharply increased productivity. Ore production was improved and paralleled by better means of extraction. As a result, machine shops with power-driven belts, relatively large machines, increased numbers of workers, and more sophisticated methods were developed and iron production was thus primitively industrialized.

Industrial capitalism was a necessary concomitant to this growth. The number and importance of capitalists increased radically and they were almost always associated with weapons production and the iron industry. Those operations were so expensive that only wealthy men participated. Early capitalism frequently involved the kings, who either borrowed money for their own iron industries or gave the capitalists monopolies. Although not the most important cause of modern capitalism, the weapons-inspired industry certainly reinforced its development.

■

The analytical and scientific study of war began with Machiavelli in the early sixteenth century. It became a discipline in the seventeenth century and institutions for the study of war were established. War began to be conceptualized more abstractly, war games were developed, toy soldiers and models were invented, and scientists were drawn into the problem to design fortifications and study ballistics and other elements of warfare.

The three decades of revolutionary change beginning at the

turn of the sixteenth century were followed by three centuries of relatively slow development. Armies grew in size, professionalization, and organization. Armies in the sixteenth century rarely exceeded 50,000 men, the armies of Louis XIV a century later comprised 200,000 or more, and the armies of Napoleon grew to approximately 1 million. They became better drilled and disciplined with trained officers, and the troops were better paid and equipped. Armies performed more sophisticated maneuvers in battle and were organized into units with a rank structure. The modern army emerged during this period, based on the pattern established during the sixteenth century.

New technological departures resolved some of the organizational problems. For example, the invention of the bayonet allowed each infantryman to be his own pikeman and simultaneously made infantry more mobile. But the bayonet charge was in a sense a step backward because it returned fighting to the level of hand weapons. Artillery became more accurate and mobile; it was used more extensively as techniques for rapid firing developed. But no fundamental breakthrough was made.

The scale of battles increased; tactics and strategy became more intricate and sophisticated. But the pattern of battle remained unchanged—an elaborate and ritualized repetition of the traditional opening artillery duel followed by infantry advances, and the use of cavalry for mopping up.

The art of fortification developed more rapidly than artillery. By the eighteenth century, fortified cities were virtually impregnable. Sieges practically disappeared from warfare and battles tended to occur in open fields where there was sufficient room for elaborate and extensive maneuvering. Further, only the richest cities could afford the luxury of security. But the high cost of extensive fortifications precluded urban expansion and restricted economic growth.

The social, political, and economic impact of these changes emerged gradually. Nobles lost more of their independence and became subordinates in the royal system, often as officers in the army, sometimes as bureaucrats and statesmen. The country house and chateau replaced the castle as a symbol of the nobility, which came to represent frivolity rather than fighting. The kings consolidated their power, extended their control, established sophisticated governing systems, found new ways to raise revenues, and generally fostered the emergence of the modern state. There were many motivations for these policies but military power was the major factor.

The impulses toward economic growth in Europe were complex and certainly not exclusively based on military aggrandizement. The drive for national power encouraged industries related to war-making. Basic to royal support of exploration and the development of colonial empires was the assumption that empires increase power. Trade and commerce were seen in terms of national competition, expressed in the economic theory of mercantilism.

The gradual changes in military technology were accompanied by correspondingly gradual alterations in European society. During the period 1500–1800, Europe was relatively stable in social, political, economic as well as military terms—requiring several centuries to adjust to the revolutionary changes of the sixteenth century.

The French Revolution resulted in an increase in the size of armies and for the first time in the modern era war became a truly mass phenomenon. Nonetheless, wars were fought in much the same way as in the sixteenth century. Modern revolutionary changes in military technology came after 1825, when European industrialization and mechanization began to alter the shape of warfare. Military technology and war after that time again reinforced the movements destined to revolutionize European institutions.

The history of early modern Europe suggests that war and society are interdependent. Military technology affects warfare, which in turn affects political, social, and economic institutions. Conversely, institutions determine what is technologically feasible. The relationship seems to be a kind of pendulum: existing technological advances allow military technological changes; these changes foster adjustments in the conduct of war; changes in war alter society; the altered society facilitates new technological advances, and so on.

This analysis also seems to indicate that military and other changes do not occur at a constant rate. The revolution of the early sixteenth century was followed by a long period of gradual change, after which another revolution occurred. This history of war and society therefore seems to be characterized by infrequent but rapid revolutions followed by long periods of adjusting to those changes and, in the process, preparing the way for a new revolution.

# PART *III*

## The Military
## in Industrializing Countries

# Introduction

The essays in this section are linked by concern for the military's role in nineteenth- and twentieth-century industrial societies and are arranged in roughly chronological order. They are distinguished by their interests in different cultures: four are clearly Western (the United States, Great Britain, Germany, Russia), one is partially so (Argentina), and one is Asian (China).

Each of the essayists examines a particular case. Thomas J. Pressly discusses the profound effects of military-political interrelationships during the U.S. Civil War. Aldon D. Bell argues that despite considerable change in their view of war during the nineteenth century, the British remained deeply suspicious of the military institution. Jon M. Bridgman suggests that the popular preconception of Germany as the prototypical military society ignores the drastic changes in the role of the military in German society during the last three and a half centuries. Donald W. Treadgold asserts that Soviet military power is real and an important consideration in the Cold War but remains entirely subordinate to civilian control. Carl E. Solberg contends that despite a significant, frequently disruptive role in Argentine politics, the military is less ideologically homogeneous than is sometimes assumed. James R. Townsend examines the army as a significant socializing force in Communist China. The degree of military independence runs from considerable (Germany and Argentina) to slight in the other societies. The nature of the military institution and its relationship to society are conditioned by specific cultural

■

realities. In some cases (e.g., the Communist regimes) the army is first a tool of governmental policies; in others it reflects social class. These distinctions in the role of the military are indicators of broader differences and demonstrate that each society is unique.

The distinctions among societies and their military institutions should not, however, obscure fundamental similarities. The comparability of military institutions is perhaps all the more noteworthy when one considers the diversity of societies discussed in these essays. In all cases, the military cannot be fully understood unless seen as an integral part of the society. In many instances in the development of these societies, war has altered, indeed revolutionized, the social structure and political authority. While the military and war are common features of these societies, an equally general characteristic is the minimal influence of the military in politics. If these societies are typical, the fear of military domination may be a myth which should be laid to rest.

The low incidence of the military's political influence should not, however, be equated with insignificance. The military clearly plays an important role in the domestic affairs of at least two cases studied here (Germany and Argentina). In all the societies examined (except Argentina), the military plays significant roles in national defense. There may indeed be an inverse relationship between internal and external roles of the military: the internal political influence of the military is largest in Argentina, where its external role is probably smallest.

# Civil-Military Relations in the United States Civil War (1861-1865)

## Thomas J. Pressly

The United States Civil War is a prime example of warfare between two societies, both of which were almost entirely "civilian" in outlook and composition, devoid of a military caste or ideology. The Union and the Confederacy, however much they differed in other respects, were similar in that neither contained a separate and highly developed social institution or group which could be designated as "the military."

The limited size of United States military forces in the nineteenth century may both reflect and explain why the military was not a force in politics or society at large. In April 1861, the regular army contained only 16,113 officers and enlisted men out of a total population of approximately 31,500,000. The officer corps, which presumably would have constituted the heart of a distinct military caste, numbered only 1,108 in the army (December 30, 1860) and 1,565 in the navy (December 1, 1860). Because of the security afforded by geographical location and the fortunate (for the United States) distribution of military and diplomatic power in the world, there developed in the United States the tradition of relying on the militia and other citizen soldiers, while employing conscription only in wartime.

There were of course individuals who became widely known through their military exploits and subsequently achieved political success. One thinks of the elections of George Washington, Andrew Jackson, William Henry Harrison, Zachary Taylor, and Ulysses S. Grant. These former generals were president for almost a third of the

■

Republic's first ninety years, but none came from a military family or identified himself primarily as a soldier. With the possible exception of Andrew Jackson, these soldiers-turned-politicians apparently accepted and stressed the supremacy of civilian over military authority as provided in the Constitution, and all—again with the possible exception of Jackson—avoided conflicts with civilian authorities when they were military leaders.

Another, quite different, type of political general nonetheless emerged. This type includes Alexander Hamilton (an officer in the American Revolution and a major general in the undeclared war against France in 1798), Civil War general George B. McClellan, George Patton, and Douglas MacArthur. All emphasized that they were military figures and thus different from civilians—one thinks of Patton's pearl-handled revolvers and MacArthur's conflicts with Truman. Yet the presidential bids of McClellan and MacArthur were notably unsuccessful. Thus the presidency has been achieved by generals who (except perhaps for Andrew Jackson) had fundamentally civilian outlooks.

Underlying and reinforcing the dominant civilian orientation was a pronounced egalitarian spirit, hostile to the concept of any elite —whether military or civilian. It fostered the view that individuals were equal, "one person as good as another"; the governing principle should therefore be "majority rule," "the will of the people," whether in the realm of culture, social patterns, politics, or military affairs.

When war came in 1861, it accordingly brought into conflict two societies which, despite their differences and disagreements, were both essentially civilian and egalitarian in character.

These characteristics became evident immediately at the outbreak of armed hostilities in April 1861. When Union troops garrisoning Fort Sumter were attacked by Confederate forces and surrendered the fort, the overwhelming public sentiment in the Union and the Confederacy supported their respective governments. Observers described large, excited crowds in the streets, men marching and drilling in impromptu volunteer groups, and women sewing uniforms and flags. According to many accounts, business came to a virtual standstill, as public attention became focused upon war and preparation for battle. In short, the populations of both sides were deeply engaged in the conflict from the start. This mass engagement was essential to the conduct of war waged by societies which lacked large professional military establishments and which assumed that government policy reflected the popular will.

A second indication of the profound influence of those characteristics was the way the armies were organized and commanded. The criteria for selecting and promoting officers were in many cases more civilian than military. Lincoln consciously used appointments and promotions in the Union armed forces, particularly at the beginning of the war, to win support from various constituencies. On one occasion, when Lincoln and Secretary of War Stanton were considering a list of possible appointees to the rank of brigadier general, a staff officer heard Lincoln urge the appointment of a man named Schimmelfennig: "There has got to be something done unquestionably in the interest of the Dutch, and to that end I want Schimmelfennig appointed." Stanton protested that there were German officers who were recommended more strongly than Schimmelfennig, but Lincoln was unmoved: "No matter about that, his name will make up for any difference there may be." As Lincoln walked off, he reportedly kept repeating the name with obvious enjoyment: "Schimmelfennig, Schimmelfennig, Schimmelfennig." This incident indicates the pressures and traditions of a civilian society at work in military matters.

A third reflection of the egalitarian and civilian character of both the Union and Confederacy is the interrelationship between political and military events throughout the war. Ostensibly military decisions—such as moving an army forward to engage the enemy forces—might be made less on strategic considerations than on political grounds, i.e., to gain or maintain public support for the government's war policies or to weaken the enemy public's support for its government. If the original military decision which was taken for "political" reasons resulted in victory, rewards accrued to the government in the political sphere, such as winning elections or votes in Congress. If it resulted in a military defeat, the government suffered accordingly in the political sphere.

This pattern rested on the requirement in egalitarian and civilian societies that government actions—even military actions in wartime—be in accord with the "will of the people." In the Union states, the political-military interrelationship reflected the further tendency in modern industrial societies for wars to become "total," requiring the mobilization of all facets of society.

■

During the first eighteen to twenty-four months of the war, the Confederacy held the military initiative. Public attention was focused on the eastern military theater between the two capital cities, Washington and Richmond. The Confederate army was commanded by the outstanding team of Robert E. Lee and Thomas J. ("Stonewall") Jackson. Lee was a professional soldier who had graduated from West Point and perhaps could even be said to have come from a military family. But he pictured himself neither as part of a military elite nor in the pattern of generals like Hamilton and McClellan. He did not emphasize his military status or become involved in serious conflicts with his civilian superiors. Jackson like many of the generals in the Civil War, was not a professional soldier.

Lee and Jackson led the Confederate forces to a series of military victories, beginning in the Shenandoah Valley (May-June 1862), continuing in the defense of Richmond (Battle of the Seven Days, June-July 1862), moving northward (Second Battle of Bull Run, August 1862), and then taking the offensive and pushing into Maryland toward Pennsylvania. Although the Maryland invasion was checked (Battle of Antietam, September 1862), the Confederate forces continued to win battles (Fredericksburg, December 1862, and Chancellorsville, May 1863, where Jackson was killed). Once again, Lee led his army on an offensive into Union territory, this time invading Pennsylvania (June 1863).

Lee's strategy was dominated by political considerations. Before he embarked on offensives into Union territory during the late summer of 1862 and the spring of 1863, Lee's communications with Jefferson Davis set forth a beautifully clear analysis of the interrelationship between military and political events. Writing in August 1862, and knowing that elections for the Union Congress would be held that autumn, Lee suggested that, if Confederate troops invaded the Union and remained there, the Union public would become dissatisfied with the war effort, would conclude that the Union could not win, would put pressure on its government to stop the war, and thus the Confederate states would gain their independence. Lee added that it made no difference whether the Union public in fact wanted such a result—once the war was stopped, it would not be resumed. It is difficult to imagine a more direct linkage of military and political developments.

Confederate military victories in the eastern theater in 1861 and 1862 were accompanied by political successes. President Davis and Vice-President Alexander H. Stephens had been selected in February 1861 as provisional officials, and in the first regular elections in the Confederacy in autumn 1861, no one ran against them, and a majority of the congressmen elected were supporters of the Davis administration. Moreover, the administration was given important war powers in 1862 by the Confederate Congress, including the authority to draft persons into the armed forces and to suspend the writ of *habeas corpus.*

These same victories, however, brought political difficulties for the Union administration. Lincoln understood that the Union needed military victories to sustain public support. One friend who was also a newspaper reporter quoted Lincoln's anguished exclamation when he learned of a military defeat: "My God, my God, what will the country say! What will the country say!"

Despite his intensive search, Lincoln was unable to find a military commander who could lead the Union troops in the east to victory. He tried a succession of generals—Scott, McDowell, McClellan, Pope, McClellan again, Burnside, Hooker. He suffered the political consequences of military defeat in an egalitarian society, most notably during the midterm congressional elections of 1862, when his war policies were severely criticized and his Republican party lost many seats in the House of Representatives, including some from Illinois. The *New York Times,* which had supported Lincoln, interpreted the results as a vote of no confidence in the administration and Lincoln referred to the election as a "defeat." If the United States had had a parliamentary system of government, Lincoln might even have been removed from office.

Lincoln was eventually rescued from his political troubles by a reversal of military events. Lee's invasion of Pennsylvania was checked at the Battle of Gettysburg (July 1863), with such heavy Confederate casualties that he never mounted another invasion of Union territory. Meanwhile, the steady advances of Union forces in the western theater since early 1862 were capped with success in July 1863, when Vicksburg fell. This victory gave the Union control of the Mississippi River, thereby cutting the Confederacy in two and bringing more public attention to the western theater.

Success in the western theater likewise brought the team of U. S. Grant and W. T. Sherman to the fore, thus ending Lincoln's search for successful military leaders. With the appointment of Grant as commander of all Union forces in spring 1864, Lincoln found a general who could win and who shared an awareness of the interrelationship between military and political considerations. Grant was a graduate of West Point and a professional soldier until 1854, but few high-ranking generals during the Civil War were less military in outlook than he.

The military victories in summer 1863 greatly eased political pressure on the Lincoln administration, as was reflected in the victories of pro-administration candidates in the local, offyear elections that autumn. A spirit of defeatism surfaced once more in the Union when a military stalemate developed in the summer of 1864. One Union army was apparently stalled on the outskirts of Richmond and a second outside Atlanta. The capture of Atlanta by Union forces early in September subsequently restored public support for the war. Lincoln was reelected and the new Congress contained a solid majority sympathetic to him.

For the Confederates, the months after July 1863 brought increasing gloom and political opposition to the Davis administration. Now it was Davis's time of political troubles. After the Confederate congressional elections in autumn 1863, he could no longer count on

a congressional majority. His own Vice-President Stephens became
one of Davis's most vocal critics and led a vigorous group of state's
rights localists, who maintained that the administration's legislation
was more centralized and hence more despotic than that of the
former United States government. Some of the most extreme members of this opposition even urged that their states secede from the
Confederacy. Thus military defeat and political defection went hand
in hand in the Confederacy's last few months before the surrender
at Appomattox in April 1865.

■

To what extent did the characteristics and patterns revealed in the
Civil War persist in the United States following Appomattox? A close
interrelationship between military and political developments continued during wars involving the United States since 1865. Military
successes in the Spanish-American War and World Wars I and II,
were frequent and military setbacks sufficiently rare to ensure that
several administrations would avoid crippling political defeats during the conflicts. All three wars ended in military victory. Disillusionment came in each instance *after* the fighting had ceased, primarily
because of the peace terms rather than the conduct of war. In contrast, the Korean and Vietnam wars resulted in military stalemate
which caused political dissatisfaction and varied difficulties for the
administration in power. President Lincoln was rescued from his
political difficulties by military victories; Presidents Truman and
Johnson were not so fortunate.

Whether the United States after 1865 remained an essentially
civilian society or whether it developed a military elite is a matter
of debate and disagreement. The United States became more industrialized and mechanized in the twentieth century and so did its
armed forces. Huge industrial establishments became necessary to
produce weapons and equipment for the armed forces. Early in
1961, President Eisenhower warned the nation against a "military-
industrial complex," a segment of society which seemed analogous to
the military elites in nineteenth-century societies. There is no agreement so far in the 1970s concerning whether a military-industrial
complex has indeed exerted much influence upon public policies.
Whether or not Eisenhower's warning is valid it is worth noting that
it was voiced by a graduate of West Point who spent most of his adult
years as a professional soldier but whose instincts and demeanor
seem fundamentally and unmistakably civilian. If such a complex has
developed it is poetic justice that it was called to the nation's attention by a classic representative of the long-standing civilian tradition
reflected in the Civil War.

# War and the Military in Nineteenth-Century Britain

## Aldon D. Bell

War seemed incredibly remote to most Britons during the generation after the great effort against Napoleon. The empire in 1815 included possessions on every continent and many strategic islands in between, and most Britons took pride in the empire despite their disagreements about its real value. Nonetheless, the average literate Englishman usually had little awareness of the military implications of empire, and was scarcely touched by military obligations or international conflict during the period.

The striking benefits of world power and insular security enjoyed by Britain were made possible by the overwhelming strength of the Royal Navy. At Trafalgar, Britain lost Nelson but gained control of the high seas. The Congress of Vienna in 1815 did not entertain discussions about maritime law or related matters—since no other nation could dispute Britain's preeminence. France in the 1880s and, more significantly, Germany in the 1890s constructed battle fleets which troubled the Admiralty and strained the resources of the British fleet but a one-to-one confrontation with British sea-power was unthinkable.

Naval strength combined with foreign policy and good fortune to keep Britain out of a European war for nearly four decades after Waterloo. During this period, British forces fought engagements all over the world, but the public was not overly concerned about frontier squabbles in such remote areas as China, Nepal, the Punjab, Natal, the Gold Coast, New Zealand, Burma, or Upper and Lower

■

Canada. Naval actions received more attention even when significant numbers of ground troops were involved in battles elsewhere. But newspapers reported military engagements sparsely; such "excitements" became known weeks or even months after the events—they seemed very far away.

The navy and the army contrasted sharply in social status and subnational origin at midcentury. Englishmen were enormously proud of their navy. English policy, English considerations, English traditions, and English sailors bound the navy to that part of the United Kingdom. The officers were mostly English, and many families of lesser peers and squires maintained commissions in the "Senior Service" for generation after generation. Over three-quarters of the seamen were English, mostly from the south.

The army, despite its success against Napoleon, was notably inferior to the navy. Except for a few brilliantly successful officers (above all, Wellington) and a handful of heroes, army men had little status. The officer corps attracted Anglo-Irish landlords looking for an escape; hard-driving Scots seeking the main chance; unimpressive English peers or younger sons of peers who had to be acceptably employed somewhere; less well-endowed squires; and some socially underprivileged on the make. Since Anglo-Irish Protestant landholders could not live comfortably as squires, they sought income and position in the army. Success in the army promised suitable marriages in England, estates, further opportunities, perhaps extending to politics, and sometimes English, as distinct from Irish, peerages. The English landed nobility considered the army less acceptable for younger sons, but still better than utter dependence upon the charity of the oldest son. The growing English middle classes contributed men who had failed elsewhere to the army, since their sons preferred business, government bureaucracies, politics, the Anglican clergy, or the nonconformist ministry.

The prime recruiting grounds for the rank and file were Ireland, Wales, and Scotland—poverty-stricken, overpopulated, and bleak regions that lacked the benefits of England's industrialization. The prospect of being stationed in India meant flogging, bad food, little medical care, and a risk of death by disease but army life nonetheless was more appealing than the gruesome poverty of Ireland and the economic problems of the Scottish Highlands. The empire's "second" army in India was comprised of troops with distinct racial and socioeconomic differences; there were 30,000 Europeans and nearly 150,000 non-Europeans (sepoys) in uniform in 1850.

Thus at midcentury men-at-arms in service to the Crown or the East India Company numbered about 65,000 in Britain, 40,000 in the colonies, and 30,000 in India—135,00 European troops and 150,000 sepoys. England, with about 68 percent of the population of the

United Kingdom, enjoyed economic and political power and staffed the prestigious navy; the army was largely manned by Catholic Irish peasants, Highlanders, Welsh, and Indians.

The army's inferior socioeconomic status was reinforced by the traditional English admiration of the navy and suspicion of the army. The army was generally respected at moments of great need and profound success—notably during Marlborough's campaign against Louis XIV and following Wellington's defeat of Napoleon. Otherwise the English distrusted the military, which reminded them of things French, despotism (Cromwellian or czarist), the Catholic Church, fawning courtiers, and irresponsible aristocrats.

The national prejudice was reflected in the relative positions of the army and navy in government. The army's position within the cabinet was weak, since the secretary of state for war also served as the secretary for the colonies. The two positions were finally separated in 1854, but neither enjoyed prestige and both were filled by ambitious men looking for better things (the Irish peer Palmerston, for instance) or by unimpressive men on the way down. Treasury officials controlled the commissariat and treated colonial, military, and home affairs with scant respect. The bureaucratic elite of the treasury extended its control late into the 19th century and often failed to consult the commander-in-chief about decisions with military implications.

In contrast, the navy maintained a strong political base in the Admiralty. The Lords of the Admiralty were usually respected because of their knowledge of naval matters or because of family tradition. The treasury dealt with the Admiralty on equal terms and scrupulously consulted the naval staff even on minor questions involving naval disbursements. The views of naval officials influenced other cabinet officers and the growing civil service while the army point of view mattered hardly at all.

The army's difficulties were compounded by the need for reform. Wellington's success at Waterloo and prestige after 1815 rendered change and adaptation to lessons learned in India or observed in Europe difficult at best. The hero of Waterloo perpetuated his Peninsular success and the techniques used in the last great set-piece battle against Napoleon. He did not represent military interests as prime minister (1828–1830; 1835), and he subsequently opposed any real change as commander in chief. His influence loomed over an army ignored or despised by most until his death in September 1852. The practice of purchasing commissions (except in the engineers and artillery), flogging, inadequate support units, poor training, insufficient weaponry, and confused lines of responsibility to civilian authorities were typical of the army during the first half of the century.

■

The British public remained indifferent to empire and unperturbed by the Continental powers (with the possible exception of Czarist Russia) and regarded war as something remote from their national destiny. Most people believed the navy would suffice in any eventuality. Britons were only slightly uneasy over the rise of Napoleon III in France, but the Crimean War shocked them into an awareness of Britain's military weakness.

Britain went to war with Russia in 1854 almost gleefully. But the result was a tragic undistinguished "victory" notable only for the exploits of Florence Nightingale. The army quite possibly suffered no more in the Crimea than it had during the previous imperial skirmishes and provincial wars of 1815–1854 and lesser wars from 1856 to 1914. The mess in the commissariat, deplorable conditions in field hospitals, inadequate training, inept tactics, and general unpreparedness only partly describe conditions in the Crimea. For the first time, however, a war had shattered the public's illusion that conflict was remote.

The press brought war to public attention during the period 1854–1856 and treated the Crimean War much like the way television news covered the Vietnam War. Britain did not have a popular, "mass" press until the 1880s and 1890s but the papers began to have a sense of power. The *Times* was innovative technologically, grew steadily in circulation, and was associated with power and influence; it thus was preeminent. John Thaddeus Delane was its great, long-term editor and W. H. Russell became the first notable war correspondent. Russell collected news as he chose, evaded the officers who tried to thwart his efforts, and wrote dramatic reports that reached London with stunning rapidity. Russell's gory, brutal descriptions of action at the front were received skeptically by Delane, who thereupon went to the Crimea himself. The *Manchester Guardian* and other newspapers unable to afford war correspondents borrowed or reprinted dispatches from *The Times.*

The public's new awareness led to the establishment of a separate secretaryship in the cabinet and a civilian bureaucracy to deal with military affairs. The commander-in-chief was officially responsible to the secretary of state for war but in fact the intricate relationship between the "C-in-C" and civilian officials was not resolved until 1895, when the Duke of Cambridge (the Queen's cousin) died. Parliament and the bureaucrats firmly held the purse strings and maintained control, but the Queen insisted that selection of the commander-in-chief was her prerogative so the creation of a relatively efficient, modern army was deferred until the period 1895–1918.

■

The Victorian public was shocked again almost immediately, at the outbreak of the Sepoy Mutiny in India (1857). Sepoys had been hired by the East India Company since the seventeenth century, had usually fought well and were loyal to European officers in support of European units. As a result, no Indian power contested British hegemony. Based on the assumption that the Sepoys were loyal to the British the ratio of European men-at-arms was allowed to decrease from 1:3 early in the century to about 1:5 in 1857. European troops were withdrawn to the Crimea and to engage in a "minor" affair in China (the Second Anglo-Chinese War, 1856).

The mutiny took Britain by surprise and reports from India outraged Victorians: the "unreliable" natives had gone berserk, slaughtered European men and—beyond all thinkable horrors— women and children. The public was mostly unaware of the atrocities committed by Europeans against the mutineers and rebellious towns and the little that was known seemed justified in view of the rebels' behavior. British power, limited as it was, was reasserted in the following year in India. The Sikhs, Gurkhas, most Muslims, Parsis, and virtually all the southern three-fifths of the subcontinent remained loyal or quiescent. Britain did away with the anomalous rule of the East India Company and established Crown authority through a government firmly in the hands of a viceroy. Disraeli declared that Victoria was the Empress of India in 1875.

The Indian mutiny probably had more profound consequences than the Crimean War. The Victorian assumptions about the empire and Britain's colonial mission were shaken and resulted in a perception of "unenlightened," "decadent," or "primitive" non-European societies. The mutiny instilled in some Britons the belief that the nonwhite races were inferior, untrustworthy, incapable of humanely governing themselves, beastly, and irrational. A few, mostly politically weak Britons were persuaded to respect non-Europeans more.

The British received still another shock in 1870–1871 when Prussia, recast as the German Empire, defeated and destroyed the French Second Empire and ended the assumption that the French army was preeminent. Britons, for the first time since Napoleon, were confronted by the possibility that a single power could dominate the European continent. The *Fortnightly Review* published "The Battle of Dorking," a fictionalized account of a successful German invasion of England. The public sensation was brief, but politicians, writers, and strategists referred to it for the next two decades.

The Crimean, Indian, and Franco-Prussian wars caused basic reforms. During the period 1870–1874, Edward Cardwell initiated some important military changes. He patterned the changes after the successful German model and territorialized all infantry of the line by dividing the kingdom into 69 districts and assigning at least one regiment to each. Cardwell emphasized unit traditions and past battle honors in an attempt to instill local pride in each regiment thus intensifying support, attracting local recruits, and in general creating an awareness of territorial military obligations. Each regiment had at least two battalions, one maintained at the regimental base in its British district and the other deployed overseas. Cardwell's intentions were realized within a quarter of a century and the public spoke of the "Derbyshires," "Dorsets," and "Suffolks." The possibility of European wars accordingly were brought closer to the British home.

British naval strength guaranteed sufficient time and security to effect Cardwell's changes, but the Navy's role was threatened after 1880, when France and Germany built superb, small battle fleets which could be deployed in the North Atlantic or in the Channel. That threat coincided with a dramatic increase in Britain's far-flung naval obligations and forced Britain to accelerate its technological improvements, the origin of the expensive and tense Anglo-German naval armaments race after 1890. The buildup strained Britain's fiscal resources since there were simultaneous demands for an extension of social reform. Britain was thus forced to make an awkward choice between guns and butter.

The Anglo-Boer War increased the strain. Britain needed a superiority of 7:1 to subdue the stubborn, innovative Afrikaaners. The British public initially applauded the British victory despite hostile world opinion but later Kitchener's concentration camps and brutal destruction of food sources resulted in a change in the configuration of partisan politics at home.

■

By 1900, the British faced the probability of a major European war in which the navy would no longer be supreme and which would require larger numbers of troops to be returned to the Continent. Few Britons—or other Europeans, for that matter—could conceive how many might be required. The British public nonetheless began to face the uncomfortable realities of economic difficulties at home and increasing demands for expensive welfare reforms. The costs of empire, the naval race, the growing army, and the likelihood of Continental war ended English aloofness. The United Kingdom could no longer escape the growing tension which made domestic problems as difficult as those overseas.

# The Changing Role of the German Army, 1618 to the Present

## Jon M. Bridgman

Before the seventeenth century, German military propensities were like those of other Europeans. German knightly crusading orders carried out a vicious policy of conquest and colonization in eastern Europe and carved out what became the state of Prussia. German behavior was not, however, unique—it was replicated by the Spaniards in Granada and the New World, the British in Ireland, the French during the Albigensian Crusade, the Americans against the Indians.

Germany was one of the sources for recruiting mercenary soldiers throughout the eighteenth century. Hessians fought against the British during the American Revolution. The availability of German mercenaries was, however, due less to their innate soldiering tendencies than to a poor and overpopulated Germany.

The beginnings of a German military tradition can be traced to the Thirty Years' War (1618–1648). The conflict was frightful, it involved civilians as well as soldiers, devastated the cities and countryside, and disrupted economic and agricultural activity. The economic destructiveness of the war was exacerbated by the simultaneous economic crisis in central Europe. The fabric of German society was torn and there is evidence that cannibalism—itself a barometer of barbarism—apparently recurred. The other belligerents lost soldiers but the Germans suffered most, since the war was fought almost exclusively on their territory. Estimates of casualties among the German population vary from one-third to one-half—

■

most probably died of starvation and disease rather than as a result of military action. The feeling grew among Germans that they had no portection and no control over their own destinies.

The war made it clear that Germany would have to create a strong state to escape domestic chaos and a strong army to defend against invasion. The most successful effort to accomplish these goals was made by Brandenburg-Prussia from 1640 to 1740 under Frederick William (1640–1688), who accordingly became known as the Great Elector of Brandenburg. Frederick believed that violence had to be controlled to ensure the survival of civilization and concluded that his state and throne depended on the creation of a strong army. Germany, of course, did not lack armies; indeed, a surfeit of armies was precisely its problem. Frederick saw the need for a disciplined force, an instrument of violence under state control. He reduced the army to a few thousand men he though were reliable and established discipline through sheer terror, making his men more afraid of him than of any enemy. The resulting small military force allowed Frederick William to control a minuscule area which he could readily protect from external chaos. Thereafter, he was obsessed by the need to expand his army and he devoted virtually all his resources during the remainder of his long reign to that purpose.

Even more remarkable, Frederick's policy was pursued by his two successors, until 1740. Brandenburg-Prussia, despite its small population and resources, managed to maintain an army comparable to that of France. This achievement required the devotion of almost all state activity to the army. The tax system operated to maintain the army and the first successful peacetime conscription was developed to increase recruitment. After four years of brutal training which ensured permanent susceptibility to military discipline, recruits were returned to the agricultural labor force during planting and harvesting seasons. Desertion became the central problem for the Prussian army—forests were avoided on marches since the soldiers deserted when out of sight of their officers. The army became a prison and even suicide promised no escape since unsuccessful suicides were beaten in a gauntlet until they were nearly dead, then they would be hospitalized until they were well enough to run the gauntlet again, repeatedly for the rest of their lives. As a contemporary French comment put it, "Prussia is not a state but a barracks."

The system probably gave Prussia greater security and order than existed in most other societies. But the army became virtually an end in itself. Prussian rulers, increasingly fascinated by the army as an institution, forgot the Great Elector's original rationale and expanded their armies simply for the sake of expansion. Frederick William I (1713–1740) actually refused to use his elaborately trained and uniformed army. He was obsessed with tall soldiers and created a palace guard of outsized men to parade about.

■

When Frederick the Great took the throne in 1740, the Prussian army, previously employed to provide internal order and protection from invasion, became an instrument of expansion. He wanted Prussia to become a great state and that required increased population and more territory. He consequently began his reign by predatorily grabbing the province of Silesia from Maria Theresa. For the next twenty-three years, he fought against most of Europe to keep his acquired territory. Prussia was outnumbered at times ten or twenty to one, but almost miraculously, Prussia survived and kept Silesia, and so maintained a basis for Great Power status.

The new Prussian army was formed in the crucible of those wars between 1740 and 1763. Its success in war gave the army a mystique and identity of its own. Army officers became a brotherhood which shared terrible ordeals and demonstrated exceptional tenacity summed up in Frederick's motto, "Hold on." Believing that the Prussian army was unconquerable, the officer corps developed a sense of moral superiority and separateness, a paramonastic military order which functioned to maintain the state's highest ideals—loyalty, service, and obedience. Those military virtues were inculcated into civilians during military training. Thus the army became educator of the nation, and military service became desirable in civic as well as military terms. In achieving this lofty position, the army became semi-independent and self-governming during the reign of Frederick the Great. The officers selected their own members, established their own legal system distinct from civil law, and made most of the decisions concerning manpower and equipment. By the end of the eighteenth century, the Prussian army had established a popular stereotype which remained until 1945.

■

The Prussian army's function was altered at the beginning of the nineteenth century. In 1806, within twenty years of the death of Frederick the Great, it was shattered by Napoleon's forces. Paradoxically, defeat did not destroy the army's mystique and prestige rather, it was envisaged as an instrument of German rather than specifically Prussian policy. Defeat also made it clear that the army was outmoded, poorly equipped, trained, and led. Consequently, a group of reformers emerged who thought in German rather than strictly Prussian terms and advocated a more modern army and broad civic reforms. In 1813, the new army leaders renounced their oaths to the king, who was forced into an alliance with Napoleon, and thereby became heroes of national liberation.

The army's reputation as national liberator and unifier persisted through the nineteenth century and subsided following Napoleon's defeat. By then reactionary particularism reasserted itself in Germany. The ideal remained, however, and eventually was justified when the army became the instrument of national unification between 1863 and 1871. Bismarck's prediction was fulfilled—the problem of German unity was resolved not by speeches and parliamentary debates but by blood and iron.

After the wars of unification, the army reached a pinnacle of power and prestige unparalleled in any other Western society. Middle-class families considered a daughter's marriage to an officer, particularly a noble officer, to be the highest social attainment. A son in the reserves was thought desirable, but one in the regular army was the peak of professional achievement. The uniform itself became endowed with mystical powers.

The status of the military was demonstrated by a delightful satire, *The Captain from Köpenick*. The story involves a fifty-year-old jailbird who decides, on his release from prison, to emigrate but he also wants to return to Germany to die. He could leave illegally but it would be impossible to return without the proper papers, which he could not get because of a "no residence permit, no job, no residence permit" paradox. Disconsolate, he bought and donned an army captain's uniform, apparently without any clear intent. But when he walked down the street, everyone saluted this unshaven, bandy-legged social outcast. He orders all the soldiers he meets to fall in behind him and decides to use his little army to get the passport denied him. On arrival at the Berlin suburb of Köpenick, he arrested the mayor and everyone else in the town hall and sent them off to Berlin in taxis he had commandeered. No one questioned his authority—when an army captain told people they were arrested, they obeyed, even when they knew they had done nothing wrong. Ironically, there was no passport office in Köpenick. The old man finally turned himself in, but was freed after a personal interview with the kaiser, who found the incident amusing. Many sensible Germans were astonished and disturbed to note that uniforms blinded people. The prestige of the military had become too great.

The army became the model and school of the nation. Universal conscription made all male citizens liable to military service. The military officials believed that army training inculcated the highest civic virtues of service, loyalty, and, above all, obedience and thus produced better citizens. The army's success in this respect was demonstrated by *The Captain from Köpenick*.

The tension between society and the army increased as Germany grew rapidly more prosperous and materialistic after 1871. The army was increasingly regarded as a repository of traditional virtues, exemplified by the officers of the General Staff who were distinguished by special uniforms and a rigorous selection system. General Staff officers frequently remained unmarried, they were diligent and rarely took vacations—puritans who frowned upon frivolity. These selfless, secular monks believed they embodied the national honor.

The army's increasing isolation from civilian society was dramatically demonstrated by the so-called Zabern Affair in 1913. Germany annexed the French provinces of Alsace and Lorraine in 1871 and they constituted a political problem, since the inhabitants spoke German but wanted to belong to France. The affair erupted in the town of Zabern when a German officer beat an inhabitant in response to taunting. The officer was commended by many of his fellow officers but the affair became a national scandal because of government protests and outrage in the Reichstag. Minister of War von Falkenhayn asserted that the army's behavior was not the Reichstag's business and that was only of concern to the kaiser and army officials. The emperor was surrounded by soldiers and largely inaccessible to civilian ministers. He increasingly deferred to the army in the decade before the war. The reaction of the German government, Reichstag, press, and many civilians to the Zabern Affair demonstrated that many Germans were opposed to the army's dominance, however, the acceptance of von Falkenhayn's point of view rendered these elements impotent in military affairs.

Germany's defeat in World War I did not reduce the army's prestige. During the war, the army achieved greater actual power over German society than before or since, it virtually displaced the kaiser and civilian government and assumed control over policy-making. Army leaders shifted blame to civilians for the defeat and surrender in 1918 and 1919 and thus preserved the army's reputation for invincibility. Many, indeed most, Germans apparently accepted the contention that Germany had not been militarily defeated. This acceptance was partially based on the myth of army superiority reinforced because the average German was unwilling to believe that the huge price of the war had been paid in vain. The war elevated the army relative to civilian components of the society and the army was more than ever perceived as the repository of German virtues. The civilian government came to be associated with defeat and Germany's enemies.

Nonetheless the war fundamentally changed the army's role in German society. From the seventeenth century on, the army was largely nonpolitical, seldom engaging directly in politics by choosing ministers or determining nonmilitary policies. German soldiers were generally unconcerned with civilian matters until the 1920s when they departed from precedent to become political—that departure proved to be a fatal error.

The German army became involved in politics in a desperate effort to preserve its own institutions, the old social order, and Germany's national greatness. These goals could not be achieved in postwar Germany without the support of the masses. The army therefore sought an alliance with a party capable of winning popular support yet one that could be controlled. The soldiers sought a charismatic obedient drummer and they mistakenly assumed Adolf Hitler would fill their need.

The traditionalists among the army leadership mostly doubted the wisdom of entering politics and supporting Hitler, but their reservations were overcome by some political generals who saw in Hitler only what they chose to see. Hitler was popular and seemed controllable he thus appeared to be an instrument of national revival. The generals initially failed to perceive Hitler's cleverly concealed, violent, nearly pathological hatred of them but Hitler soon disabused them of their illusions. He demanded and received an oath of total obedience that most German officers later found to be a barrier to revolt which few were psychologically able to cross. Hitler replaced the army leadership, undermined its prestige, and extended his control by assuming direct command over military operations in 1941. By 1945, the army was Hitler's tool.

The collapse in 1945 shattered the army and the defeats in battle merely confirmed the political defeats already conflicted. Complete subordination to Hitler and its humiliation after the 1944 assassination attempt destroyed the officer corps as an independent element in German society.

■

The role of the army was altered again in 1945. The two German states maintained separate armies, each rooted in a different tradition. The army of the German Democratic Republic (East Germany) has a discipline and esprit closer to the Prussian model. It resembles the firmly controlled army of Frederick the Great more than it does the domineering army of the late nineteenth century. The army of the German Federal Republic (West Germany), however, its troops may join a trade union and could hypothetically strike. The West German army apparently has little discipline and few regulations. Both armies are civilian-controlled and in that sense are quite untypical of the German experience. Each army is modeled on the army of its patron: the GFR's on the U. S. Army, the GDR's on the Red Army. The best measure of any revolutionary change in German society may be a search for precedents outside of German history.

The stereotype of Germany as the ultimate military society is only partially valid. The stereotype applied to part of Germany

(Prussia) for much of its history but to all of Germany for only a short period (1871–1945). The army's role has frequently changed in the last three centuries and the military was controlled by the state most of that time. The stereotype in any event no longer applies. Germany and Japan, the major defeated powers of World War II, are now among the least militaristic societies.

Militarism is frequently condemned because it is assumed that large armies cause wars. The German experience challenges that assumption. The Prussian kings of the early eighteenth century demonstrated that large armies can be maintained without being used. Further, the Prussian army was used because of decisions made by civilians, Frederick the Great and Bismarck, and not by their generals. The German army influenced events before and during World War II through weakness rather than strength. Paradoxically, the Nazi experience suggests the need to reevaluate the role of armies in politics. War-making may be too serious a business to be left in the hands of civilians.

# The Military in Soviet Russia

## Donald W. Treadgold

In relations between the Soviet Union and the United States, the ultimate determinant is their relative military strength, sometimes called "the balance of terror." A vital element in this equation is clearly Soviet military strength, which in turn is related to the Soviet military establishment. An understanding of the Cold War consequently necessitates an examination of the Soviet army and its role in Soviet policy-making.

A useful starting point is the generalization offered by Carl J. Friedrich and Zbigniew Brzezinski in their book *Totalitarian Dictatorship and Autocracy.* In the typical nontotalitarian dictatorship, the dictator characteristically takes power through the army, which then retains independent power, perhaps sufficient even to depose the man it put into office. In a totalitarian dictatorship, by contrast, the government is able to make the army into a mere subdivision of the party.

The army's role in nontotalitarian dictatorships is frequently significant. Such leaders as Marshal Pilsudski in Poland, Kemal Atatürk in Turkey, General Franco in Spain, General Perón in Argentina, and Yüan Shih-k'ai, one of the earliest presidents of the republic, as well as Chiang Kai-shek in pre-Communist China, all rose to political power through the army. Since none was able to divorce himself entirely from it, the army remained an integral part of the power bases.

The generalization seems less widely applicable to totalitarian

■

dictatorships. In Communist China the relationship between army and regime is far from clear. The Nazi government certainly sought to subject the army to its control, but the army retained a modicum of identity and power until very near the end, as demonstrated by the July 20, 1944, coup against Hitler.

The generalization does apply, however, to the Soviet situation. The Soviet army is a subdivision of the Russian Communist party. It is necessary to investigate how this situation came about.

■

During the period of the Russian Empire (1721–1917), the military —or, to be more precise, the officer corps—was clearly and unequivocally under state control. The officers were members of a service nobility, totally dependent upon the czar for rank, privilege, and property. The situation altered somewhat after the mid-eighteenth century, when the so-called upper class in Russia was relieved of the obligation to serve from the age of fifteen until death. Many returned to their estates and frequently became the degenerate, incompetent, unproductive characters depicted in Russian novels of the nineteenth century. Those who continued to serve as members of the civil and military bureaucracy failed to develop the characteristic cohesiveness and solidarity of their west European counterparts. One Russian general, for example, asked the czar to make him a German, which would have been preferable to being a general. The quality of the nineteenth-century Russian officer corps was uneven but perhaps not unlike its counterparts in western Europe, except for the Prussians. The Russian army's record during the period was mixed: initial failure but eventual success against Napoleon, general success against the Turks, a draw against the British and French during the Crimean War, and a disastrous failure against the Japanese. Its great and final test occurred in World War I.

That war was a terrible ordeal for the armies of all the belligerents. Initially, few commanders distinguished themselves, perhaps because none were trained for the modern, mass war they were forced to fight. The Russian army had several outstanding generals, such as Alekseev and Brusilov. The assumption of field command by Czar Nicholas II in 1915 is frequently condemned but it actually resulted in an advantage; control of strategy was put in the hands of Alekseev and he did an excellent job. Brusilov conducted a successful offensive in 1916 against Austria-Hungary, so successful that Rumania was persuaded to join the Allies. That victory turned out to be a disaster for Russia after Germany defeated Rumania and Brusilov was obliged to extend his front and halt his offensive. There were some daring generals, like Kornilov, who appealed to the imagination of many soldiers, officers, and rightist politicians after the February Revolution. Other generals were downright incompetent, corrupt, unscrupulous, or constantly inebriated. Perhaps as important as the mixed quality of generalship was the low standard of the czarist army's organization and supply. That combined with the inadequate productive capacities of Russian industry, reduced the army's ability to conduct mechanized warfare below that of the other belligerents.

The army's leadership was not worthy of its rank and file, a point dramatically made by Aleksandr Solzhenitsyn in *August 1914.* The average Russian soldier fought well, indeed remarkably, considering his lack of equipment and supplies, and frequently incompetent commanders. The army maintained its cohesion despite incredible defeats, privation, and even political disturbance. The frequent claim that it collapsed immediately after the February Revolution is incorrect: in fact it held its position against the Germans and actually launched a new offensive in July 1917. Only after this offensive failed and after the total disruption of Russian society the following autumn did the czarist army collapse.

The February Revolution first and then the October (Bolshevik) Revolution did, however, alter the army's role in Russian society. The army was forced to enter the political arena for the first time in its history. Officers fought on both sides in the ensuing civil war. The outstanding military leaders on the White (anti-Bolshevik) side after the October Revolution—e.g., General Denikin, Admiral Kolchak, and Baron Wrangel—were not political reactionaries but republicans or at least were committed to a popular decision on the question of retaining the monarch as a figurehead. The problem for such men was less the nature of their politics than their political inexperience, due largely to their training as officers. The Whites ultimately failed, however, because of military strategy. Denikin allowed his forces to be penned up in the Crimea and thus lost British, French, and American support. Many czarist officers joined the Bolsheviks, but most of them probably supported the Whites and created the impression that the army was anti-Bolshevik. Whatever their abilities or motives, many czarist officers loyally defended the institution which had created them.

The czarist officer corps was divided on the Bolsheviks, but the Bolsheviks were unified in condemning the czarist army. The Bolsheviks applauded the army's collapse and like many other European revolutionaries and Socialists they advocated complete destruction of the old regime, including the police and bureaucracy as well as the army. The Bolsheviks however, recognized that a new army was necessary to preserve their power against the Whites. Creation of the so-called Red Army was entrusted to Leon Trotsky, who had no military experience and who as a journalist had never met a payroll or been elected to political office. His accomplishment was outstanding—an army built from the bottom up, starting in early 1918, and victorious by 1921. The new army's rank and file remained the traditional peasant draftee. It was staffed largely by former czarist officers sympathetic to the revolution if not specifically to the Bolsheviks. The new and critical element was the establishment of the political commissar system comprised of party agents who observed the officers to ensure their loyalty to the regime. This system reflected the Bolsheviks' awareness of the precedent of military coups after revolutions, along the lines of Napoleon. Thus from the start, the Bolsheviks were determined to control the army rather than be controlled by it.

Between the two world wars the Red Army passed through three fairly distinct stages. Once the Civil War was won in 1921, Lenin and a number of his supporters sought to decentralize the army and create in its place the popular militia envisaged by many prophets of socialism. But Stalin, who eventually took over after Lenin's death in 1924, opposed such a transformation and built instead during the late 1920s and early 1930s a traditional, rigidly disciplined military force policed by political commissars. Stalin may have become concerned about his own success, for, from 1936 to 1948, he purged almost the entire higher officer corps, as well as trade-union and party leaders. The purge eliminated most of the best generals, including former czarist officers as well as early revolutionaries, such as Marshal Tukhachevsky. Stalin thereby ensured his control over all elements of Soviet society but at the price of weakening the Red Army.

These internal convulsions make it more possible to understand the crisis caused in Russia by World War II. Stalin's collectivization of agriculture during the early 1930s—which involved killing, starving, or incarcerating millions of people and profound economic disruption—produced a situation Stalin described to Churchill as even more dangerous than World War II. Collectivization, however, never seriously threatened the regime with internal revolt or external invasion. The results of the Stalin era were graphically illustrated by the response of Russian civilians and soldiers to the German invasion in 1941. The peasants rejected as propaganda the government's warnings about the Nazis and welcomed the Germans as liberators; Russian soldiers surrendered in vast numbers, twice in lots of 600,000 —mistakes for which they paid dearly later.

The course of the war was ultimately determined more by Hitler than by Stalin or the Allies. Hitler rejected a massed offensive in favor of a stately, broad advance extending from the Gulf of Finland to the Black Sea. At the crucial moment, he denied the center the armor which might have allowed it to take Moscow, disrupt the entire transportation system of European Russia, and perhaps thereby win the campaign against Russia. In addition, Hitler, instead of responding to and exploiting the friendliness of many Russians, applied the view expressed in *Mein Kampf* that Russians were subhuman. Thus he gave the Russian people no alternative but to support the Soviet regime. Hitler's military and political stupidity, the Allied decision to support Stalin, and Stalin's adroitness combined to reverse the situation. The Russian people fought for Mother Russia, perhaps in the vain hope that Stalin would reward them after victory. Despite the disastrous beginning, Soviet forces performed well, suffered terribly, and contributed mightily to winning the European war. (Russian losses at the Battle of Stalingrad alone were greater than American losses during the whole war on both fronts.) The Russian national state and the Soviet regime thus survived their most serious test.

The Red Army was also tested and changed by the war. This transformation began with Russian victories at Stalingrad in late 1942 and at Kursk in 1943. Two clusters of generals developed separate identities because of their roles in the defense of Moscow and Stalingrad, a distinction which exists today. The Stalingrad group, not as able or well known as the Moscow group, was nonetheless formidable; one of their representatives is Defense Minister Marshal Grechko. The Moscow group tended to prevail in the postwar conflicts among the top military leaders. Only once has a fighting—as distinguished from a political—general been appointed to the Politburo. Marshal Zhukov who directed the defense of Moscow was appointed but removed by Khrushchev after a few months, one of the shortest tenures. After the dismissal of Khrushchev, the Moscow group briefly achieved more power than any generals in the Soviet Union had ever had, then remain prominent though less powerful today.

Soviet civilian leaders doubtless consult the generals on the technical capabilities of the Russian military establishment, which then set limits on and thereby affect Soviet policy. Soviet military policy, however, remains firmly in civilian hands. Behind the distinction that some have sought to draw between Soviet military and civilian leaders is the implication that they reflect fundamentally different viewpoints, i.e., the soldiers would presumably pursue a more aggressive policy than the civilians. This is probably a misleading assumption since it is highly doubtful that the Soviet military is anxious to launch an aggressive war. Like all Generals the Soviets are less influenced by humanitarian scruples than with the practical consideration of fighting wars that might be difficult to win. The prominence of generals in Soviet leadership consequently does not necessarily threaten the peace.

The military under the Soviet regime **is** subordinate to civilian control. In this sense, the Soviets resemble not **only** other totalitarian systems but also their capitalist-democratic rivals more than they do other nontotalitarian dictatorships. The Soviet army is effectively a subdivision of the Russian Communist party.

Civilian control and the apparent disinclination of Soviet generals to launch an aggressive war should not, however, be interpreted as weakness. The Soviets have a mighty military arsenal, for the first time on a par with that of the United States and the political and military implications of this development remain unclear. In seeking to clarify the situation, however, we should examine Soviet civilian leadership or, better yet, Soviet leadership as a whole, rather than to focus exclusively on the Soviet military.

# The Army
# in Argentine Politics

## Carl E. Solberg

The purpose of this essay is to analyze the political movement constructed by Juan Domingo Perón (Peronism), which attempted to reconcile military aspirations for industrialization and economic independence with organized labor's quest for economic and social justice. This essay focuses on the period 1943–1955 and on an analysis of Peronist policies and bases of support during those years. The analysis suggests that the Peronists faced a complex problem in mediating the divergent demands of Argentina's two most powerful political groups—military officers and organized labor.

Long before 1943, when Perón first appeared in the national political arena, the army was a powerful political institution in Argentina. It was the product of an ambitious foreign policy dating from the 1880s. That policy was founded on the assumption that the federal government at Buenos Aires should dominate the Paraná-Paraguay river basins and be capable of defeating the combined forces of Chile and Brazil, the republic's two principal potential enemies. Implementation of that foreign policy obviously required large, well-equipped, and professionally trained armed forces. Although they were bitter enemies on a number of issues, the conservative, elite-dominated governments which ruled until 1916 and the middle-class Radical party regimes (1916–1930) basically agreed on those foreign policy objectives and the need to finance a modern military establishment. Prior to World War I, the government imported German advisors to instruct Argentine officers, but eventually

■

the republic's own military academy, founded at the turn of the century, produced a professionally competent officer corps. The academy attracted able candidates, ambitious sons of the immigrant-born middle class who viewed the military profession as a vehicle of upward social mobility as a means of demonstrating their identification with Argentine nationalism.

By the 1920s, the officer corps contained a large and growing body of well-trained engineers and technicians who were beginning to resemble a development-oriented national intellectual elite. Many officers were alarmed by extreme shortages of fuel and manufactured goods and the lessons of World War I that proved the close relationship between integrated economic development and effective military power. Those officers therefore questioned the republic's traditional economic policy. Exports of rural products dominated Argentina's economy and, by the mid-1920s, nearly 40 percent of total goods produced were shipped abroad, primarily to Britain. Argentine manufacturing industries remained undeveloped, for the politically dominant exporting interests opposed protective tariffs. Moreover, British capitalists owned most of the railways, port works, electric power plants, telephone networks, and, in some cities, the water works. United States investments, in contrast, were smaller and concentrated in light manufacturing and meat packing. In the early 1920s, nationalists proclaimed that British ownership kept railway and utility rates too high and impeded Argentina's economic development. Within the military, nationalistic officers began to express similar views. Army officers were convinced that the federal government, controlled by export-oriented cattlemen and their urban allies, would never support economic nationalism and industrialization, and they believed that the existing economic system potentially threatened Argentine security. "Our economic organization is absurd," wrote Colonel Luis E. Vicat, a metallurgical engineer. Should an enemy blockade the republic's ports, "they would defeat us practically without firing a shot."[1]

Aside from the industrialists, few in number and relatively weak politically, the army was the only significant pressure group which worked for industrialization and economic nationalism during the period between World War I and the Great Depression. During the 1920s, military strategists emphasized that steel and petroleum industries, under state ownership if necessary, were crucial to Argentine security. The Radical party governments, whose economic policies were strongly free trade, gave in to military pressure and in

1. Luis E. Vicat, "Ideas sueltas que creo útiles al progreso del norte argentino," in Benjamín Villafañe, ed., *El atraso del interior* (Jujuy, Argentina, 1926), p. 179.

1922 created a state oil corporation (YPF) to administer its rich petroleum lands. The first head of YPF, Colonel (later General) Enrique Mosconi, worked tirelessly to transform the inefficient and unproductive state oil fields into a thriving enterprise. Since then, nationalists within the army have promoted and identified with YPF as a powerful symbol of Argentine economic independence.

By the 1930s, the Argentine army had an economic development program as well as the administrative and technical capacity to carry it out. But this strong orientation toward industrialization and economic nationalism brought many officers into conflict with the political elite, especially when World War II began to isolate Argentina economically from the United Kingdom. Discontent among military officers grew rapidly under the inept and corrupt conservative governments of the early 1940s. The national congress, controlled by large landowning interests, was relatively unconcerned with industrial development, economic diversification, and fiscal reform. When Brazil began to construct South America's first integrated steel mill in 1942, the Argentine government, to the military's dismay, failed to follow Brazil's example in promoting heavy industry. The army's unrest was brought to a head, however, not by corruption or economics, but by the question of entering World War II on the Allied side. The issue was raised when President Ramón Castillo and his conservative political allies attempted to engineer (largely by fraudulent means) the election of Rubustiano Patrón Costas, a well-known admirer of the British and advocate of Argentine cooperation with the Allies. Nationalist officers, however, saw neutrality as the most viable course for Argentina, partly because of pro-German sentiment, but mainly because they regarded British economic policy with deep suspicion and often outright hostility.

In 1943, the republic's vast expanse of over one million square miles contained a population of only 14 million people. The Argentine economy still relied upon agriculture and stockraising, but about 60 percent of the population was urbanized, and over 3 million inhabitants crowded into Buenos Aires, essentially a commercial and bureaucratic center but also the focus of Argentina's light industry. In the countryside, a small elite monopolized ownership of the best land, while the rural masses, condemned to a dreary existence as tenant farmers or seasonally employed wage laborers, found few outlets for upward mobility other than migrating to the cities and entering the unskilled labor force. Disdainfully called *descamisados* (shirtless ones) by the upper classes, this rapidly growing, unskilled migrant group constituted a potentially powerful but still unorganized political force. Labor unions remained weak, partly because the early anarcho-syndicalist traditions of the Argentine labor movement prevented attempts at centralized leadership and partly because governments, especially after 1930, openly opposed labor organization.

■

After a group of colonels, including Perón, seized power in the coup of June 1943, bitter internal disputes, largely centering on the government's labor and unionization policies, broke out within the army. For the next three years, a succession of generals occupied the post of provisional president. Meanwhile, the populist-oriented faction around Colonel Perón struggled to isolate a large group of more traditional officers who advocated a government which would continue to support established Argentine social and economic policies. Perón and his friends, however, understood the potential for building a powerful government based largely on the laboring masses and Perón began a highly successful organizational campaign in 1944. He became secretary of labor in the military government and assumed the mantle of populist leader. Perón's appeal was strongest among the unskilled working classes, and when their unions, organized under his protection, went on strike, they found that the ministry of labor supported their demands.

Perón's reputation was favorable among younger army officers throughout the period 1943–1946. Perón made numerous and influential friends within the officer corps while a student at the military academy and after graduation. During his rise in the army hierarchy, he was careful never to cross the wrong people. Regarded within the army as an intellectual, Perón had read widely and had traveled extensively in Europe, where Mussolini's Italy had impressed him. He was a man of considerable intelligence who understood Argentine cultural traditions, and the art of public speaking. He possessed characteristics which appealed particularly to the working classes, above all, an attractive public image enhanced by his reputation as a *macho.*

Perón strengthened this *macho* image by identifying with a charismatic woman. Eva Duarte, probably the most important woman in Latin American history, was a radio actress who married Perón in 1946. Still considered akin to a saint among the Argentine masses, Eva Duarte was an effective liaison with labor for Perón, since she came from the unskilled migrant working class. The upper classes, particularly women, feared and despised her because she upset their polite image of a president's wife to become a powerful symbol of social justice among the Argentine masses. Eva Perón, who was a gifted public speaker, could raise audiences of a half a million to heights of emotional indignation never before experienced on a mass scale in Argentine politics. Eva Perón never incited the masses toward revolutionary violence but instead urged mass political organization to support Peronism, which, she promised, was working to improve the lot of the *descamisados.*

By October 1945, Peronism had gathered such momentum that conservative military leaders became alarmed. Consequently, they announced Perón's exile and imprisoned him on an island in the River Plate. The process of mass mobilization was, however, far too advanced for the conservative generals to quell. On October 17, 1945, labor leaders throughout metropolitan Buenos Aires organized a massive protest demonstration and threatened to literally tear the capital apart if the generals did not allow Perón to return. The military chiefs capitulated. That very night, Perón announced his candidacy for the presidency in the forthcoming (1946) elections. Supervised by the military, these elections were honestly conducted and produced a smashing Peronist victory. The factional struggle within the army was at least temporarily over and the populist-reformist group led by Perón was solidly in power. In just three years, Perón revolutionized Argentine politics by politicizing the working classes and by basing a government largely on their support.

The military, however, remained crucial to Perón's regime, and from 1946 to 1950 he spent huge sums to modernize and reequip the armed forces. This policy was popular, for during World War II the rival Brazilian army received over $200 million in United States aid, mostly Lend-Lease arms and equipment, and the wily Brazilian dictator Getulio Vargas, as part of his price for Brazil's participation in the war, extracted a United States commitment to finance construction of an integrated steel mill. The Argentine generals were alarmed at the growth of Brazilian military strength and embittered at the United States for intruding in South American power politics. Perón's military policy—including high officer pay scales, new jets for the air force, and a general commitment to parity with Brazilian military strength—gained him considerable backing throughout the Argentine armed forces. Moreover, Perón did not try to establish political control over internal military affairs.

Perón formed an alliance with the Catholic Church in 1946 on the basis of the election-year issue of divorce. Further, he emphasized that Argentina ought to model its culture on national tradition rather than on imported models from the United States and northern Europe. This policy meant that the Church, the family, and Argentine national symbols such as the gaucho received priority from the Peronist government, at least in the first few years. Most important for the Church, Perón retained religious instruction in the public schools, a policy instituted in 1944.

The Perón regime received limited backing from some sectors

of the middle class. Small-scale industrialists, employing a few dozen workers making clothes or shoes, frequently did well under Perón, in part because of high import tariffs. Yet middle-class support for the regime never became a cohesive or well-organized political force and some sectors remained implacably hostile.

The largest power base was organized labor. The General Confederation of Labor (CGT), whose leadership became militantly Peronist, exercised sufficient power to extract from employers considerable benefits for its three million trade-union members. Largely because the wages of workers who belonged to CGT unions rose rapidly, labor's share of national income rose from about 40 percent in the mid-1940s to over 50 percent in 1952.[2] Other labor unions not associated with the CGT and generally led by Socialists or Communists found themselves isolated and sometimes persecuted. Perón consolidated his working-class power base by instituting the first effective public welfare and social security systems in Argentine history. Eva Perón took personal responsibility for the vast welfare system. She made it her duty to ensure efficient communications between the government and those who required public assistance. Moreover, she was not above going into the streets to distribute largesse in highly tangible fashion.

Perón spent large sums on welfare, but he also shared the military's traditional interest in developing Argentina's industrial strength. Peronist governments utilized the state's Industrial Bank (founded in 1944) to extend credit to private industrialists. The regime also began to form state-owned corporations, generally administered by top military officers, for the production of steel and petrochemicals. In addition, this policy symbolized for the working classes a path to rising living standards.

The government's expensive programs of nationalizing foreign-owned enterprises absorbed much of the money that might otherwise have been employed to construct the factories Perón promised. But public hostility to British capital in Argentina meant considerable support for the nationalization policy. It is important to note that the government did not expropriate the British properties but purchased them, often at high prices, using funds the country's exports had earned during World War II. This policy reflected the Argentine military's commitment to the principles of economic nationalism and private property. Apart from the railways and utilities, no significant expropriation of land or industries occurred during the Perón regime.

Perón called his theory of economic nationalism "justicialism."

---

2. James R. Scobie, *Argentina: A City and a Nation,* 2d ed. (New York: 1971). p. 250.

Denouncing both the United States version of liberal capitalism and the Soviet version of communism as inimical to Argentina's traditional cultural values, justicialism envisaged a mixed economy in which both state and private capital would play important roles, partially directed by government planners. On the international scene, justicialism emphasized Argentina's "third position" allied with neither of the two principal post–World War II power blocs. Implicit was the promise that Argentina under Perón was on the verge of sustained economic development and Great Power status.

■

It is clear in retrospect that Perón's neglect of the rural sector was his principal economic failure and eventually undermined the stability of his regime. The government's expenditures on welfare programs, military equipment, industrialization, and economic nationalism were financed partially through IAPI, a state monopoly which controlled the export of all major commodities and had the power to fix prices to producers. Following World War II, IAPI's planners paid farmers and cattlemen too little for their produce even though Argentine exports fetched high prices in European markets. Rural producers were therefore cut back, and exports fell. Perón apparently assumed that a third world war would ensue and that a neutral Argentina exporting food to a hungry world would flourish. Given this assumed prosperity, the government thought it could afford to exploit agriculture in the short run. World market prices for Argentine exports slumped after 1950, however, and production plummeted when the landowners refused to produce at IAPA's low prices. By 1952, the Argentine economy, still excessively dependent on two or three rural exports to earn foreign exchange, entered a period of serious recession.

Eva's death in 1952 was Perón's great misfortune; she died just as economic difficulties were forcing the government to postpone or abandon some of its major programs. Perón's most effective link to the working classes was gone, inflation was beginning to reduce the workers' real income, and he mistakenly adopted a series of policies which weakened the military-labor alliance.

The military's disillusionment with Peronism became evident in 1951, when the army hierarchy prevented Eva from announcing her candidacy for the vice-presidency. The position of Perón himself in this episode remains unclear, but the military elite clearly indicated its distrust of populist policies. The government launched an anti-clerical campaign, which further unsettled the generals and admirals since many of them were devout Catholics. Possibly intended to distract working-class attention from economic difficulties, this program ended religious instruction in public schools, eased curbs on prostitution, and proposed the legalization of divorce. Perón also advocated sainthood for Eva and hinted at constitutional changes to separate Church and state. Millions of Argentine Catholics, particularly middle-class and elite groups which never had accepted Perón, responded with suspicion.

By 1955, Perón's bases of support were seriously eroded. The CGT unions were still loyal, but their fervor had cooled. Anticlericalism failed to arouse mass support for the government and turned many influential Argentinians against Perón. Finally, in 1955, Perón signed exploration and development contracts with United States oil companies, traditionally distrusted in Argentina, particularly in the army. Argentine nationalists regarded the contracts as a potential threat to YPF's existence and expressed dismay at Perón's policy shift.

As the foundations of the regime weakened, military conspiracy recurred, in the traditional Argentine pattern. After an unsuccessful coup in June 1955, navy and army leaders plotted to isolate Perón and his working-class power base in Buenos Aires. The military chiefs revolted in September 1955, and Perón was faced with a bloody and probably hopeless civil war should he choose to rally worker resistance. He resigned and fled to exile.

The overthrow of Perón could not, however, destroy the working-class movement he had helped create. The military thoroughly and brutally purged its officer ranks of Peronists but could not erase the conviction, widely held among the working class, that Perón was the only president in the country's history who really cared about them. For eighteen years after his overthrow, Perón and Eva continued to be idolized by the masses. During this period, the military suppressed Peronist candidates in elections and Peronist leadership within the CGT, and carried out mass executions of Peronists. But the conservative military chiefs seriously erred when they tried to end inflation and raise funds for economic development by reducing the real income of the working-class which fell at least 20 percent between 1955 and 1970.[3] The workers, in close contact with Perón in Madrid, finally rebelled during the Cordobazo, a massive and bloody insurrection which demolished much of the industrial city of Córdoba in May 1969.

With the working classes virtually in open revolt, the military hierarchy reluctantly considered Perón's return to power. After lengthy negotiations, during which the exiled leader agreed not to take reprisals against military leaders who had opposed him, Perón returned to Argentina in November 1972. After two interim govern-

3. Scobie, *Argentina*, p. 250.

ments, he was elected president with over two-thirds of the popular vote in September 1973.

From his election until his death in July 1974, Perón again attempted to forge a strong military-labor alliance as a power base. Many conservative officers retired when Perón returned, but most of the military hierarchies accepted Peronism as the only practical alternative to the Marxist social experiments advocated by Argentina's vigorous guerrilla movements. Perón discarded the anticlerical policy which marred the period 1952–1955 and appealed to Argentina's millions of expectant trade-union members by emphasizing economic nationalism and industrialization coupled with welfare populism and a rhetorical Third World foreign policy.

While Perón lived, he was able to contain working-class aspirations for rapid economic gains. Wide schisms in the movement have, however, appeared since his death between the relatively conservative trade-union bureaucrats and entrepreneurs and students, intellectuals, and working-class militants. Clearly Peronism's most significant political legacy was to endow the Argentine working classes with a profound sense of their potential power as an organized force. No Argentine government can succeed without recognizing this essential fact.

■

Twentieth-century Argentina provides a revealing case of civil-military relations and the military's involvement in politics. It demonstrates that the military is not necessarily a monolithic or exclusively conservative force but rather a group with divergent, sometimes conflicting political tendencies. The military certainly included a large conservative element whose primary objective was to preserve the traditional elements of Argentine society. But to Perón and his supporters the military was populist rather than elitist, mass rather than narrowly based, progressive rather than traditional. The Argentine case also demonstrates the military's commitment to national power. In the case of an underdeveloped society like Argentina, this concern meant support for industrialization and economic nationalism. In this sense, even the conservative military fostered change. Their dual concern—at once to industrialize but preserve traditional Argentine society—may prove to be the conservatives' dilemma as well as the ultimate problem of Argentina.

The recourse to populist mass movements in the name of progress will doubtless be one alternative for developing societies throughout the world. Because Peronism is a model, it must be evaluated accurately. Perón was frequently charged, particularly in the English-language press, with being a fascist in the mold of World War

II European dictators. Perón refused to align Argentina with the World War II Allies or with the United States during the Cold War. The charge is, however, incorrect in at least one important respect. The European fascists tended to preserve the established socioeconomic structure, whereas Peronism redistributed income in favor of the rural and urban masses and to the detriment of the traditional upper classes. Peronism should thus be analyzed in the context of traditional, authoritarian, populist Latin American military regimes, rather than in that of European fascism. This approach promises more accurate understanding and suggests insights into the general problem of the military's role in developing societies.

# The Military
# in Modern China

## James R. Townsend

Wars and military mobilization have had a profound impact on modern China. From the mid-nineteenth century—when the Taiping Rebellion (1850–1864) claimed tens of millions of lives and laid waste vast areas of the country in one of the most destructive wars in human history—down to the present, wars and preparations for war have been salient features of Chinese life. Nonetheless, the character of military hostilities and their economic, social, and political consequences have changed significantly during this period. The most important shift occurred in 1949 with the establishment of the People's Republic of China (PRC), an event that failed to bring peace to China and introduced a new era in Chinese military history. This essay analyzes the major differences between pre-1949 and post-1949 military phenomena and suggests that an unusual if not unique civil-military relationship has evolved in contemporary China.

No brief description can do justice to the level and variety of military hostilities that engulfed China during the century preceding 1949. There were multiple rebellions and revolutionary civil wars; national wars against foreign countries that ranged from resisting limited military action by Western imperialism to fighting the attempted Japanese conquest of China; and innumerable contests among Chinese military elites—particularly during the "warlord" period (1916–1928)—that often seemed to have little meaning beyond plunder and the acquisition or defense of territorial power.

■

If the details defy simple description, it is relatively simple to point out some general characteristics and consequences.

One of the most obvious consequences was the direct cost in material and human terms. For several decades in the early twentieth century, military expenses frequently claimed approximately half of the central government's budget. Since provincial governments in this period had considerable political, financial, and military autonomy, they also devoted large shares of their revenues to maintaining armed forces. Taxes multiplied endlessly as lower levels of government sought to pacify the demands of higher levels and yet satisfy their own appetites for funds. Of course, much of the cost of maintaining scores of large armies and probably hundreds of small ones never appeared in government budgets, since the troops lived to a large extent off the populations and countryside. Looting was a primary form of remuneration for common soliders, and many commanders simply pocketed their governmental allocations. Actual hostilities were less frequent than the level of mobilization might suggest—warlords viewed their armies as assets to be saved rather than squandered—but the cumulative loss of life and property as a consequence of military action was still substantial.

It is important to note that nearly all the military engagements during the period prior to 1949 were fought on Chinese territory. Obviously this was true of contests between Chinese for regional or national power. In addition, foreign powers obligingly brought their forces to China to settle their grievances.

Chinese military mobilizations of this period were essentially exploitative and even parasitic. The extraction of resources from society for military purposes was carried out without a corresponding mobilization of the population to support the cause in question. Most military institutions secured compliance to their demands by force, threat, or bribery; most citizens viewed them as alien factions to be resisted or avoided and certainly to be feared. Of course, many Chinese armies served what their leaders regarded to be important national goals. The cases in which significant numbers of citizens were mobilized to support these goals—for example, the Nationalist campaign to unify the country in 1926–1928, the early stages of resistance to Japan after the 1937 invasion, the Chinese Communists' long revolutionary effort—were, however, exceptions rather than a rule. Military hostilities appeared primarily as a burden on an impoverished population for whom the costs were far more immediate than projected benefits.

These circumstances inevitably imbued military elites with immense political power. Political leadership was frequently nothing more than recognition of military power, conferral of a civilian title on the commander of the strongest army. Whether actually led by military elites or not, governmental structures depended on their armies, since constant threats from domestic and foreign enemies seemed to make military preparedness the primary condition for political survival. Military requirements as articulated by military officers tended to take precedence over long-range plans and programs for socioeconomic development.

The Chinese Communist party (CCP) was a product of this environment. It was organized in 1921 during the warlord period, and soon discovered that military power was essential to political survival and success. The Communist movement lacked armies of its own and was almost wiped out in 1927 by Chiang Kai-shek. Thereafter, the CCP shifted its revolutionary strategy from urban insurrection to the development of rural bases defended by armed forces. The People's Liberation Army (PLA) emerged and grew as a result of conscious efforts by the CCP to provide a military arm that would protect its territorial strongholds and ultimately defeat its opponents in the field. The PLA's growth was slow and erratic, but by 1949 it had grown to a force of 5 million which then decisively defeated the Nationalist armies to establish CCP control over all of China.

This long process fused the PLA and the CCP within the Communist movement. Where the army was strong, the movement flourished; when it retreated, the movement's political and administrative structure normally retreated with it (although the CCP maintained some underground political operations). A high percentage of soldiers and almost all officers were party members; most party members had military experience, including—for senior party elites—actual command of or service as political commissars in combat units. The commissars and party committees ensured political control over the army and maintained a regular program of political education within its ranks.

The fusion of party and army laid the foundation for a successful conquest of the mainland and for much of the pattern of civil-military relations in the PRC after 1949. It is particularly important to note two significant points. First the army created by a broader political movement was loyal to the political goals of the revolution. With rare exceptions, the CCP was not faced with the constant bargaining, shifting alliances, and revolts among military commanders that had plagued governments during the warlord and Nationalist periods.

Second, the PLA was unique because of its discipline, morale, and relatively harmonious relations with society. Soldiers joined the PLA mainly out of political commitment, reinforced by intensive organization and education within its ranks. Guerrilla tactics necessitated close contact with and dependence on the peasants. Most other military forces lacked the PLA's reputation for national service and dedication. Troops helped build community organization rather than destroying it. Personal relationships within the army and between army and people were relatively egalitarian, emphasizing primarily tasks of national defense and reform. Hence, the military mobilization that accompanied the Communist revolution rested not on forced extractions from the population but rather on party, army, and citizens participating in what they perceived to be a common effort.

■

War and the threat of war have played a prominent role in post-1949 Chinese affairs. The new government faced a difficult mopping-up operation against scattered Nationalist forces and their supporters in 1949. The PLA's occupation of Tibet in 1950, viewed by the CCP as part of its consolidation of national territory, was also a major military undertaking, although it involved little fighting. Chinese intervention in the Korean War in effect put the PRC at war with the United States for nearly three of its first four years. Continuing hostilities with the Nationalists on Taiwan occasionally resulted in brief but tense engagements (in 1954 and 1958). The Tibetan revolt of 1959 was quickly suppressed but that area continued to simmer until the brief Sino-Indian border war in the latter part of 1962. American escalation of the Vietnam War in 1964–1965 created new commitments for the PRC which were particularly acute because the Sino-Soviet conflict made China the only nation with real reason to fear war with either or both of the superpowers. By the late 1960s, the threat of war with the United States lessened, but there were numerous military clashes along the Sino-Soviet border, and rumors of Russian plans for a nuclear strike against China. In the early 1970s, the Chinese continued a variety of construction and relocation projects designed to guard against a possible Soviet attack.

The military and national security considerations prominent in post-1949 China provide important contrasts with the pre-1949 period. First, the wars since 1949 have been less frequent and more limited. The Korean War, the PRC's greatest military effort, strained the PLA and the Chinese economy but it was kept within limits and there were no attacks on China itself. The other hostilities referred to above had less impact on China. The years since 1949 may be viewed, therefore, as relatively peaceful.

Second, China's military engagements since 1949 were confined to the country's periphery—to Korea, the Straits of Formosa, the Himalayas, and the Sino-Soviet border. the end of civil war and the new government's capacity to keep hostile foreign powers at bay have spared the PRC the destructive military movements and battles of the past.

Third, since 1949 there has been a significant reversal in the cost of military activities relative to the financial capabilities of the system. The PRC's early years were marked by high levels of military mobilization, but PLA strength was reduced from about 5 million to about 2.5 million after the Korean armistice of 1953. That force level remained constant until the late 1960s, when there were reports of increases in army size—and the budget for the military was cut. Massive state-sponsored programs brought rapid economic growth and great increases in governmental revenue, and military claims on national resources dropped to relatively modest levels. By the early 1960s, the ratios of army size to total population and of defense expenditures to national product for China were substantially less than half those ratios for either the United States or the Soviet Union. The PRC's nuclear development program gathered momentum during the 1960s, and this financial burden increased the military share of national product in China to a point probably comparable to other major countries. Nonetheless, the PRC's military costs have not been excessive relative to those of other powers and are significantly lower than those incurred by previous Chinese governments.

■

The PLA may be the world's "cheapest" army in terms of cost-benefit. Its capabilities have clearly been sufficient to meet its military responsibilities, but material benefits to both officers and men are modest. The organization is pervaded by a strong sense of egalitarianism and frugality especially since the abolition of insignia of rank and titles of address in 1965. PLA recruitment is technically based on universal conscription, yet the number of eligible recruits is so large that the PLA is quite selective in its choice of new members. Once enlisted, recruits serve at least four years to maximize the return on the training provided. The PLA has undergone periods of "modernization" to acquire essential new weaponry and skills, but it remains basically an army of footsoldiers whose training and logistical needs are relatively inexpensive.

Moreover, most PLA units raise some of their own food and produce some of the supplies they need. Troops have been heavily employed in large-scale construction projects, especially in frontier areas, and many state farms and defense-related enterprises are run by PLA units. The training of millions of young peasants in the PLA has been an important supplement to the country's educational system. Soldiers and former soldiers frequently receive administrative and political assignments at all levels of government.

In short, the PLA's style and role have kept its real cost to society at a minimum. It would, however, be foolish to assume there has been no internal conflict and misgiving, particularly on the part of career officers who fear a weakening of combat effectiveness. The PLA's role of "serving the people" nonetheless has produced economic benefits and the populace seems to hold a high opinion of the PLA.

One of the great strengths of the Communist movement arose from its mobilization of the peasants to positive support of the revolution. The CCP came to power by means of a military superiority largely derived from a common purpose that united party, army, and the people. Since 1949 popular mobilization has been maintained through the basic institutions of the PRC, supplemented by mass movements which focused popular energies on national targets in a political atmosphere suggestive of wartime.

The Korean War, following so closely on the revolutionary war itself and coinciding with sharp class struggle in domestic programs, gave a pronounced martial quality to the mass movements of the early 1950s. Thereafter, the CCP continued to use military themes and symbols. During the Great Leap Forward of 1958–1960, basically a drive for accelerated economic development, one of the goals of the communes was to make militia service universal under the slogan "Everyone a Soldier." The Cultural Revolution of 1966–1969 was also marked by an emphasis on military preparedness. That campaign centered on domestic political conflicts within the CCP leadership, but the PLA became increasingly prominent.

It is difficult to assess the effects of campaign rhetoric, but there can be little doubt that martial elements in the mass movements have helped perpetuate an atmosphere of national struggle and crisis. This is not to suggest that the sense of urgency is artificial or that the foreign threats to the PRC are unreal. China might have been attacked or it might have failed to progress if the population had not been so well prepared for extraordinary collective efforts. Yet China's avoidance of the destructiveness of actual warfare coincided with the government's increasing capacity to mobilize the population in pursuit of nonmilitary goals. The population's evident preparedness for national struggle permitted the government to limit its commitment of resources to the defense establishment without appearing weak or vulnerable to potential enemies.

■

What happened since 1949 to the direct political power of military elites so conspicuous in pre-1949 China? As might be expected, the PLA is prominent in the politics of the PRC, however, with important distinctions and qualifications.

One of the most interesting aspects of the PLA has been its role as a symbol of the traditions, spirit, and ideals of the Communist system. Beyond the use of military models, terminology, and style in mass movements, the PLA has figured prominently in more general cultural and educational activities. Films, dramas, popular literature, and stories in school textbooks have drawn heavily on the history of the PLA (particularly the "Long March" and the Anti-Japanese War), its exploits in the Korean War, and its defense and construction activities in frontier regions in more recent years. The heroism and selfless dedication of individual soldiers are widely publicized as models of behavior for other citizens, and the PLA has been portrayed as an institutional embodiment of patriotism, discipline, militancy, and willingness to sacrifice. The use of the PLA as a national political symbol added an element of romanticism to its very real services that has enhanced its prestige and made military careers more desirable.

The PLA is a primary source of the political elite. Young discharged soldiers move into positions of local leadership and many senior party officials have experience as military commanders. Moreover, the PLA has assumed important governmental responsibilities. From 1949 to 1953, Communist armies acquired administrative powers over the areas they occupied until the new governmental institutions of the PRC came into being. During the Cultural Revolution, the PLA was called upon to support Maoist "rebels" in attacking "revisionists" and it provided *de facto* government for most of China. Many observers concluded that a military takeover had occurred.

Local commanders assumed political leadership in their areas and military officers gained nearly half of the seats on the CCP Central Committee elected in 1969. Minister of Defense Lin Piao was named in the 1969 Party Constitution as Mao's successor. The newly won power and arrogance of the PLA was apparently confirmed in 1971 by reports that Lin conspired to assassinate Mao and seize control of the country. The argument that the PLA was similar to other armies in a desire to seize power from civilian elites, however, overstates the case.

Maoists ordered the PLA to intervene in the Cultural Revolution, and the evidence suggests that many military commanders were reluctant to accept such direct and controversial political and administrative responsibilities. Moreover, once the turmoil of the Cultural Revolution was over, the CCP began to rebuild and to reassert the basic principle of party supremacy. Military officers, heavily represented in the new government and party organs, did not openly contest party rule or its implementation. Lin Piao's coup failed (he died in the course of it) and it is clear in retrospect that he acted on behalf of his own faction, not on behalf of the PLA as an institution. The ensuing purge of Piao's supporters apparently weakened military representation to some extent, but the incident was not treated as an indication of PLA disloyalty or untrustworthiness.

The Cultural Revolution undeniably created a crisis in civil-military relations and raised a specter of party disintegration and a revival of warlordism among regionally based military commanders. But the system overcame the threat of outright military rule and reestablished the primacy of party authority. Army officers hold many high political positions but that is not, in itself, proof of a military takeover since most of them are long-standing party members who had held political office—not necessarily at such high levels. Furthermore, military commands are dominated by political figures. The fusion of party and army that emerged in the revolutionary war persists although it shows signs of strain.

Contemporary China provides interesting and paradoxical lessons for students of war and military institutions. China is in the midst of its most peaceful era but its population is thoroughly prepared for war. The military establishment has met the needs of national defense, including the development of nuclear capabilities, without limiting socioeconomic development and retaining an ethic of egalitarianism and service to society. The army enjoys immense prestige and is deeply involved in the political life of the country, but it is not itself a competitor in the struggle for power. How long this pattern will persist—as the revolutionary tradition fades and new international and technological pressures emerge—is open to question. Yet the PLA will certainly continue to play a central role in Chinese affairs.

# PART *IV*

# War in the Industrial Age

# Introduction

The essays in this section share a concern for war in Western industrial societies and the implications of total war.

The essays formulate these general problems in specific terms. L. L. Farrar, jr., analyzes the outbreak of World War I in terms of long-term (institutions and forces) and short-term (individuals and situations) causes. Marjorie M. Farrar interprets World War II as a total war which had profound political, social, economic, and psychological effects on Europe. Edward A. Stern argues that American defense policy during the Cold War is less a result of the so-called military-industrial complex than of the American political structure as a whole. Judith A. Thornton contends that American prosperity is not dependent on massive military spending. Otis A. Pease suggests that contemporary American notions about war should be viewed as part of a historical pattern of fluctuating American attitudes.

Several themes run through these essays. All reveal an interdependence between modern war and society. The effects of war—particularly total war—on these societies are probably the more obvious aspect of this relationship; the influence of the military and military questions is similarly clear. But all these essays likewise suggest that society has an equally profound effect on the conduct of war. Total war is possible only in twentieth-century society and that may indeed symbolize modern society's tendencies toward centralization, dehumanization, and reliance on technology. War and society may become more closely integrated as society becomes more industrialized, but the basic relationships are not altered by modernization.

■

# The Causes of World War I

## L. L. Farrar, jr.

The long-term causes of war can be explained in terms of the general international system in which war occurs. The cause of war can be associated with international and national institutions and forces. International institutions include states, such organizations as the United Nations or the League of Nations, alliances among states, international law, treaties, etc., as well as widely accepted but infrequently formalized assumptions such as spheres of influence, the balance of power, and some notion of the proper role of a state. National institutions involve political constitutions, law, political parties, economic and social structures, intellectual and cultural organizations, race relations, etc. International forces include nationalism, imperialism and colonialism, and militarism. National forces are political change, public opinion, social and psychological impulses, and economic development.

These generalizations become more meaningful in examining the long-term causes of World War I. The basic international institution was the so-called Great Power system, characterized by alliances which divided Europe into two fairly clear camps by the beginning of the twentieth century. There was no international organization at that time but a considerable body of international law had been accepted. Some spheres of influence were generally recognized, others were openly contested. Perhaps the most striking international institution was a shared attitude about the operation of the state system. Survival was the ultimate objective of the Great Powers and

■

power was the means. In this context, war became a natural and necessary demonstration of power. The outcome of such a system was not whether but when war would occur. An explanation of the causes of World War I in these terms therefore emphasizes alliances, international frictions over disputed spheres of influence (especially in the Balkans and the colonial world), and above all a commonly held view of what states, primarily the Great Powers, were supposed to do.

National institutions were indirectly causal in the sense that they resisted the forces of change. Thus it is argued that the war resulted from the elitist (nonpopular and socially narrow) control of foreign and military policy; European conservative governments duped the masses into war under the guise of national emergency to preserve their political power. American President Woodrow Wilson and other liberals concluded that the common man was peaceful and generous but that traditional governments were belligerent and selfish. If so, it follows that democratic control over diplomatic and military policy—Wilson presumed this was true in the United States even though he dominated policy-making himself—would remove one basic cause of war.

Most explanations of the long-term causes of World War I are based on the influence of international forces and emphasize the effect of nationalism. Nationalism usually means an increasing rivalry between nations, frequently related to the growth of mass politics. Some historians argue that nationalism affected only the richest, the most powerful and articulate European societies. Others, considering the behavior of political parties, labor unions, schools, and churches on the eve of World War I, argue that most people were imbued by nationalism.

Imperialism, broadly defined in terms of a rivalry among the Great Powers over colonial areas, is the basis of arguments that attempt to explain the war in economic terms. Lenin perceived imperialism to be the last stage of capitalism leading irrevocably to war. The most persistent colonial conflicts during the half-century before World War I were, however, between Great Powers allied during the war, and there were relatively few conflicts between nations that later became enemies. Nonetheless imperialism may well have been a major cause of the war, though less an economic than a psychological factor. Imperialism reflected the view that the state system was essentially competitive and that view perhaps prepared people to accept war as an appropriate, indeed necessary, policy outcome.

Militarism is usually perceived in terms of those policies which are inclined to resort to war, policies dominated by the military and frequently measured in terms of arms races. The arms buildup among the Great Powers occurred on the eve of war so militarism fails to explain previous international behavior, e.g., the French and Russian naval buildup during the 1890s was directed at Britain which was later allied with France and Russia during World War I. There was, in addition, a mutually reinforcing cause-and-effect relationship —international tension caused the arms races, the race augmented tension, which in turn accelerated the race. Militarism implies that the military plays an important if not overwhelming role in policy-making. The military was prominent in determining policy in general and in the arms buildup in particular but it is difficult to prove that the military role increased or that it actually dominated policy. None of the military establishments in Europe unanimously supported either the arms race or the war. Thus, "international forces" proved to be awkward in explaining the cause of war but they were symptomatic of the prevailing frame of mind.

The most striking national force was the rapid growth of mass politics, public opinion, and the press during the half-century before the war. The masses were politicized as never before except during brief periods of revolution. Some historians argue that there is no relationship between politicization and World War I and counter that the common man was interested in paychecks, not international affairs. Most historians, however, see nationalism as an international reflection of domestic politics. When the masses were interested in politics and nationalistic, they were not peaceful—as liberals like Wilson suggested. In that case democratically controlled foreign policy might prove to be more aggressive than non-democratic diplomacy.

Socialism, which spread rapidly and widely during this period, hardly seemed to provide a direct stimulus to war. The Socialists opposed war more openly than other parties and did little to encourage it, but when it came to the crunch, Socialists unanimously voted for declaring war and war credits. The Socialists may have been too weak to oppose war; socialist leaders may have opposed war while feeling that their supporters favored war, Socialists might have been more nationalistic than socialistic and thus may have opted for nationalism but there is little evidence to indicate it was a direct cause of the war. Some observers have suggested that socialism indirectly encouraged class conflicts causal to the war. The Socialists threatened the upper classes with revolution, in turn the upper classes created a national emergency to preserve their privileged status—ergo, the war was the result of an international conservative conspiracy. This appealingly simple thesis has little evidence to support it. A few conservatives advocated war but many cogently argued that war would lead inevitably to revolution and socialism.

The argument supporting social and psychological pressures as national forces which led to war suggests there was a compulsive

activism among the ruling class in Europe that was reflected in imperialism, industrialism, social Darwinism, "muscular Christianity" and
an emphasis on emotion in contemporary art and music that appealed to basic elements. European society was also viewed as decadent, materialistic, and lazy, i.e., fundamentally passive. It is difficult
to prove that either of these clearly antithetical views was true of
prewar Europe. The evidence for both is not provided by politicians
and statesmen—i.e., the decisionmakers—but from artists, musicians,
dramatists, and novelists. Their assertions may be accurate but cannot be rigorously tested.

This categorization of possible long-term causes of the war is
necessarily general and it fails to consider the behavior of individual
states and statesmen. For example, the differences among the various
forms of nationalism are de-emphasized or even obscured. Such generalizations also fail to note that if the forces and institutions are
critical factors, then individuals are not. The term "forces" as used
here implies the application of pressure, "institutions" suggest resistance to pressure. It may be possible that wars result when irresistible
social forces meet immovable institutions.

Long-term causes provide a general explanation of war. For
several hundred years of existence, there was an oscillation between
generations of war and generations of peace in the European state
system. If that pattern is more than merely coincidental, it suggests
that war and peace were essential to the survival of the European
system. Therefore the establishment of national and international
institutions merely reflected the particular need of the time. Europe
was a dynamic civilization, so new forces impinged on increasingly
anachronistic institutions, which had to adapt thus creating circumstances conducive to war. Therefore it seems that war will recur so
long as there are forces for change and institutions devoted to continuity. Can it be that permanent peace requires a renunciation of
either change or continuity?

■

Short-term causes of war are traditionally called international crises.
There is usually little agreement concerning the interpretation of
specific prewar events but there is a general consensus regarding the
kinds of issues typically involved. The short-term causes of war tend
to involve questions of political responsibilities and situations. If a
statesman's decisions led to war and if other options were available
that might have avoided war, he was "responsible." On the other
hand crisis "situations" sometimes tend to constrain effective decision-making and are themselves causal.

The crisis on the eve of World War I is a useful case study for this type of analysis. The individuals commonly accused of being responsible for the war were, of course, the rulers and decision-makers of the Great Powers. The Austrians, Germans, and Russians were most widely criticized (certainly by Anglo-American historians), followed by the French and then more distantly by the British. Some historians actually listed the decisions made by European leaders during the crisis and argued that some or all of them might have been made differently, thereby avoiding war. Rulers and statesmen were alleged to be guilty as a group. Some historians argue that European leaders of that era were below par and suggest that if another Bismarck had been available, war might have been avoided.

The military has been generally criticized for allowing the generals to take over and turn the crisis toward war. This argument is clearly incompatible with the view that civilian leaders were responsible. Conservatives in and out of government have been accused of seeking war to preserve their privileges and the public in one or more countries was cited for mass demonstrations favoring declarations of war. The common man has been accused of wanting and perhaps even demanding war. The emphasis on individual and group responsibility is typical of most of the historiography of World War I and must therefore be taken seriously.

The crisis situation can be analyzed to produce a variety of causal explanations. It involved decisions made by many individuals and the critical question is how they were made and by whom. It is essential to determine whether the war might have been avoided if a particular decision had been made differently and then to determine whether a different decision was possible under the existing circumstances.

It was the duty of European statesmen in 1914 to preserve and, when possible, to extend the power of their respective states. They employed peaceful means if possible but were prepared to use war if necessary. No statesman long remained in office if he put the preservation of peace above his own state's interest and power. There were, however, hypothetical alternatives to all the decisions taken during the 1914 crisis. For instance, Austria-Hungary might have avoided giving an ultimatum to Serbia and Germany might have chosen not to support Austria-Hungary. But it can also be argued that each decision was logical, even necessary given the existing circumstances.

The responsibility of specific groups can also be questioned. Rulers and statesmen generally reflected the attitudes and conditions of their respective societies but the available replacements would probably have made the same decisions. It can also be argued that the military played a relatively small part. The critical decisions leading to the war were made largely by civilians and the military was involved only when war was nearly inevitable. The view that soldiers favored war while the civilians preferred peace is thus questionable. Further, the records left by conservatives suggest more of them were opposed rather than in favor of war. Businessmen consulted by government officials—infrequently during the crisis—were against the war because it would be bad for business. The rulers asked politicians and parliamentarians to rubber-stamp their declarations of war. Public opinion was mobilized following the crisis but it was seldom consulted as the war approached.

The term "crisis" suggests circumstances which reduce choice and diplomatic maneuverability. The personal idiosyncrasies of leaders seemingly lessen under crisis conditions when perceptions of national interest force leaders to play certain roles. Leaders, despite their national origins, frequently use similar language, particularly as crises develop. Consequently, crises often create circumstances wherein individual "responsibility" cannot satisfactorily be determined to be a cause of war.

The long- and short-term causes of war are interdependent—if one is emphasized, the other must be de-emphasized. The relative emphasis depends on the specific historical situation and the particular interpretation of the historian. Both are necessary to a convincing explanation of war.

# World War II as Total War

## Marjorie M. Farrar

A discussion of World War II in Europe as total war raises the problem of definition. The term "total" is absolute: only total and nontotal exist and degrees of totality are, strictly speaking, illogical. The term is thus inapplicable to most human behavior, including war. Totality can, however, be interpreted as one extreme in a spectrum of possibilities. Distinction is then made among degrees of totality, rather than between totality and nontotality. In other words, an absolute term can be applied in a relative sense: war is total in the degree to which it approaches the extreme of totality. The degree of totality can be determined by the characteristics of destruction and mobilization.*

Although World War II was exceptionally destructive in human and material terms, it was clearly not total in the sense that every individual in every participating nation was killed and all territory laid waste. Nor was the damage permanent, since populations revived and the ruin was repaired. Nonetheless, in terms of scope and destructiveness, the war can be regarded as the nearest approach to total war the world has experienced.

Mobilization can be measured by the number of nations or people involved and the degree to which populations or resources were affected. Obviously some nations were not belligerents, entire popu-

---

*The essential work on this subject is Gordon Wright, *The Ordeal of Total War 1939–1945* (New York: Harper & Row, 1968).

■

lations were not conscripted and resources were not exhausted. The war, however, involved many nations and most people in the belligerent states were mobilized as soldiers or workers in factories, on farms, and in government. Hence mobilization was a reflection of the war's overall impact and the degree to which the war encroached upon and altered individual lives. Food was rationed; homes were bombed; loved ones were killed and wounded; political, social, and economic structures were changed; psychological strains were imposed. In short, life was disrupted, if not destroyed by the war.

■

The European belligerents had quite different political institutions and wartime experiences. France was a multiparty, parliamentary democracy. Great Britain had a two-party, parliamentary democracy. Nazi Germany was a totalitarian, single-party regime with a rightist, fascist ideology. Russia was also a totalitarian regime but with a leftist, communist ideology. The belligerents' wartime experiences were likewise contrasting. Germany, the aggressor, conquered most of Europe and was overwhelmingly victorious until 1942, after which it was generally on the defensive. German cities were extensively bombed, the population suffered, its resources were depleted, and it finally surrendered unconditionally. France was humiliatingly defeated in 1940, occupied or controlled by German forces until it was liberated in 1944. Great Britain was the only state which opposed Germany from 1939 to 1945. Britain was heavily bombed but it was never invaded and England became a symbol of resistance to Hitler. Britain joined the United States and Russia to engineer the final victory. Russia, initially a German ally, was later invaded by German forces and suffered greater human and material losses than any other belligerent. Finally allied with the Western democracies the Soviet Union gradually repulsed the German armies, invaded eastern Europe, and finished the war as a member of the victorious coalition.

Notably these distinctions in political systems and wartime experiences made little difference in the war's profound political effects on these states. In Nazi Germany, the Reichstag remained and formally confirmed Hitler's arbitrary powers during the war, but it had no political power. Germany became a single-party state in which individual freedom was severely restricted—a police state in every sense. For a totalitarian state like Germany, the loss of individual freedom and the extension of governmental authority leads to the question of whether any elements within the society retain any freedoms. Clearly the average German citizen had little. The military increased in power during the war, but never achieved an independent position; it was subordinate to Hitler as commander-in-chief. The decline in German military fortunes can actually be traced from the date of his increased interference in military matters. The war reinforced the existing authoritarian tendencies and caused Germany to become more totalitarian than before.

The situation in the Soviet Union was similar. Individual rights had largely disappeared before the war. The Communist party was in full control and the Supreme Soviet was merely its vehicle; political dissent was virtually nonexistent. The Russian military, subordinated to the state before the war, suffered severely during the great purges in the thirties. The generals nonetheless were increasingly responsible for conducting the war, Stalin heeded their counsel, temporarily removed political commissars from the army, and generally gave a greater voice to the military. Ultimately however, the power of the Generals proved to be brief and mostly honorific; they never had an opportunity to control Russian society. Stalin formalized his position as absolute dictator by assuming dual roles as head of state and supreme military commander.

Britain provides an interesting example of the political implications of total war. An electoral truce was declared in 1939 and the prewar parliament remained in power until 1945. A coalition government was established and Clement Attlee, head of the Labour party, became vice-premier achieving political consolidation. Political dissent and criticism of governmental policies declined largely by parliamentary consent. Political power was centralized when Churchill became minister of defense and commander-in-chief; he interfered with military decisions almost as much as Stalin and Hitler and ran his war cabinet virtually as a dictator.

Similar developments, largely unprecedented in democratic societies, occurred in the United States and France. Roosevelt basically ran the war with the Joint Chiefs of Staff and the role of civilian leaders was vastly diminished. In France, Daladier was given extensive wartime decree powers in 1939 and Pétain, as head of the Vichy regime after the defeat in 1940, became a virtual despot. Although France had no military forces after the German occupation, Pétain was at once chief of the military and head of the domestic government.

Thus governmental authority was centralized and increased at the expense of individuals, parliaments, and the military in all of the belligerent states. As a result institutional and ideological distinctions among the belligerents were reduced and the democratic regimes increasingly resembled their totalitarian counterparts.

■

Notably World War II produced several great wartime leaders each of whom displayed unique characteristics and perhaps a special kind of genius. The successful leaders demonstrated an ability to exploit, sometimes even to mold, developing situations. In particular, they aroused the masses and identified themselves with national causes; they accepted setbacks with remarkable fortitude; took risks in the face of uncertainties (what Churchill called the "terrible ifs"); and imposed their will on potential rivals and unruly subordinates.

The situation, however, also contributed to the emergence of great leaders. Total war induced general centralizing pressures which subordinated agencies, parliaments, and armed services to an ever-narrowing decision-making group. The individuals who assumed power in wartime certainly tended to be power grabbers, but the need for efficiency produced smaller decision-making groups. The war also polarized choices, the rewards of unconditional victory or the danger of unconditional surrender.

The psychological motivations for the emergence of wartime leaders originate in the total war mentality which equated dissent with disloyalty, conformity with loyalty. These alternatives induced the masses to accept great sacrifices and provided many with a sense of commitment seldom felt in peacetime; these emotions were brought into focus by the leaders. The desire for a savior in desperate times and a celebrator in victory also required leaders. In short, wartime leaders satisfied a need and it is likely that, had they not existed, the masses would have invented them. Wartime leaders became dictators at least partially by consent.

Leaders and masses were consequently symbiotic. The leaders repressed opposition and dissent, exaggerated their own roles, and generally exploited the situation, and the war created a public desire for precisely those qualities. Total war thus produced total leaders which reduced differences among the several regimes. Dictators appeared everywhere. A dictator remains in the one successful totalitarian state (Soviet Russia), but the dictator disappeared in the unsuccessful totalitarian states (Germany and Italy) and the democracies (Great Britain, France, and the United States).

■

Regardless of political or economic system, governments intervened to mobilize their economies for war and attempted to reduce or destroy the economic power of their enemies.

Germany's transition to a war economy was unencumbered by ideological readjustments and scruples like those which plagued the democracies. The conversion to a wartime economy began at the latest by 1936 with the Four-Year Plans and great armaments buildup but the general impression of Hitler's extensive and thorough economic preparedness is inaccurate. He shifted priorities among industries according to the needs of a particular campaign instead of converting the whole economy to full-scale war production. This approach succeeded for a time until the invasion of Russia proved that it was no longer possible. Hitler introduced rationing and comprehensive wage and price controls, but German industry continued to produce consumer goods at prewar levels until 1941 and *autobahn* construction continued even though their military utility proved less than expected. The transition to a total war economy was finally made in 1942. The Nazi organization and lack of resources also produced deficiencies in the war economy. The competing and overlapping authorities within the Nazi power structure impeded the centralization of all aspects of the economy. Even after Speer assumed leadership of the ministry of armaments and munitions in 1942, certain areas were outside his authority. For example, he never controlled manpower allocation, which remained under Sauckel. Other organizations such as the SS, which decided economic questions for the conquered territories, were outside Speer's jurisdiction. In addition, Germany simply lacked the raw materials essential for a prolonged war, deficiencies only partially alleviated by stripping conquered countries.

The Soviet government had amassed considerable experience in comprehensive planning since 1928, when the Five-Year Plans for agriculture and industry were introduced. The Plans continued into the war period and the two years of the Russo-German alliance coincided with the last two years of Russia's third Five-Year Plan. Russia put those years to good use, building up industries in the Urals and western Siberia which proved essential after the German invasion, when economic mobilization was vastly intensified. A massive transfer of industry occurred, as approximately 1,300 plants were demobilized, moved behind the Urals, and rebuilt. Russia's most important industrial centers were overrun by the Germans but Russia still managed to set and maintain high production levels. The United States supplied vehicles and clothing but the armaments used by Russian troops were produced almost entirely in the Soviet Union. Problems of management and morale were also amazingly well handled. Further, although the richest 42 percent of the land was occupied by the Germans and the total farm labor force was reduced by 33 percent, agricultural production was maintained. Rigid control over the economy was established through rationing consumer goods and consumption, high taxes, and manpower allocation. The Russian wartime economic achievement demonstrated tremendous ability to improvise and sacrifice.

Great Britain lacked the Russian advantage of experience with a planned economy and, unlike the Germans, made few preparations before 1940. The British were confident that time was on their side, as it was in World War I. They felt that if they could hold out long enough, their factories would produce what was necessary, but the defeat culminating at Dunkirk made it clear that a drastic reorganization was required. Churchill assigned general supervision of the economic effort to the Lord President's Committee, a small ministerial group, headed by a civil servant, Sir John Anderson. By the end of 1941, just eighteen months after the beginning of the war, Britain had the most thoroughly coordinated economy of any warring nation. A system of points rationing was established, the distribution of food and other consumer goods was strictly limited. Imports and exports were rigidly controlled, and raw materials were allocated according to national priorities. From 1940 on, the British suffered from a labor shortage which they partially resolved by mobilizing previously unemployed groups, women and older people. Labor mobility was restricted, as people were drafted into the military services or given jobs in specific factories. A scientific budget plan, increased taxation and compulsory savings, allowed the British to cover about half of governmental wartime expenditures out of current revenue. No other nation achieved such a financial record.

The belligerents mobilized at different rates and with varying degrees of success. Despite their tradition of control, the totalitarian states were less organized by the end of the war than democratic Britain. This suggests that consent may be a more successful organizing principle than compulsion. But the differences may be partially attributable to other factors. Great Britain's economy, certainly in the financial area, was more sophisticated than Germany's and Russia's. Furthermore, Britain continued to have access to the world's resources, the "tight little Island" was never invaded and it was seriously bombed only briefly. The European powers mobilized gradually and mobilization became thorough only during 1941–1942 for reasons that were partially technological: mobilization for total war is a complicated process involving considerable trial and error. But it is also likely that few political leaders wanted to confront the prospect of total war. The Germans hoped war would be brief and successful, the British hoped someone would come to their rescue, and the Russians hoped to postpone it as long as possible. The degree of success in establishing war economics differed but the effects were comparable. Governments controlled their economies, sought efficiency and coordination, disrupted both market and planned economies, and redistributed wealth through tax and rationing. The war was a traumatic shock for all economies.

The belligerents engaged in economic warfare to reduce the effectiveness of their opponents' economic mobilization. Although generally overrated, these campaigns were not insignificant. They included attempts to prevent materials from reaching the enemy, as in the Anglo-American blockade of Germany and the German submarine attacks on Allied shipping, as well as preclusive purchasing of neutral goods. They also involved efforts to disrupt enemy economies through strategic bombing. The Germans sought to destroy British industrial potential but their bombing campaign was designed primarily to terrify the British into surrender. The Allied bombing campaign was intended to force Germany to surrender through starvation and industrial strangulation. Postwar studies have, however, indicated that the Allied expectations were exaggerated. For example, at the height of the bombing in 1944, German industrial production was reduced only 17 percent. Even so the heavy bombing of oil refineries may have kept some German planes out of the air during the Normandy landings. The results, marginal at best, were achieved at a high cost and the resources devoted to strategic bombing might have been more productively employed in other areas. Economic warfare was an auxiliary tactic which may have supplemented the more standard military weapons but could never have replaced them.

■

Militarization produced the most obvious effect on European society. Greater social discipline and the regimentation of civilian lives created hierarchical relationships. The military values of courage, daring, and self-sacrifice took precedence over traditional civilian standards. Channels of social mobility were altered. The most obvious access to higher social status was offered by the military. Yet military prestige and the military's increased official capacity did not result in the replacement of civilian leaders by soldiers.

Class distinctions became less pronounced in wartime. Most people were subjected to rationing and were liable to military service or war production work. Shortages of goods, austerity standards, and increased social discipline blurred class distinctions. Government concern for the health and morale of the whole population led to free social services such as medical care and social security. Since government intervention characterized the totalitarian states, the notable changes occurred in the democracies—total war tended to diminish distinctions between them. Government work and war industry provided opportunities for social mobility and the socially and economically underprivileged benefited most. Women achieved great gains and specific groups, e.g., British scientists, played unprecedented roles. The greatest gains, however, were made by the least commendable—social dropouts and misfits achieved positions of power within the Nazi regime and its puppets in occupied countries.

The war dramatically and fundamentally altered values and relationships between social groups in the occupied and defeated nations. Whole intellectual and professional elites were eliminated in some countries—the most horrible example was the extermination of Jews in Poland and occupied Russia. The social structures of German occupied areas were totally changed by the importation of a German ruling class. In western Europe the failures and has-beens of the prewar period, notably Quisling, Pétain, and Laval, were elevated to positions of power. Different elites emerged, only to be discredited and replaced following the war by new individuals, frequently from resistance movements.

Government psychological policies paralleled economic policies to mobilize the population. The media were used to propagandize the masses and win support for the war. For example, German Minister of Public Information Joseph Goebbels played upon such themes as the "crusade against bolshevism" or "justice for Germany" to augment popular support for the German war effort. Later, German propaganda sought to maintain civilian morale in the face of defeat. The British made similar use of broadcasts and pamphlets and though difficult to measure, they were probably successful in mobilizing the populations for war.

Both sides tried to weaken the morale of enemy populations. The British, for instance, told the German people that their position was "brilliant but hopeless." Subversive forces within enemy occupied countries were aided by radio broadcasts. These policies doubtless had some effect but it was probably marginal.

The psychological impact of the war is most difficult to establish. Millions of individuals suffered traumatically from the prolonged strains and terror of modern warfare but it is difficult to evaluate the effect since studies of certain types of victims yield only tentative data. Society continued to function in heavily bombed cities without extensive mass hysteria or serious disruption indicating that people in such situations can sustain serious pressure for long periods without collapsing. The study of concentration camps provides quite different evidence. Individuals were totally adapted to their environment and there was no possibility for resistance and adjustment. The evidence indicates that when people remain in familiar social groups and retain a sense of hope, however narrow, they apparently survive psychologically. When people are isolated without hope, they lose the capacity for survival. Victims of bombing were widespread and they provide a better gauge of the effects of war. The concentration camps nonetheless provided insights into the potential for total control, and they are the ultimate symbol of war's tendency to obliterate political, economic, and psychological distinctions.

Like the political and economic systems, science and technology were also mobilized. Scientists turned to weapons development and produced startling new weapons systems—radar, magnetic mines, demagnetizing devices, powder rockets, and ultimately the atomic bomb. Medical science developed sulfa drugs and penicillin, and improved care for the wounded. Churchill clearly recognized the importance of science and appointed as his closest advisor the controversial Oxford science professor F. A. Lindemann, later Lord Cherwell. Lindemann had no well-defined responsibilities but he by-passed normal channels of command to reach Churchill directly. He was largely responsible for strategic bombing decisions, the effects of which he greatly overrated. In Germany, however, science was used in ad hoc projects; and scientists were drafted and sent to infantry units. Hitler failed to utilize German scientists efficiently or to mobilize science for total war until it was too late.

■

World War II was not a total war in terms of destructiveness or mobilization, but nonetheless it deeply affected the lives of most Europeans. The victorious states were extensively affected by the war and the effects were often revolutionary in the defeated nations. The experience demonstrated that modern war involves political, economic, social, psychological, and technological dimensions far beyond strictly military events.

The cost in human lives and material destruction was horrendous. The trend toward government power, sometimes dictatorship, and away from political liberty and individualism was encouraged universally during the war and in some cases afterward. State control of national economies, social disruption, and sometimes revolution, occurred everywhere. The psychological strains were traumatic; rationalism and humaneness were often displaced by bestiality and opportunism. Technology was harnessed to war-making and produced the most destructive weapons ever devised. The war pushed Western civilization toward totalitarianism.

There were some positive, less obvious, outcomes. The necessity to win general support for the war involved groups formerly outside political power. Government intervention in the economy sometimes resulted in efficiency as well as disruption. Increased social mobility and leveling tended to loosen rigid societies and Europe became more socially and economically egalitarian with a higher standard of living than ever before. Perhaps the most striking benefit is an apparent disinclination on the part of Europeans to resort to a new war.

# The Military-Industrial-Academic-Congressional Complex

## Edward A. Stern

The notion of a military-industrial complex, popularized and perhaps even legitimized by Eisenhower in his farewell address, has become part of American culture. More important, it summarizes for many the process by which American defense policy is made. It is clear that both the military and industry are engaged in this process but it is less well recognized that two other groups are also essential parts of the "complex." Academics at universities and experts in think tanks (e.g., the RAND Corporation and the Hudson Institute) and other technical persons comprise one group; Congress is the other.

The original purpose of the coalition was altogether valid: to increase American security by maintaining and expanding military strength. The grouping emerged during World War II and culminated a tremendous effort by developing atomic weapons. The group grew in cohesiveness and size and reached a peak in late 1967, when Secretary of Defense Robert McNamara announced that the United States was about to deploy antiballistic missiles, the Sentinal System. Reaction to that decision led to a breakup and decline of the coalition.

It is tempting to ascribe sinister and conspiratorial motives to the MIAC complex. Members are sometimes characterized as heartless merchants of death. Those views are appealingly simple and suggest obvious solutions. A closer look indicates, however, that the situation is not so simple, since the basic motivations of most participants seem to have been honorable. The judgment of some was, however, cor-

■

rupted by unlimited power gained because of a breakdown in the American governmental process and its system of checks and balances.

That fundamental system is frequently forgotten when American defense policy-making is discussed. The MIAC complex expanded its powers because the system of checks and balances failed to function. This failure must be strongly emphasized because certain groups instrumental in the breakdown now deny participation and claim to be innocent of the resulting excesses—the accumulation of power within the executive branch (e.g., within the Pentagon), uncritical judgments on policy questions, and corruption.

Congress was responsible for the primary failure because it seldom evaluated requests for authorization of military appropriations critically. Indeed, some members of the House Armed Services Committee complained that they were not provided a means of analyzing military budgets. Pentagon people would simply appear at hearings with an army of technical experts to produce elaborate testimony indicating why their programs should be approved without question. The only operative question in Congress was political, i.e., would the American people accept the costs of the programs? Cuts were made, based only on questions of economy rather than of merit. Congress tended to reflect the generally prevailing Cold War mentality, i.e., high defense budgets were seen as necessary to maintain the security of the Free World. Nevertheless, congressmen should have more critically evaluated Pentagon proposals.

The result was predictable. The Department of Defense gained approval for essentially all its programs for a quarter-century and easy approval led to a laxity of standards, poor programs, excessive expense, and corruption. The development of personal relationships between military men and congressmen fostered the process. Thus the military was corrupted by its own apparent success. Congress and other agencies did not require the military services to defend their programs rigorously, so they produced less defensible programs.

The academic community was also victimized by the process. The intellectual independence essential to a critical analysis of Pentagon programs was lost by many academics who became involved. Those academics were not necessarily weak or evil but the process of absorption into a large system was nearly irresistable. Those academics tended to become totally involved in making the system work and accepted the prevailing view that national security required ever-larger accumulations of military hardware. They failed, however, to continuously evaluate other desirable alternatives such as negotiations and they neglected domestic problems which did not fall within their purview. Gradually many academics concerned with problems of national defense were co-opted as Pentagon experts.

Their experience replicated the military's failure to make critical and independent judgments and to suggest departures in policy.

Large military budgets encouraged industry to produce military hardware. Contracts, in many cases awarded without genuine competitive bidding, fostered shoddy proposals and discouraged efficiency. Allowances for cost overruns protected contractors against their own mistakes, and personal relationships between congressmen, military men, and industrial representatives reinforced the whole process. It should be recalled, however, that industry performed its assigned function in American society of achieving economic profit by producing what society demands. This role was open to criticism in the matter of military contracts but it was unrealistic to expect industry would police itself. Congress, the military, and academics, alike should have demanded efficiency and honesty.

Inter-service rivalry was minimal as long as sufficient funds were available to support programs advocated by all three services. Funds were divided indiscriminately from 1945 to 1970 and the services got relatively comparable shares of the budget. As a consequence, the air force had its own intercontinental ballistic missile system and the navy its Polaris missiles on nuclear submarines. The army had no missile system and felt it needed one to meet the competition for talented career officers. The result was a proposal to develop an antiballistic missile under army command—the Sentinal System was initiated in the Fall 1967. The Sentinal program proved to be a stumbling block for the army and the whole MIAC complex when it was revealed that missile sites would be located near populated areas. The public became involved in the debate and then in the whole domain of defense policy-making.

The tenor of public involvement was best exemplified in Seattle, Washington when a largely unused army base, Fort Lawton, was designated as a missile site. Residents expected that the base was to be given to the city for use as a regional park. The army's plans precluded that use and the public also felt that the city would become a military target. The city administration suggested that the missiles be sited elsewhere but army officials refused and argued that Fort Lawton was the only technologically feasible site. The city apparently had little recourse, and the matter seemed closed until a group of scientists at the University of Washington[1] examined the Sentinal System and its role in defense strategy. They concluded that the Sentinal System was a bad mistake, that the reasons for its deployment were not those which had been publicly stated, and that its siting in Seattle should be further evaluated. The evidence con-

---

1. Professor J. Gregory Dash, Professor Edward A. Stern, Mr. Newell Mack, Mr. Phil Ekstrom, and Miss Diane Hartzell.

vinced the public in Seattle that the army could not defend the Fort Lawton site on the basis of national security. Citizen groups pressured their congressmen, who compaigned against siting at Fort Lawton. The army was finally forced to withdraw its proposal, particularly through the insistence of Senator Henry Jackson.

The army subsequently proposed to site Sentinals on nearby Bainbridge Island and the inhabitants followed the lead of Seattle residents. The opposition and resistance to proposed sites elsewhere in the country forced a temporary postponement of siting decisions at the end of 1968.

The period of reassessment traditionally associated with the inauguration of a new president resulted in a drastic alteration of the Sentinal System in early 1969. The location of defensive ABMs near missile sites reflected a domestic political decision and a fundamental change in nuclear strategy. Their placement near population centers —which the Sentinal System could not effectively defend in any case —would tend to induce the Russians to build missiles capable of destroying those population centers. The relocation of the ABM system to defend American offensive missiles was not a threat to Soviet deterrence capabilities and would consequently not escalate the nuclear arms race. The proposed redeployment actually reduced the likelihood of increased human casualties in a nuclear exchange. The adjusted system, now named Safeguard, was less objectionable but it was still only barely approved by Congress.[2]

The modification and defeat of the ABM program broke up the MIAC complex. Academics knowledgeable about nuclear strategy but not deeply involved in the complex recognized that the system was corrupt as evidenced by the army's attempt to deploy the Sentinal System. A receptive public, in turn, utilized the scientists' arguments to win the support of congressmen. As a consequence of the Sentinal episode, Congress was inclined to more critically consider Pentagon requests and the checks-and-balances system began to function. The Vietnam War reinforced the public's inclination to question military decisions and encouraged Congress to reassert the role it had virtually renounced with the Gulf of Tonkin Resolution.

Mistakes made by the military, industry, Congress, academia, and the public at large contributed to a breakdown in the system of checks-and-balances and the experience should be correctly interpreted, to avoid drawing false lessons. An overreaction against the military would be genuinely dangerous since the existing international situation renders national security to be an unfortunate neces-

2. Indeed, subsequent events have vindicated the opposition. SALT I and II agreements halted further deployment of the ABM beyond the presently ineffective single site in each country.

sity. The military properly advocates programs to ensure security and it is up to Congress to evaluate those programs in relation to other national concerns and oversee the performance of industry in fulfilling military contracts. Corruption and excessive profits can be avoided through competitive bidding, critical evaluation of bids, and discouragement of cost overruns. It must be recognized, however, that many new weapons systems are so near the frontier of technological knowledge that costs are frequently hard to predict and it will be difficult to distinguish between honest and negligent mistakes. The public should nonetheless insist that its representatives evaluate military proposals. That public pressure demands increased concern, more involvement and sufficient education on the issues if we are to reach valid conclusions.

Academics and other experts on national security needs cannot become so closely involved in decision-making that they lose their independence. Yet the universities should not be totally precluded from involvement in military problems. Indeed, the Sentinal System episode suggests that academics should be involved, yet sufficiently independent to allow detached, objective, and sometimes unpopular judgments. Furthermore, academic experts in strategic matters must enter the political arena when they feel such action is required. Their expertise will remain ineffective unless they are willing to do so.

The general lesson to be drawn from our recent experience is that our success and perhaps our survival depend on the proper function of all the elements of the American system—above all, the general public. But this is more easily suggested than achieved since the military tends to exaggerate its needs; industry short-sightedly pursues profits; Congress puts short-term political goals before the national interest; the public leaves policy-making to others; and academics are either absorbed into the governmental machine or disappear into ivy halls. Yet, an informed and aroused public is being effectively institutionalized by various lobby groups. Hopefully, effective public involvement may extend past brief moments of crisis.

# War, Peace, and Prosperity

## Judith A. Thornton

The economics of war and peace is a complex issue, one aspect of which is the relationship between military spending and peacetime prosperity. Marxists assert that capitalist societies require high military spending as an antidote to inevitable business crisis and that war is promoted by profit-seeking capitalists eager to expand control over foreign markets and just as eager to get profitable government contracts for the production of munitions and military hardware.

Those who argue that American prosperity requires high military spending often note that wartime tends to produce high demand and low unemployment. Economists suggest that is a misinterpretation of historical evidence. Actually measured production and employment rise during war while real standards of living are adversely affected and may even decline. The per capita consumption of real goods and services is reduced by transferring resources away from peacetime activities. Leisure is reduced. Many members of the labor force become involuntary employees of the government on terms that are generally inferior to those formerly enjoyed in the civilian economy. As civilian investments and educational enrollments decline, society depletes its civilian capital. In wartime more people work harder in exchange for less, and the burden of sacrifice falls disproportionately on draftees and their families. In terms of civilian output wartime is a period of economic depression.

Economists recognize that society has limited resources, and

■

that resources devoted to military use have alternative uses elsewhere in the economy. The loss of those alternative uses of labor
force and capital stock represent the real social cost of maintaining
the military services. The decision concerning the allocation of resources to national defense is made through the political process.
Taxes and budget deficits transfer purchasing power from private
households to the federal government and congressional allocations
divide government expenditure between military and domestic uses.

The share allocated to defense from the national income has
varied from as little as .8 percent in 1929 to as much as 47.9 percent
in 1944. After World War II, demobilization reduced defense expenditures to 4.5 percent of the national income, but the Korean and
Vietnam wars raised military expenditures to peaks of 16 and 11
percent in 1953 and 1968 respectively. Defense spending was 5.9
percent of the national income in 1975. Table 4 indicates that this
represents a relatively small national income and total government
spending, but 6 percent of an aggregate GNP (1975) of $1,397 billion
represents a large allocation of resources in an absolute sense.

How would these resources be used if some were available for
transfer to a peacetime economy? They would probably be divided
among domestic expenditures in roughly the same proportions in
which total current expenditure is divided . For example, according
to the *Economic Report of the President, 1970,* 42 percent of GNP
was spent on food, clothing, and housing; 10 percent was spent on
transportation; 6 percent on health; 4 percent on construction of new
housing; and 11 percent on business investment.

Some resources might be used to augment direct governmental
spending at the federal, state, and local levels, and some might be
used to expand welfare and income transfer programs. However, by
1975, the military budget was dwindling in comparison to the massive budgets of government funded social welfare programs. Military
expenditures cost about $400 per capita for every person in the
United States; social welfare spending at all levels of government cost
nearly three times as much, well over $1,000 per capita.[1]

But do government budgets for defense accurately measure the
real sacrifices involved in supporting the military? In 1975 it was
possible to answer "yes" with more conviction than in the past, since
the military moved toward a voluntary army. During the years of the
draft, the portion of military budget devoted to manpower under-
stated the true social cost, i.e., the loss of goods and services incurred
when society transferred workers out of the peacetime economy.
The difference between the compensation of draftees in the army

1. Jonathan Spivak, "The Soaring Cost of Social Welfare," *Wall Street Journal* (12
March 1974).

TABLE 4
GOVERNMENT SPENDING AS PERCENTAGE OF NATIONAL INCOME

| | Total Spending[a] | Defense Spending[b] | Domestic Spending[c] |
|---|---|---|---|
| 1929 | 11.9 | 0.8 | 11.1 |
| 1933 | 26.6 | 1.5 | 25.1 |
| 1939 | 24.2 | 1.6 | 22.6 |
| 1944 | 56.4 | 47.9 | 8.5 |
| 1949 | 27.2 | 6.1 | 21.1 |
| 1953 | 33.2 | 16.0 | 17.2 |
| 1959 | 32.8 | 11.5 | 21.2 |
| 1960 | 32.8 | 10.8 | 22.0 |
| 1961 | 34.9 | 11.2 | 23.7 |
| 1962 | 34.9 | 11.3 | 23.7 |
| 1963 | 34.6 | 10.5 | 24.1 |
| 1964 | 33.9 | 9.7 | 24.2 |
| 1965 | 33.1 | 8.9 | 24.2 |
| 1966 | 34.2 | 9.8 | 24.4 |
| 1967 | 37.2 | 11.1 | 26.1 |
| 1968 | 38.0 | 11.0 | 27.0 |
| 1969 | 37.6 | 10.2 | 27.3 |
| 1970 | 37.8 | 9.3 | 28.5 |
| 1971 | 37.5 | 8.3 | 29.1 |
| 1972 | 39.1 | 7.9 | 31.2 |
| 1973 | 38.6 | 7.0 | 31.6 |

[a] Expenditure of federal, state, and local government as defined in national income accounts.
[b] Purchases of goods and services for national defense as defined in national income accounts.
[c] Total spending minus defense spending.
SOURCE: G. Warren Nutter, "Where Are We Headed?" *Wall Street Journal* (10 January 1975), p. 8, data taken from *Economic Report of the President, 1974*, pp. 249, 265, 328.

and the full money cost of recruiting them under a voluntary system comprised a heavy tax in kind paid by draftees. Manpower costs in the defense budget rose from 33 to 55 percent with the shift to an all-volunteer army, in spite of substantial reductions in manpower. Between 1968 and 1974, the armed services decreased from 3.5 to 2.2 million personnel and total Department of Defense employment, including civilian, civil service, and employment by industry, dropped from 8 to 4.9 million.[2] The reduction in military effort after the Vietnam War released substantial resources potentially available for civilian uses, contingent only on governmental economic policies consistent with a healthy domestic economy.

2. *Economic Report of the President, 1974*, p. 878.

The decline of military spending in 1975 (to 17 percent of total public spending) allayed the fear that the United States was becoming a garrison state, but the efficiency of the political process in determining the level of military spending was still in question. The extent to which lobbying by groups with economic interests in the defense establishment—the armed forces, defense contractors and their employees—might inflate military expenditure at the expense of other programs.

The term "military-industrial complex" was used as early as January 1961, in President Eisenhower's farewell address. That concern seems today to be only a part of the whole problem of the relationship between the government as a major spender of money and all the civilian sectors of the economy that stand to be affected by governmental spending. In 1975, 22 percent of GNP went to direct governmental purchase of goods and services at all levels.

The purchase of a public good like national defense is different from the purchase of consumer goods. Households signal how much income they want to devote to various goods by making purchases in the market sector. Families buy different quantities and mixes of commodities. In the public sector, however, households express a demand for national defense by participating in the electoral campaigns for congressional candidates and by lobbying their congressmen.

The essential decisions on tax levels and allocation of the federal budget between military and civilian uses are made by Congress, often after extended public debate. All members of society are then supplied the same level of national defense; those who wished to buy more and those who wished to buy less are protected by the same army. Small groups are motivated to pretend to want less defense than they actually desire in hope that other groups will tax themselves more. There are, however, strong political reasons for military and congressional leaders to err on the side of extra protection. Political leaders are especially susceptible to arguments that suggest they have made the country vulnerable to attack. The alleged missile gap played a crucial role in the Kennedy-Nixon debates and in John Kennedy's narrow presidential victory. An informed public debate on national security issues is difficult because governmental agencies are the main source of information on U.S. defense needs and the capacity of other countries to threaten our security.

Both sides of the military-industrial complex need careful scrutiny. The Department of Defense is the largest single governmental employer. In 1975, it employed 4.9 million men, including 2.2 million men in the armed forces. The defense budget (approximately $85 billion) comprised some 28 percent of federal expenditures and 17 percent of total governmental expenditures. Military personnel,

operations and maintenance, and military procurement each constituted approximately 30 percent of the budget while research and
development represented less than 10 percent of defense cost.

Defense procurement tended to be heavily concentrated in a
few firms in a few industries. For example, Murray Weidenbaum
found that 72 percent of the value of military prime contracts went
to 100 companies and institutions in 1962. Fifty-six of those companies were in aircraft, missile, and space related industries or in electronics and research and development work closely related to
aircraft and missile programs. Ten supplied aviation gasoline and
other petroleum products, seven were automotive, shipbuilding, am-
munition, and service companies; five were construction firms; and
one produced rifles. Weidenbaum estimated that 90 percent of the
material procurements for defense consisted of equipment for specific purposes produced in special facilities.[3] He also found that the
four major defense-related industries—ordinance, aircraft, shipbuilding, and electronics—employed one-fifth or more of the workers engaged in manufacturing in Kansas, Washington, California,
New Mexico, Connecticut, Arizona, and Utah. Defense-generated
employment was less than 10 percent of total employment in all
states in 1966. In that year, the most defense-oriented states were
Alaska with 9.7 percent defense-generated employment; Utah, 9.1
percent; Hawaii, 8.3 percent; District of Columbia, 8.3 percent; Vir-
ginia, 7.7 percent.[4]

The Pentagon is not an ideal customer from the point of view
of the industrial supplier. Defense-related industries show greater
variations in sales and employment than consumer-oriented industries. The defense industries risk instability and unpredictability of
demand, loss of independence in decision-making, and a tendency to
lose their ability to compete in nongovernmental markets. In addition, industrial suppliers frequently complain that congressional
pressure often induces letting defense contracts on the basis of political rather than economic grounds.

There is no evidence that defense-oriented industries are more
profitable than civilian production. George Stigler's major historical
study, *Capital and Rates of Return in Manufacturing Industries,*
concludes that business investment moved rapidly to eliminate
differences in industrial rates of return. Over the long run, the rate
of return in manufacturing (measured as earnings on total assets) was
just over 7 percent, and Stigler was unable to find convincing evidence that riskier industries, as measured by variability of sales,

3. Murray L. Weidenbaum, "Obstacles to Conversion," *Bulletin of the Atomic Scientists* (April 1964): 11.
4. As cited in James L. Clayton, *The Economic Impact of the Cold War* (New York:
Harcourt, 1970), pp. 366–37.

earned higher rates of return. The stocks of major defense suppliers tend to sell at lower price-earnings ratios on the stock market than the average for all manufacturing, indicating that investors discount the expected earnings of these firms as riskier than others.

Some evidence suggests that major defense suppliers differ substantially from other large-scale manufacturing firms. They hire four to five times the number of scientists and engineers per sales dollar than other manufacturing firms. In part this reflects the technical characteristics of their products, but it also reflects governmental guidelines that base the award of contracts on indices like the number of engineers employed by the bidding firms. Defense suppliers are relatively undercapitalized and undiversified. Cost-plus contracts make it profitable to subcontract production and to hold little invested capital. Thus, when a large share of purchasing power is held by governmental agencies, the market system generates firms relatively well-adapted to supplying government customers, whether they demand high-technology military hardware, urban mass transit, ocean-floor mining, or liquid hydrogen power plants.

The argument that military producers do not determine the level of demand for national defense does not ignore the effect of lobbying. Interest groups will continue to lobby for or against the construction of every new military base and weapons storage depot. Potential suppliers will make the strongest case possible on behalf of any new weapon system. At the same time, other groups affected by government programs will lobby on behalf of their interests.

In sum, the serious problem of determining a desirable level of military spending does not lie mainly in the Pentagon or in industry but in the very nature of the congressional decision-making process. The Pentagon is responsible for drawing up military programs that can be executed if Congress votes the resources. The Department of Defense is not responsible for determining how a given increment in taxes might be better spent. There is mixed evidence concerning how effectively Congress carries out its function of allocating governmental expenditures among programs.

■

Most economists agree that the market economy is capable of transferring resources from one use to another, but they question the costs and speed of those adjustments. Economic theory includes formal models which characterize the market adjustment process, but nothing in economic theory tells us how fast a system will adjust from one resource-use pattern to another. The answer to this question at any point in time depends largely on the actual institutional arrangements and constraints of the system.

The transition from wartime to peacetime at the end of World

War II marked the largest transfer of resources in the U.S. economy during the last century. At the peak of the war, military production took 47 percent of U.S. national income; in August 1945, 36 percent. A year later military spending was cut to 8.9 percent of national income; by 1947, to 3.7 percent. The armed forces were cut from 11.5 million to 1.5 million men during the same period and one-sixth of the working population was returned to the peacetime economy. The economy showed relatively little disruption despite that enormous shift. The resources used to produce tanks, planes, battleships, and ordnance were shifted to the production of automobiles, new housing, home appliances, and other peacetime goods. Unemployment rose from 1.9 percent in 1945 to 3.9 percent in 1946 and to 3.6 in 1947, well below the rates usually accepted as normal. The transition from wartime to peacetime after World War II was eased by the high level of accumulated savings, which provided strong demand for consumer goods. The three years following the war were prosperous and large-scale adjustments were accomplished with a minimum of disruption.

Demobilization following the Vietnam War involved a relatively small adjustment. In 1968, military spending amounted to 9.3 percent of our national income, with a little over one third going directly to the war, and the armed services numbered 3.5 million. Between 1970 and 1973, the armed forces were cut from a force level of 3.2 million to 2.3 million returning nearly a million men into the labor force. During the same period, the civilian labor force grew from 82 to over 90 million. The unemployment rate, 5.9 percent in 1971, did not differ significantly in 1974 for veterans (5.3 percent) and nonveterans (6.0 percent) ages 20 to 34 years.[5] As resources were transferred from military to civilian uses, real GNP rose at rates well above long-term trends. In 1972, real economic growth was 6.2 percent; in 1973, real GNP rose 5.9 percent, but in 1974, the economy moved into a full-fledged recession and the decline in production was the largest since the Great Depression. This development raises a question concerning whether the termination of the Vietnam War was related to the recession and, if so, how.

The government intervenes in the economy to divert resources from civilian to wartime use and the increase of governmental expenditures during our major wars has never been covered by tax receipts. Total federal tax receipts during the Civil War were one-fifth of total expenditures; during World War I about two-fifths; during World War II about three-fifths.[6] That government deficit added

5. *Economic Report of the President, 1975,* pp. 108, 276.
6. Milton Friedman, "Price, Income, and Monetary Change in Three Wartime Periods," *American Economic Review* 42:2 (May 1952).

to the aggregate demand for goods and services, thus exerting an upward pressure on prices. Further, much wartime government borrowing was financed by government money creation. Since World War II, this expansion occurs through open market operations of the Federal Reserve System. When government borrowing becomes large relative to the private capital market, the Federal Reserve intervenes and purchases government bonds for its own account. It pays for the bonds by setting up a new credit balance on its books, in effect causing the money supply to increase by a multiple of the initial credit balance. Once established, inflation tends to compound like interest until a change in government policy with regard to money stock reverses inflationary expectations. The cost of ensuring against the uncertainty of future rates of inflation is very high, and the housing industry and long-range capital investments are thus adversely affected by high nominal interest rates. Consumer confidence is also hurt by rising price levels. Eventually, the process of squeezing off inflationary pressures and reversing inflationary expectations dampens economic activity for a period of time, generating a downturn or recession in the economic cycle.

This line of argument indicates that a diversion of resources away from peacetime production as well as government financing of large-scale military spending both contribute to an inflationary-recessionary process that is difficult to control. It is, however, an oversimplification to say that war causes inflation. More accurately it is apparent that government financing of large-scale expenditures is often inflationary, and wars have been a major cause.

Attempts to control inflation tend to dampen economic activity, so the end of wartime expenditures may be related to slowdowns in monetary growth and the onset of recession. Historical data on the business cycle compiled by the National Bureau for Economic Research facilitates study of the timing of wars and recessions and permits us to test the notion that the ending of war "causes" recession. Those data indicate that "slumps" occur more frequently than wars. The U.S. has experienced seven wars and 31.5 boom-and-recession cycles since the Mexican-American War. The conclusion that every war is followed by recession is thus trivial—every war is also preceded by recession and occasionally interrupted by recession. More recessions are preceded by periods of "not-war" than by periods of war. The Great Depression actually followed a period of peacetime economic expansion.

The duration of the business cycle measured from trough to trough averaged 49 months. In terms of war-interrupted business cycles, the mean period from trough to trough was 61 months. This observation apparently suggests that the occurrence of war postpones the next expected recession. However, statistical analysis reveals a variance in the cycle so great (plus or minus 21 months) that there is little significant difference in the timing of peacetime and war-interrupted business cycles. The differences in the two samples may have occurred simply by chance.

In a second test, recessions and booms were partitioned to determine whether they began during war or peacetime and the results are shown in Table 5.

TABLE 5

|                    | Recessions | Booms | Total |
| ------------------ | ---------- | ----- | ----- |
| "Not-War" Periods  | 27         | 25    | 52    |
| War Periods        | 4          | 7     | 11    |
| Total              | 31         | 32    | 63    |

The booms apparently occur slightly more often during wartime but there is no significant difference in the wartime and peacetime samples.

The historical data were analyzed to determine whether war, when compared to other traditional economic variables, explained changes in price level and unemployment.[7] These tests suggest that changes in the stock of money were a significant factor in cyclic behavior. War, as an additional (test) variable did not aid in predicting the concurrent or lagged values of price change or unemployment.

These results suggest that war affects the economy by affecting traditional economic variables. The government pursues inflationary policies during wartime but it is not necessarily the only time. Finally, it should be noted that periods of major wars are true recessions when the real standard of living (in terms of civilian goods and services) and real civilian capital stocks both decline.

The notion that capitalist, and particularly American, prosperity is tied to war or a high military budget is fallacious. The resources devoted to military production can be utilized in the civilian economy. Actually, there is reason to believe that the allocation of resources among alternative uses occurs more efficiently in the market sector than in the public sector of the economy.

The commitment of large scale economic resources to military use is sometimes attributed to the operation of a military-industrial complex. Closer examination, however, reveals that the efficiency of the political process in choosing a desired level of military spending is only part of a broader question. How efficiently does Congress

---

7. The technique employed (multiple regression analysis of time series data) was used in an attempt to predict the unknown values of one variable from the known values of another.

make all of its tax and expenditure decisions? The effect of wartime spending on the economy also depends upon the kinds of governmental policies pursued by Congress. The market economy is apparently capable of transferring large quantities of resources from wartime to peacetime use providing government policies are properly made. Ill-conceived and restrictive policies disrupt the economic system, even in peacetime.

The use of economic resources for military purposes is intended to enhance the security of U.S. citizens and to safeguard their legitimate interests. But national security is not based entirely on military protection. It is dependent on a healthy and growing economy, a populace that enjoys social and economic opportunities and a measure of consensus on public policies. It is also dependent upon a reduction of international tensions through the operation of nonmilitary institutions.

# The American Experience
# with War

## Otis A. Pease

America has symbolized both war and peace. The Union Army's
William Tecumseh Sherman was one of the first generals in modern
times to define and illustrate the concept of total war. After announcing that he would make Georgia "howl," he marched his army three
hundred miles through a nearly defeated Confederacy and ripped its
patchwork economy apart. Yet the boundary between the United
States and Canada is the longest, most enduring, and most famous
unfortified border in the experience of nations. Over fifty years ago
Secretary of State Charles Evans Hughes hammered out what was
possibly the most effective pact for the reduction of armaments in
modern history. It led to the scrapping of seventy battleships and
cancellation of plans for building new ones. The pact succeeded
mainly because Hughes, through the skillful use of diplomacy and a
willingness to commit the nation's enormous prestige to the outcome, imposed it on the two major naval powers. Five years later
Hughes's successor, Frank Kellogg, in response to a proposal by
French Foreign Minister Aristide Briand, persuaded most of the
nations of the world to renounce offensive war as "an instrument of
national policy." Twelve years later, however, the American government took the lead in developing nuclear weapons and in perfecting
the strategy of mass bombing. Yet by 1960, President Eisenhower
believed that one of his most important achievements was persuad-
ing the Soviet Union to open talks on nuclear arms limitation. The
paradox is familiar. The American people were well known in the

■

nineteenth century for the surpassing excellence of their small firearms and for their small organizations devoted to universal peace.
America's ingenuity in war and its dedication to the elimination of
war are two themes that seem to run through American history.

Indeed, Americans have fostered the contradictory ideals of nationalism and internationalism. Their struggle for independence established the supremacy of modern nationalism yet Americans
founded international bodies to avoid war and to check nationalism
in the twentieth century. Woodrow Wilson's dream of the League of
Nations was rejected, yet the United Nations was supported primarily by American elected officials and their advisors. The United States
continues to be one of the few nations that support the United Nations financially. These contradictory ideals can be drawn to an even
finer point. The revolution in 1776 and the war for union in 1861
involved the liberalism that regards the state as the servant of the
individual, and the kind of nationalism that subordinates the individual to the state.

The American paradox is further emphasized in the behavior of
its electorate. In a democracy which subscribes to the principle of
civilian supremacy in government, the people have elected six generals as President, primarily in recognition of their records as wartime military leaders. (Taylor, Grant, and Eisenhower were career
officers; Washington, Jackson, and Harrison stood more in the tradition of civilian generals.) None of the nation's wars or major military
operations was launched during their administrations, and two of
them explicitly proposed to end the fighting begun in a previous
administration or to prevent its recurrence. President Grant said,
"Let us have peace." "I shall go to Korea," promised Eisenhower.
Eight years later, in his farewell address President Eisenhower
warned the nation against the danger of what he called a military-
industrial complex. Few nations have blended and obscured the roles
of civil and military authority more persistently than the United
States. American history is thus an apparent contradiction—our
elected leaders were often trained primarily to conduct war but they
pursued peace more ably than their civilian counterparts.

War has played a central role in shaping American history but
historians pay relatively little attention to that role. The historiography of American foreign relations and diplomacy is competent, complex, and penetrating, and studies of the causes of war have
multiplied impressively during the past fifty years. Investigations of
the economic consequences of war for the United States are comparatively recent and rare. Few scholars have attempted to synthesize
the social and intellectual effects, or the meaning of war for Americans. There is information, almost unmanageable in quantity, and

preliminary studies available from which to build generalizations and a comprehensive theory.

■

It is difficult to accurately state the costs of war to the United States. Historians do not agree on the issue but the evidence suggests that except for personal losses of dead and wounded, wars have seldom been more than an inconvenience to the American people. Ordinary goods and services became less abundant, but employment mounted, personal income generally outpaced inflation, and farmers usually prospered. Governments gained economic experience and approval for policies bound to stimulate national growth after the war, thus generally resolving doubts about the wisdom of expanding public authority in peacetime.

The American Civil War, presumably retarded industrialization but on closer examination it caused only a temporary dip in the rising curves of national production, income, and social growth. World War II ended the severest depression in American history and within five years the unprecedented growth in peacetime income, spending, and investment allowed the income of the lower two-thirds of the population to increase significantly.

War also produced advantages in the social realm. The Civil War established a constitutional framework for the legal, political, economic, and social equality, of black citizens. Eighty years later, World War II provided employment opportunities for women, a significant step in their quest for social independence and equality of treatment. To a degree of irony too cruel to contemplate, the health and salvation of the American system has been a result of both peace and war.

■

Americans have displayed a marked ambivalence toward the purposes and ultimate wisdom of all but one of their wars. Popular opposition to military preparedness in peacetime often reflected the refusal of some citizens to anticipate the future intelligently. At other times, however, it was due to an awareness of a future they could anticipate all too well. Even after entering war, the American people have frequently been divided over the nation's policies. Indeed, the degree and extent of public criticism and opposition have sometimes astonished citizens of other nations, even those with comparable traditions of public dissent. A free press, however, did not account necessarily for the issues raised or the forms they took.

During the American Revolution, possibly a quarter of the inhabitants of the thirteen continental colonies opposed independence. Many fought against the patriot militia and left the new nation as Loyalists to the Crown in voluntary or involuntary exile. The War of 1812 generated bitter and implacable opposition in New England, where some men and women talked openly of separation from the United States. The war against Mexico in 1846 suited the aims, strategies, and temper of southern and western citizens and originated in part with the political amibtions of Democratic party leaders. New England and midwestern free-soilers, including young Abraham Lincoln, denounced the war as the product of pro-slavery expansionists. They formed an anti-Southern political coalition which eventually became the Republican party.

Some citizens in half a dozen border states opposed secession but supported the right of Southern states to protect slavery during the Civil War. Others favored a negotiated settlement on terms that would have altered the Union. Still others opposed the wartime policies of the Lincoln administration. The abolition of slavery was a persistently divisive issue for many otherwise staunch opponents of the Confederate cause. New York City workmen rioted in opposition to a draft law, and some critics of the war were jailed for voicing their opposition.

There was little open opposition to the goals and strategies of the McKinley administration during the short war with Spain in 1898. Nevertheless, after the peace treaty was signed and ratified, an anti-imperialist movement of prominent citizens questioned the necessity, wisdom, and morality of the war and demanded changes in the nation's policies toward the Philippines and the Caribbean nations.

By the time Wilson forcefully recommended a declaration of war against Germany in 1917 antiwar sentiments were commonly voiced by progressive reformers and Socialists. The reformers felt that the effects of war on domestic policies was a greater threat to American democracy than a German victory in Europe. The Socialists believed that both sides threatened the cause of the working classes and preferred that the United States remain neutral. The opposition of citizens to the war aims and policies of the Wilson administration was probably more widespread and fervent than most historical narratives have indicated. Opponents of the war suffered official repression and public hostility to a degree unmatched in the nation's history. Socialist opponents of the war were tried, convicted, and jailed for sedition. After the armistice and the nation's failure to support the League of Nations, isolationism offered a rallying point for conservatives, liberals, and radicals to oppose American involvement in international conflict. Isolationists continued their efforts to keep the nation out of the growing crisis in Europe and Asia in the 1930s.

After the United States entered World War II, critics and opponents of American involvement dwindled to the smallest number in the nation's history. Most Americans apparently viewed the war as just and necessary. During the Korean War, opponents were generally silent possibly because most Americans tended to regard the war as an unfortunate necessity.

Criticism of American military involvement in Vietnam reached unprecedented proportions and commanded wide and intense support. For the first time in American history, public pressure forced the administration and Congress to disengage from open warfare and seek a negotiated settlement. This radical shift was particularly noteworthy because it occurred when the influence of the military "establishment" was commonly considered to have reached a peak.

■

American culture reflects an ambiguous relationship between military and civilian institutions, behavior, and modes of belief. Until 1940 the United States had no significant military establishment in the sense of a permanent organization with major influence, social continuity, and independence. It is therefore easy to underrate the importance of military institutions and modes of thought in the century and a half before 1940 and to overrate their importance since then. Actually, military and civilian affairs have been intricately bound together from the beginning.

The traditional colonial (and English) mistrust of standing armies made it likely that the new nation would attempt to build civilian supremacy into every one of its institutions of authority. In an era of continued insecurity, stemming from the physical presence of armed enemies on three sides of a decentralized young republic, fine-drawn distinctions between civilian and military affairs were difficult to maintain in practice. The citizen-soldier concept was the key to the success of the movement for independence, it survived every war that the nation fought, and it powerfully affected the conduct of those wars. The concept was exemplified in the Civil War by businessmen, craftsmen, and professionals in private life who received wartime commissions and responsibilities which they fulfilled as knowledgeable amateurs (sometimes well, sometimes badly) before returning to their civilian careers at the end of the war.

The influence of the chief executive conspicuously determined the strategy and conduct of American wars, and American presidents usually had no professional military training. For example, President Polk formulated the military strategy and diplomatic maneuvers that produced an American victory over Mexico. Aside from the political and moral dimensions of that war, it can be argued that Polk fused military and political considerations more effectively than anyone trained solely in the military might have.

The record of President Lincoln was similarly noteworthy. In effect he was the Union's principal military strategist for about half of the Civil War. Lincoln's sense of military affairs was so much more effective than that of Jefferson Davis (a graduate of West Point) that historian David M. Potter speculated that the Confederacy would have won its independence if the two sides had exchanged presidents.

Woodrow Wilson and Franklin Roosevelt substantially shaped military and political policies in times of war, and if a war had occurred during Theodore Roosevelt's administration, he probably would have run it and would probably have ignored the advice of his military staff. In the closing weeks of World War II, Harry Truman and his civilian advisors ultimately decided to explode two atomic bombs over Japan despite the reservations of some of his military aides. Since 1940 every American president has played a crucial role in merging military and civilian thoughts about strategy and politics in ways that have made it almost impossible to distinguish between military and political considerations in foreign affairs and their domestic consequences.

The results may prove undesirable. Nonetheless, the intellectual turmoil, the mass disaffection over the American involvement in Vietnam are encouraging indications that Americans have maintained the tradition of civilian, and ultimately political, sovereignty in matters of war and peace. That tradition, deeply rooted in cultural values, was apparent in the refusal of John Quincy Adams, as congressman from Massachusetts in 1848, to vote a resolution of thanks to the generals who conducted "that most unrighteous war" against Mexico. It is embodied in Stephen Crane's *Red Badge of Courage,* Ernest Hemingway's *A Farewell to Arms,* the postwar novels of John Dos Passos, the cartoons of Bill Mauldin, the reporting of Ernie Pyle, Norman Mailer's *The Naked and the Dead,* and the corrosive visions of the antiheroes created by Joseph Heller and Kurt Vonnegut. It also is perpetuated in American war films, such as *Patton,* which is a brilliantly ambiguous epic tribute to the significantly American notion that central to a free society in a modern war is the unresolved tension between compulsive individualists (whose egos clash with the coercions of military professionalism) and moderate "GI" generals (who are more comfortable and perhaps no less professional or militarily competent "team" players).

■

The American experience with war, characterized by paradox, advantage, ambivalence, and ambiguity, has encouraged a tradition of skepticism about war and the professionals who wage it. Because of continuing doubts that aggression is an appropriate response to threats historically used to justify war, each generation can ultimately reject the demeaning apparatus war evokes in even the freest societies, the headlong accumulation of authority and the collectivization of economic and social energies. The paradox in the Americans' response to war originated at the nation's birth: the national independence needed to sustain personal liberties could not be won without waging a war which risked those very liberties. This fundamental political dilemma remains. We must preserve the tradition that recognizes the existence of the dilemma and seek continually to lessen the cost of resolving it.

PART V

The Law, Morality,
and Emotions of War

# Introduction

The essays in Parts I through IV vary in approach from theoretical to case-oriented and from causes to consequences of war but they are concerned with the general problem of understanding war. This approach implied neither acceptance nor advocacy. The essays in Part V are concerned less with understanding than with evaluating war, less with causes or consequences than with responses, less with the mechanisms than with emotions.

Responses to war are complex and difficult to categorize but four basic ones are represented among the following essays. Arval A. Morris examines the precedents established by the Nuremberg and Tokyo trials. Peter H. Merkl examines attempts to create international order out of an anarchic state system. The moral aspects of war are treated by Donald W. Treadgold in his analysis of Western pacifism and by Giovanni Costigan who presents the views of Freud and Einstein on war. The variety of emotions inspired by war is conveyed by Richard T. Jameson's discussion of the interrelationship of war and the several genres of American war films and by Giovanni Costigan's view of the profound but varied sentiments of British poets during World War I.

The previous sections are characterized by an effort to remain objective and detached as a requirement for understanding, while the essays of this section are distinctively moral in tone. Whether analyzing pacifism, the implications of Nuremberg, the dismay of Freud and Einstein, or the indignation of the British poets, these

■

essays convey abhorrence. The previous sections focused on war as a group phenomenon; this section is more concerned with individual responses and responsibility. This distinction implies a different attitude toward choice. The previous sections imply that choice is relatively unimportant, perhaps because individual options are limited and the individual's influence so insignificant. These essays generally recognize both constrictions but they imply that choice is fundamental.

The general themes treated before recur in this section. The responses of individuals, and their embodiments in international law, films, and poetry, are clearly conditioned by society as well as individual personalities. The general dismay evoked by war evolves into a criticism of society.

# International Law: Nuremberg, Tokyo, and Vietnam

## Arval A. Morris

Two arguments have been used to apply the Nuremberg principles to American participation in the Vietnam War. First, the United States is a legal entity bound by those principles. Second, Nuremberg established standards of individual responsibility which apply to citizens of all countries. These arguments are based on the statement by Chief American Counsel at Nuremberg, Robert Jackson, that while this law is "first applied against German aggressors, if it is to serve any useful purpose, it must condemn aggression by any other nation, including nations which sit here now in judgment."

Much has been written about the responsibility of the United States as a political unit for the war in Vietnam, but little has been said about the responsibility of individual Americans. Many Americans—particularly those in authority—refuse to grapple with the question and imply that talk of Nuremberg is naive and inappropriate. This attitude is unjustified in view of the American commitment to the Nuremberg principles.

Article 6 of the Nuremberg Charter, the basic statement of principles governing individual responsibility, specifies three categories of illegal acts. Crimes against peace, usually committed by those in authority, are defined as the planning, preparing, or initiating of aggressive war or war in violation of international treaties or assurances. War crimes, violations of the laws or customs of war, include, but are not limited to, the murder, maltreatment, or deportation of civilians or captured soldiers. Crimes against humanity consist of

■

systematic extermination, enslavement, deportation, persecution, or other inhumane acts committed against civilian populations on political, racial, or religious grounds. From the Nuremberg Charter one principle clearly emerges: an individual is responsible if he intentionally engages in any of the acts within these three categories.

Less direct individual responsibility is not so clearly established. Article 6 states that "leaders, organizers, instigators and accomplices who participate in the formulation or in the execution of a common plan or in a conspiracy to commit any of the foregoing crimes are individually responsible for all acts performed by any one of the persons." This principle involves a degree of guilt by association, which, depending on definition, can be found in Anglo-American criminal conspiracy laws.

The definition of individual responsibility is extended to include membership in organizations which commit the defined crimes. Article 9 asserts the authority to declare a group criminal. Article 10 states that "in cases where a group or an organization is declared criminal by the Tribunal, the competent national authority of any Signatory state shall have the right to bring individuals to trial for membership." This article provided one of the arguments for the Eichmann case. Israel, a signatory, had power to try Eichmann because he had been a member of a Nazi group found by the Nuremberg Tribunal to be criminal. This principle implies that a possibly insignificant act like joining a group is sufficient, ex post facto, to establish culpability.

The Charter focuses specifically on the responsibility of national leaders. Article 7 states that "the official position of defendants, whether as Heads of State or responsible officials of Government departments, shall not be considered as freeing them from their responsibility or mitigating their punishment." Ensuring the responsibility of officials seemed necessary because of the Act of State doctrine, according to which no external tribunal has the authority to investigate genuine acts of a national state in order to identify individual responsibility. This doctrine was argued vigorously by the United States in 1919. At Nuremberg Dr. Harriman Juarez contended that individual German leaders ought not to be prosecuted for Germany's aggressive war because individual responsibility "cannot take place as long as the sovereignty of the state is the basic organizational principle of interstate order." The Charter, however, rejects this contention and holds individual leaders responsible.

Finally, the Charter deals with superior orders. Article 8 states: "The fact that the defendant acted pursuant to order of his Government or of a superior shall not free him from responsibility, but may be considered in mitigation of punishment if the Tribunal determine that justice so requires."

The Charter established a very broad network of individual responsibility. Persons are guilty if they voluntarily and intentionally commit any one of the designated crimes; if they voluntarily and intentionally conspire to commit such crimes; if they are members of groups declared criminal; if they are officials of states which commit crimes; if they commit crimes under orders.

The Charter's broad definition of individual responsibility was narrowed by decisions of the Nuremberg Tribunal. In the matter of superior orders, the Tribunal accepted a view similar to the established notion of duress. Most of the defendants argued that they had acted under Hitler's orders and therefore could not be held responsible for their acts. The Tribunal stated that Article 8 was in conformity with the existing law of all nations preventing a soldier who violated international law from claiming the defense of superior orders. In its actual judgment, however, the Tribunal stated that "the true test which is found in varying degrees in the criminal law of most nations is not the existence of superior orders but whether moral choice was in fact possible." Two factors are involved in establishing the existence of moral choice. One is knowledge, i.e., whether the individual knew or should have known that an order was illegal. The second is coercion, i.e., whether an individual was forced to commit a war crime. It is, however, important to note that this modification did not deny that a war crime had taken place but rather shifted the locus of individual responsibility up the ladder of authority.

The Tribunal radically altered the category of crimes against humanity. The enormous Nazi crimes of persecution, incarceration, and systematic extermination were well known and beyond debate. The Tribunal recognized that war crimes had been committed on a scale sufficiently large for them to be designated crimes against humanity. But, since they had been committed during wartime, the Tribunal ruled that they were related to the execution of war and fell under the heading of crimes against peace. Thus, the category of crimes against humanity was virtually eliminated.

The Tribunal's decision to disregard the charge that "the defendants conspired to commit war crimes and crimes against humanity and [would] consider only the common plan to initiate and wage aggressive war" modified the Charter definition of conspiracy.

Finally, crimes against peace were restricted by the Tribunal's decision to require clear proof of intent to wage aggressive war. This condition was easily satisfied with regard to high-echelon Nazis, since the Germans kept meticulous records, which demonstrated beyond doubt that top Germans had planned to launch the war. The requirement was, however, harder to meet for German leaders lower in the chain of authority, and proof of guilt at the top implied less responsibility below.

Thus, in many respects, the Nuremberg principles regarding individual responsibility, especially as interpreted by the Tribunal, are similar if not identical to the previously existing international law of war.

▪

The Tokyo trials were conducted by an international tribunal set up by General MacArthur. Although the trials established no new legal doctrine, they demonstrate how general principles of the international law of war are applied in particular cases. The trial of Koki Hirota is illustrative.

Hirota served briefly as Japanese prime minister and then as foreign minister (1932–1937). When he received reports of atrocities committed by Japanese troops during the so-called rape of Nanking, he demanded and received assurances from the Japanese War Ministry that the crimes would be halted, but they in fact increased. The tribunal found Hirota guilty of war crimes because "he was derelict in his duties for not insisting before the cabinet that immediate action be taken to put an end to the atrocities" and "was content to rely on assurances which he knew were not being implemented." He was also found guilty of crimes against peace, since he had been involved in planning aggressive war against China. Koki Hirota was consequently sentenced to death and hanged.

General Tomoyuki Yamashita was tried by the American military, but the principles are the same. Yamashita took command of Japanese troops in the Philippines at a time when the collapse of discipline in the Japanese forces led them to commit extensive atrocities. It could not be proven that he had been willfully ignorant, but he was, nevertheless, found guilty of war crimes on the ground that "he had failed to provide effective control of his troops as required by circumstances." The United States Supreme Court approved Yamashita's conviction. He was also sentenced to death and hanged.

Both cases indicate how broadly the principle of individual responsibility can be applied, particularly in view of the tribunals' assumption that leaders controlled subordinates, whether that control was, or could have been, established.

▪

The principles established and interpreted at Nuremberg and Tokyo and in General Yamashita's case provide a basis for judging individual American conduct in Vietnam. The most general problem is to determine whether crimes against peace were committed. It was stipulated at Nuremberg that crimes against peace require proof of intent to conduct aggressive war. In the case of American involvement in Vietnam, this condition is difficult to satisfy. The Pentagon Papers show that Mr. Johnson's claim that the United States would not become more deeply involved in Vietnam was duplicitous. Involvement or duplicity is not, however, equivalent to aggression. Nor is the intent behind the action usually relied upon to demonstrate American aggresssion—the bombing of North Vietnam—entirely clear. No proof exists that Americans systematically sought to kill civilians or to destroy whole cities. Even if such proof existed, there is no international body that could try the United States. Moreover, it is unlikely that Congress would take up such an issue, in view of its involvement in the war.

The supremacy clause of the Constitution regards treaties as part of the supreme law of the land. Supreme Court rulings indicate, however, that treaties can be abrogated if Congress subsequently passes an inconsistent law. If the Nuremberg Charter is considered a treaty and if congressional acts—the Gulf of Tonkin Resolution, financial appropriations for the bombing of North Vietnam, etc.—are regarded as inconsistent laws, it can be argued that the United States thereby repudiated the Nuremberg principles. Thus it is unlikely that the Supreme Court would declare top American leaders guilty of conducting aggressive war in Vietnam.

American war crimes were undoubtedly committed in Vietnam. In response to guerrilla warfare by the Viet Cong American troops tried to deny them support among the civilian population through such tactics as the hamlet and free-fire zone program. In an area where civilians were suspected of harboring Viet Cong, the Americans moved the inhabitants into camps. Those who refused to leave their villages were presumed to be Viet Cong supporters, thus enemies, and were to be shot on sight whenever found in the area. Many of the resulting civilian casualties can be regarded as war crimes.

Where should individual responsibility lie? The Yamashita precedent points to General Westmoreland; the Hirota precedent to Johnson and his cabinet. Since none has been indicted, the United States has demonstrated that it does not accept these precedents. Yet the conviction of Lieutenant Calley commendably marked the first instance in history of an army condemning war crimes by its own troops.

Nuremberg principles were employed by some to justify resistance to the draft during the Vietnam War. According to this argument, it was the individual's moral responsibility to refuse to participate because the United States government was committing war crimes in Vietnam and a crime against peace by conducting the war. However, induction did not necessarily involve service in Vietnam, and service in Vietnam did not necessarily require committing war crimes. Indeed, the Nuremberg principles provide no clear precedent for draft resistance.

■

The Nuremberg principles prove more applicable to crimes against peace and war crimes than to crimes against humanity. Some crimes against peace, such as those of Germany and Japan during World War II, are more readily demonstrated than others. War crimes are absolutely clear in some cases (the Nazis), clear enough in others (Americans in Vietnam), but unclear in still others (the Hirota and Yamashita cases). The Nuremberg principles do not resolve all the legal problems involved. Nonetheless, they are the best guidelines available for judging behavior in wartime.

American involvement in the Vietnam War is regarded by many as a crime against peace, but the case probably cannot be proven by Nuremberg standards, since there is no documentary proof of an intent to conduct aggressive war. Specific American policies—especially the free-fire zone program—qualify as war crimes. The Calley conviction does not resolve the problem of responsibility or absolve his superiors of culpability, since the free-fire zone policy was ordered by the military and approved by civilian authorities. In a very real sense, the resulting war crimes were logical, virtually necessary, and perhaps even the desired result of that policy. If the United States is to exercise the moral leadership it claims, it must abide by the standards it imposes on its defeated enemies. This is nowhere more true than with regard to the Nuremberg principles concerning individual and collective responsibility.

# International Order

## Peter H. Merkl

The United Nations is undergoing perhaps its biggest crisis of public confidence. There have always been right-wing critics who wanted to "get the U.S. out of the U.N. and the U.N. out of the U.S." because they believed that the United Nations and its specialized agencies posed an intolerable threat to our national sovereignty. Others insisted that the U.N. was Communist-dominated during the very same years that the Soviet Union and other Communist countries quite rightly regarded the U.N. as an instrument of American domination of the world. In recent years, however, American control of the U.N. has obviously lapsed, and the united actions of the Arab, African, Asian, and Latin American countries have caused such annoyance in the United States that continued American financial support of and even membership in the U.N. are being questioned. Some Americans are appalled at the expulsion of the Union of South Africa and similar threats against Israel in the specialized agencies. The United States is no longer able to prevent such decisions as the recent invitation extended to Palestine guerrilla leader Yasir Arafat to address the General Assembly. Critical voices in the American press even belittle the ability and willingness of the U.N. to prevent wars and to promote the peaceful settlement of disputes among nations.

At the root of the current discontents are conceptual misunderstandings, as well as a pattern of widespread ignorance in the world about the reasoning behind the various attempts to curb the reign of anarchy among nations. And finally, there is the all-too-human

■

tendency to expect miracles of organizations such as the United Nations and then cast them out when they achieve only a part of their objectives against fearsome odds.

■

Let us begin with the supposition that prior to the development of organized societies and government, a state of anarchy existed among primitive tribes and clans. Political philosophers such as John Locke, Thomas Hobbes, and Jean-Jacques Rousseau even suggest, somewhat implausibly, that there was anarchy among individuals bent on perpetual war of all against all (Hobbes) in the "state of nature." There can be little doubt that in primitive societies, more often than not, wars, feuds, and the sheer struggle for physical survival have always taken an awesome toll of human life and happiness. In contrast to these antecedents, the rise of large-scale political units such as the modern nation-states has signified, on the whole, a considerable increase in domestic order and the rule of law. To be sure, at times these states have endured long periods of devastating civil war or domestic discord. Some of them are still threatened by revolutionary violence or just plain anarchy as long as their governments lack the legitimacy and strength to control their own citizens. In other nation-states, brutal systems of social or political oppression have at times created conditions hardly preferrable to anarchy. But on the whole, the evolution of the modern state appears to have provided human beings with a life vastly better than a "state of nature" in which, as Hobbes said, human "life is nasty, brutish, and short."

The growth of internal order and justice under the protection of the modern nation-state, however, did not at the same time make for order and tranquility among the states. Quite the contrary, the better their internal organization, the more they insisted on independence from each other and on sovereignty over internal elements, and the more effective their governments became in waging war upon one another. Under the international law of the jungle, as under conditions of domestic anarchy, the only justice was self-defense or retaliation for the strong, or trial by ordeal, that is, war. International anarchy is still the basis of the international system of sovereign nation-states, idealistic dreams of a better world notwithstanding. There are, however, some important modifications of anarchic power politics.

As strong central governments arose in Europe to unify large territories and populations and to build up powerful bureaucracies, armies, and navies, the relations among the new states became more competitive. Dynasties strove to consolidate and enlarge their respective territories at the expense of weaker competitors. The constant threat of war and shifting alliances forced countries to squander scarce resources on armaments and fortifications and, in many cases, encouraged the growth of absolutism. The objectives of war in time turned from dynastic prestige and limited gain to uninhibited conquest and subjugation.

Ideological crusades for and against the French Revolution combined with new forms of popular military mobilization (*levée en masse*) and ultimately led to the destructive world wars of the twentieth century. And yet, at the same time that Napoleon's armies and those of his opponents were marching across continental Europe, philosophers of the Enlightenment began to dream of a worldwide realm of "perpetual peace" that would give international relations the order, stability, and justice that the Enlightenment sought to achieve in the domestic sphere. The Age of Discoveries led to colonial empires built by the better-organized European states over primitive societies. It also revived ancient Roman ideas of the rule of law and equity in a multinational world. A law of the sea and of relations between nationalities, even an international law of warfare, sought to bestow upon international anarchy some of the benefits of domestic legal order.

The age of conflicting imperialisms toward the end of the nineteenth and the beginning of the twentieth century finally launched worldwide power politics on its destructive course. The growth of industrial power and of ever more sophisticated military technology translated insatiable appetites for more power into ominous arms races and far-flung alliances among nations. As powerful empires vied with each other belligerently, more concrete attempts were made to stem the lethal tide of war. There were naval conferences among the Great Powers to curb the competitive buildup of navies, and agreements to negotiate some disputes short of war. Schemes of partial disarmament or limitations on the production and use of the most destructive weapons were a logical next step. Still, World War I broke out and in its aftermath the most ambitious attempt to curb the frequency of wars was born, collective security. The problems of international anarchy are not only still with us, they have grown prodigiously with the addition of nuclear weapons, with the great confrontation between East and West, and with the many new players on the international scene, the newly independent nations of the Third World and their pressing problems.

■

How can one ever hope to curb the anarchy inherent in the national egotisms and pigheaded policies that comprise the system of sovereign nation-states? One attempt has been the concept of collective security, upon which the League of Nations and the United Nations were built. The underlying theory is that member nations have a common interest in maintaining peace and should, therefore, jointly suppress aggressive action by any power or powers against the territory of one of them. The practical weaknesses of such a system have been serious, although perhaps not irremediable. Both the League of Nations and the United Nations have suffered from a dilemma that is inescapable under the principle of national sovereignty. Coercive action to save the peace required unanimity in the League of Nations as it does among the five permanent members of the U.N. Security Council. The veto privilege of the Great Powers in the Security Council and of all states of the old League is based on the premise that a truly sovereign state must not allow itself to be coerced against its will. An enforcement action by an international organization against an aggressor nation, of course, violates the sovereign rights of that nation and can violate also the sovereign rights of other states involved in the coercive undertaking.

Another and no less serious problem raised by collective security is that condemning every design for territorial changes as a present or contemplated act of aggression automatically lends an undeserved air of saintliness to the status quo. A desire for territorial change can be legitimate, for example, for the purpose of righting previous wrongs. What is needed, therefore, is a procedure for peaceful change and a tribunal that could rule authoritatively on the merits and legitimacy of a particular claim for peaceful change. Such an authority, however, would cut deeply into the sovereign rights of the nations concerned. Let us assume, for example, that an overwhelming majority of the German-speaking inhabitants of the South Tyrol in northern Italy wished to secede from that country and join Austria. No greater interference in Italy's sovereignty can be imagined than if an international organization undertook to judge the merits of this case for secession and, perhaps, facilitated such a territorial change. Yet, short of such a violation of national sovereignty, where could a dissatisfied ethnic minority get a fair hearing? It could only resort to violence, and Austria could support it clandestinely or go to war for it. With this last alternative, the vicious circle from national sovereignty to the most stringent form of power politics, international war, is once more complete. Since small wars are so entangled with worldwide power relationships that they cannot always be confined to a given area, such a local minority problem could lead to another world war that would kill tens of millions and destroy whole civilizations.

Another means for attempting to change the system of power politics is disarmament. The underlying theory is that no major war and, in particular, no aggressive war can be fought without an ample supply of modern military equipment. Without restraint or limitation on national armaments, there can be no curbing of the mad competition between East and West or any other hostile nations for ever bigger stockpiles of ever more devastating weapons. Disarmament as an alternative to the arms race is an idea that goes back to the nineteenth century and includes the naval conferences of the 1920s and 1930s, which sought to establish a ratio among the war fleets of the Great Powers. Its history also includes the futile attempts to distinguish between "aggressive" and "defensive" weapons, or between nuclear and conventional armaments, for the purpose of outlawing "aggressive" and nuclear weapons. Proponents of disarmament generally admit the need for limited national forces capable of maintaining internal order and a measure of defense. "Total and general disarmament," such as the Soviets have repeatedly proposed, could open the door to a different kind of aggression by Communist guerrilla forces and violent overthrow of governments by the fifth columns that Cuba, Peking, and the Kremlin have sent into many lands. And the Communists are not the only ones menacing the self-determination of small countries in this fashion. Limited systems of arms control, on the other hand, such as measures to curtail the spread of nuclear weapons, and safeguards against war by misunderstanding or against the possibility of major surprise attacks, hold greater practical promise.

Disarmament and arms control may be capable of restraining the arms race between opposing military blocs, but they are no panacea for war. It is quite difficult to come to a disarmament agreement when the stakes are as high as they are today. Even a limited gesture of disarmament such as a ban on nuclear testing between East and West has time and again had to yield to considerations of military and technological advantage. It does not of itself facilitate the peaceful settlement of international disputes. Finally, and perhaps most discouraging, disarmament neither removes the economic capacity for sudden rearmament nor disarms belligerent minds. Hence, wars can still start and the arms race is only delayed until the outbreak of hostilities.

Again, disarmament impinges upon national sovereignty even where it is voluntarily entered into, for the full use of the national capacity for war and defense is an integral part of that sovereign autonomy that recognizes no limitation or obligation above itself. This becomes readily apparent if one thinks of the controversy over inspection of the extent of Soviet compliance with any plan for nuclear disarmament. It is the sovereign right of a great power to cheat on disarmament provisions for the sake of its ultimate security or even victory, just as the canons of power politics sanction spying in the national interest.

A third remedy against the reign of international power politics is logically more consistent and compelling than the stopgap measures of collective security and disarmament. If the relations between nation-states are anarchic and in striking contrast to the well-ordered life inside most modern nations, then the solution to the problem of peace in our time is to make an orderly society out of the international world. Political thinkers and practical politicans have given much thought to this process of civilizing the world among the modern states and, by implication, the external behavior of these states. As the famous Dutch lawyer and statesman Hugo Grotius (1583–1645) wrote in the midst of seventeenth-century power politics:

> Among the traits characteristic of man is an impelling desire for society, that is, for the social life—not of any and every sort, but peaceful, and organized according to the measure of his intelligence, with those who are of his own kind . . . this maintenance of social order . . . is the source of law properly so called. To this sphere of law belong the abstaining from that which is another's, the restoration to another of anything of his which we may have, together with any gain which we may have received from it; the obligation to fulfill promises, the making good of a loss incurred through our fault, and the inflicting of penalties upon men according to their deserts [*Prolegomena*, sections 6–8].

The first step in the direction of taming the international anarchy was the revival of international law by Grotius and his contemporaries. As Western society has rested securely on a basis of customary law and consensus, they believed, the international society of states ought to be based on rules derived from natural law—the law above the positive law of particular states.[1]

The idea was good, but the practice at times imperfect, as long as the observance of rules and treaties was a matter of voluntary compliance or enforcement by the aggrieved party taking justice into its own hands. At the turn of the last century, international tribunals of arbitration and a permanent court of international justice were introduced for the purpose of arbitrating or adjudicating all disputes submitted to them. This worked quite satisfactorily in cases in which small nations or small matters were concerned. The big political questions, however, were withheld from the courts and instead decided in the customary manner—by brute force. The resurgence of power politics for worldwide stakes and the brazen imperialistic drive, first of the Axis powers and then of the Communist bloc of nations, moreover, further reduced the uses of international law and the world court. Neither the Soviet Union nor the United States has accepted the compulsory jurisdiction of the Inter-

---

1. See also Majid Khadduri and Herbert J. Liebesny, *Law in the Middle East*, vol. 1 (Washington, D.C.: Middle East, 1955), pp. 349–72, on Islamic notions of international law.

national Court of Justice since World War II. The superpowers, and even small international lawbreakers, had once more restored the anarchy of naked power politics over the beginnings of an international social order.

Efforts at civilizing the savage ways of the international world did not stop with these discouragements. The idea of an international police force, on an expeditionary or permanent basis, had long been discussed before one was actually employed by the United Nations in the Middle East, in Korea, and in the Congo. Were there to be an adequate international police force, the other attempts at restraining the reign of power politics—collective security, disarmament, and international law—would take on a new significance. There would be an enforcement agency that could at least in theory restrain an aggressor, inspect compliance with disarmament agreements, or enforce treaties and covenants. Yet the idea of a permanent international police force, as a last step toward an orderly international society, was evidently premature and resulted in a deep crisis for the United Nations when several large powers refused to pay their share of the enforcement effort in the Congo. There also remain the special privileges of the Great Powers, who, in the Security Council, can veto any enforcement action against themselves, their client states, or their interests.

International society will come to resemble domestic society only when an international government completes the structure of order and law. From antiquity to this day, political thinkers, writers, and voluntary organizations have thought at great length about such a world government or world state. But there has been no serious effort in the direction of establishing such a structure, which would presumably be federal in character so as to guarantee home rule and autonomy to the constituent states. The United Nations is very far from developing into anything like a world government. It is committed to the principle of national sovereignty, which would have to yield to a world government and its new legal norms.

There have nonetheless been efforts toward the establishment of more effective international government of a federal character at the regional level, such as among the original members of the European Economic Community (EEC). The participating nations and their governments have been ready to give up some of their ancient sovereign rights to a future common government in exchange for a lasting reign of peace among such age-old antagonists as France, West Germany, Italy, and other European countries. Yet even among the member states of EEC, a single old-fashioned nationalist leader such as President de Gaulle demonstrated how easy it is to ruin the existing goodwill and cooperation by selfish demands for a preponderant position for one of the member states.

■

It is easy to ridicule these approaches to what many observers consider the most crucial problem of the twentieth century, especially as long as one either refuses to recognize that there is a problem or fails to suggest alternative approaches. The most obvious alternative, of course, is the one dictated by national egotism: we will get our way regardless of the interests of other nations because we are strong. The collapse of American power in Southeast Asia and the achievement of military parity by the Soviet Union should, however, have taught us that the dream of American invincibility and omnipotence is indeed only a dream. On the other hand, there is also a line of facile criticism of the attempts to control international anarchy. It is a cheap shot to say that the United Nations has not been able to prevent *all wars,* in view of the continual flare-ups, for example, in the Middle East. The real question is how many wars would have broken out were it not for the mediating and modifying role of the U.N. and its agencies. Only then can we measure the rate of failures against the number of successes and arrive at a balanced judgment.

# War, Religion, and Pacifism

## Donald W. Treadgold

Most conscientious opposition to war has had a religious foundation. This is true of non-Western as well as Western pacifism. For instance, despite many permutations and stages of development, Buddhism has generally opposed the taking of life, whether human or animal. Christian pacifism, however, has been associated for the most part with heresy. As used here, heresy should be taken not as a value judgment but rather as a descriptive term implying deviation from existing orthodoxy. Such beliefs can be traced back to the first or early second century A.D., when most Christians decided to come to terms with the world because they concluded that the Second Coming was not imminent, as had often been thought. Those who persisted in believing that the Last Judgment was approaching often became pacifists not because they were concerned with the war issue but because they associated pacifism with renunciation of the world. They consequently made frequent attempts to create tiny, sectarian utopias set apart from the impure, secular world of the state. This position was often accompanied by refusal to pay taxes, honor officials, perform military service, or fulfill any obligation derived from the state. Religion-based pacifism with heretical and antistate overtones is thus a part of Christian history from its beginnings.

Similar beliefs were held, for instance, by the Waldensians of the twelfth century, the Anabaptists of the sixteenth century, some Quakers of the seventeenth century, and the Jehovah's Witnesses of the twentieth century. Often such people were admired by the com-

■

munity at large for their renunciation of self-advancement, their dedication to personal values, and praiseworthy conduct. Others were, however, distinguished by behavioral peculiarities. For example, the Old Believers of Russia practiced mass self-immolation—as depicted in Mussorgsky's *Khovanshchina*; the Russian Skoptsy sect conducted self-castration. While many such communities refused any association with the state, others—such as the Quakers—managed to make their peace with the system by peforming noncombatant service.

A second pacifist tradition, which emerged in Western society in the nineteenth and early twentieth century, was socialist. In the view of many people, socialism as a whole owed much to the Christian tradition, despite its ostensible repudiation thereof, and the pacifist aspect of socialism was related to the ancient repudiation by Christian heretics of government and all organized society outside their own ranks. Marxism was never pacifist in principle; opposed only to "capitalist" wars, it urged violence in pursuit of its goals. Many professed Marxists or semi-Marxists, however, were influenced by the pacifist current in socialism or, in part, by the antimilitarist side of the radicalism or liberalism of the day.

The most notable organization that reflected such pacifist ideas was the Second International, a grouping of socialist parties in various countries. Its activities became so widespread and apparently compelling to European workers that several governments, doubting their ability to mobilize their societies for war, developed secret plans to arrest Socialist leaders. But the Second International failed to prevent either mobilization or war. Most Socialists placed national above pacifist concerns and supported their country's war efforts.

After World War I, secular pacifism became less partisan. It permeated art, music, cinema, and literature, as perhaps most notably represented by Remarque's *All Quiet on the Western Front*. It also influenced scholarly investigations of the causes of war, efforts which all too often degenerated into sterile attributions of guilt to individuals, groups, nations, or all of Western society. This spirit affected state policies, as in the Allied assertion of Central Powers' guilt and obligation to pay reparations for the war. Above all, the horror of war and hope that it would never recur were virtually universal. While most people were probably not pacifists, the basic premises of pacifism—that war is horrible, morally wrong, and should be avoided—were probably more widely accepted than ever before.

The Communists were among the most active interwar political groups concerned with the problem of war and peace. Like the earlier Marxists, they opposed only those wars they regarded as imperialist. They—in particular, Lenin—argued that war was caused by imperialism, defined as the last stage of capitalism before the socialist (i.e., communist) revolution. The only way to end war was to destroy the capitalist system. Lenin expected this to happen as a result of World War I, which he hoped would expand into an international civil war and establish proletarian control throughout Europe and the world. Lenin adjusted his schedule when that revolution did not occur, but it remains an official communist credo. The Communists joined the growing peace movement during the 1930s in western Europe, not out of pacifist conviction but because the movement was opposed to the fascist threatened "imperialist" war. The Communists reversed themselves to become staunch militarists when Russia was attacked by Germany in 1941. Following the victory over the Axis in 1945, they reverted to a policy condemning "war-mongering" American actions, including the Marshall Plan.

War and peace meanwhile became an issue in American domestic politics. Many Republicans sought to pin the label of "war party" on the Democrats who were in power during all recent wars. In the 1952 campaign, Republicans claimed that the Korean War was "Truman's war" and urged the election of Eisenhower, who would "get us out of Korea" and, by extension, keep us out of all future wars. This line, typical of American politics, did not ensue because Republicans were pacifists or agents of the communists, it merely suggested that many Americans were disinclined to participate in wars.

Indeed, since 1945 the Cold War reflects an American antipathy toward participation in military adventures. The Russo-American confrontation and the danger of nuclear war (perhaps the ultimate symbol of war) presumably threatened an end to civilization. This possibility stimulated discussion of the morality of war in which the polarizing question became whether it was "better to be red than dead." Pacifism, sometimes thoroughly militant, surfaced in other countries, most notably among young people in Germany and Japan, the powers defeated in World War II. Despite the omnipresent Cold War issue and the A-bomb debate, pacifism and war resistance were almost nonexistent in the United States, even during the Korean War. These movements attracted popular support during the Vietnam War.

A dispassionate discussion of the Vietnam War may not yet be possible. But if Americans are to learn something from that experience the Vietnam War issue must be confronted clearly.

American opposition to the war was characterized by its variety. Some pacifists based their opposition on ancient religious grounds and more recent philosophical tenets. Other opponents represented various groups of the political Left: Communists with connections in Moscow and Peking who were not opposed to the war but wanted the Viet Cong to win; leftist pacifists opposed to all wars and leftists opposed to this particular war. Some extreme rightists like members of the John Birch Society also opposed the war. Self-styled political realists opposed the war on the grounds that it was unnecessary, useless, and could not be won.

Some opposition to the war reflected a broader philosophical rejection of society as a whole. There were people who wanted to secede from an imperfect world, specifically an imperfect American system. Some people were prepared to underscore their views by enduring jail, self-imposed exile, even suicide. More aggressive opponents of the war shocked the middle class by "confronting them with their life-style." Some, thoroughly conventional opponents, adherents of Senators Fulbright and McGovern did not want to destroy "the establishment," American governement or society—they did not oppose the war by using drugs, throwing themselves in front of troop trains, or even wearing long hair.

Opposition to the war did not fit into the traditional political spectrum, it was neither Republican-Democrat nor conservative-liberal. Liberal politicians like Johnson, Humphrey, and Henry Jackson; labor leaders like George Meany; journalists like John Roche; and academics like Robert Scalapino supported the war for a substantial period. The opponents included strange bedfellows, Communists, members of the John Birch Society, and Bertrand Russell. Opposition sometimes seemed to require renunciation of liberal principles, as when columnist Joseph Kraft attacked serious efforts to institute reforms in South Vietnam on the grounds that they would protract the war. Advocates of liberal policies were sometimes exposed to criticism, as in the case of Professor Roy Prosterman of the University of Washington, who was labelled "hawk" for promoting land reform in Vietnam. Individual attitudes toward the war were unreliable guides to their political philosophies.

Opposition to the war and tensions created by the war itself intertwined to produce an unprecedented domestic turmoil. The New Left developed an extremism reinforced by the war. The youth culture, and accelerated drug use, blossomed during the 1960s. The minorities—blacks and other ethnic groups—and women's liberation raised other social and political issues. These movements altered the American political climate and probably reinforced opposition to the war. Despite the government's pursuance of the war and the passive support of a considerable portion of the public there was no rightist backlash. Indeed, the antiwar movement apparently had a subtle and profound effect on the officer corps—which might have been expected to defend the war most. For example, officer students (mostly colonels) at the Army War College in 1972 were concerned lest they appear to be anti-Communist, anti-Russian, anti-Chinese, or anti-anything.

Opposition to the Vietnam War passed through three fairly distinct stages. It was limited to a fairly small circle before 1965. It grew rapidly until the downfall of President Johnson, and reached a peak in reaction to the Cambodian incursion (spring 1970). Opposition finally declined upon the American withdrawal in early 1973. It was an eccentric position prior to 1965 and almost a nonissue since 1973. The stance of most Americans during that period was directly proportional to the American involvment as measured by troop commitments and casualties.

■

The morality of war is an issue as old as war itself. Historically, most people have accepted an obligation to fight for their societies but many men have also evaded military service for reasons of conscience. Pacifism, generally associated with religious beliefs, evolved into secular opposition in connection with specific wars during limited periods of time. Pacifism is frequently motivated by a world view critical of the state and existing societies.

These elements appeared in the opposition to the Vietnam War. The politics and character of people opposed to the war varied widely and defied traditional political and social classification and the war issue was involved with other problems and movements. The Vietnam experience suggests that reactions to war are not monolithic but heterogeneous, not permanent but changing, not simple but complex. The reactions are motivated by several interests varying from the most sincere to the most devious and pragmatic. The aspirations of the people involved are sometimes specific and limited or they can involve programs of total systemic and spiritual reconstruction.

The long history of the war debate suggests that it may not be easily resolved or readily dismissed. The case for a just war was eloquently made in the Greek reply to the Persians, who bade them surrender: "A slave's life thou understandest, but, never having tasted liberty, thou canst not tell whether it be sweet or no. Ah! Hadst thou known what freedom is, thou wouldst have bidden us fight for it." The case for pacifism is based on humane considerations, the preservation of life and the pragmatic conclusion that war is no solution to social problems. Between these extremes other variations argue in favor of some wars and against others and this spectrum of views is likely to persist. We should not denounce or dismiss any particular position and thus obscure the basic issue, rather we should seek to understand the motives, applicability, and implications of every point of view.

# Einstein and Freud on War

## Giovanni Costigan

When war broke out in 1914, it was traumatic to a degree that few people alive today can appreciate. The nineteenth century was the most peaceful in the history of Europe, reminiscent of the Augustan Age of ancient Rome, an age that Gibbon called the happiest period in the history of mankind. Nineteenth century wars were of short duration: the Austro-Prussian War lasted only six weeks, the Franco-Prussian War only six months, and the Russo-Japanese War only about eighteen months. Most intelligent people in Europe regarded war as unthinkable since it would ruin European civilization. The eruption of war in 1914 consequently was viewed with horror and despair by Einstein and Freud among many others.

Einstein left Germany and went to Switzerland to escape military service at the age of fifteen—submission to a drill master was unthinkable. He was in Switzerland when the war broke out and in 1915 he wrote:

> When posterity recounts the achievements of Europe, shall we let men say that three centuries of painstaking cultural effort carried us no further than from the fanaticism of religion to the insanity of nationalism. It would seem that men always seek some idiotic fiction in the name of which they can hate one another. Once it was religion; now it is the state.

Einstein's pacifism deepened and in "The World as I See It" (1930) he denounced militarism:

■

This shameful stain on civilization must be wiped out as soon as possible. Heroism on command—senseless violence and all the loathsome violence which goes by the name of patriotism. How passionately I despise them; how vile and contemptible war seems to me. I would rather be torn limb by limb than take part in such an ugly business.

A young Swiss wrote Einstein in 1931 to ask what a conscientious objector should do if conscripted. Einstein's reply was revealing:

Let me express my respect for your courage and dignity. A man like yourself acts like a grain of sand in a machine. It is my hope that by such means and such grains of sand, the war machine will be destroyed or at least the degrading system of conscription will be abolished.

Later, Einstein seemingly changed his mind. Two Belgian conscientious objectors refused military service and a pacifist friend wrote to Einstein for advice. In his reply of July 20, 1933, Einstein wrote:

What I shall tell you will greatly surprise you. Were I a Belgian, I should not in the present circumstances refuse military service. Rather I should enter such service cheerfully in the belief that I would thereby be helping to save European civilization. This does not mean that I am surrendering the principle for which I have stood heretofore. I have no greater hope in my life than that the time may not be far off when refusal of military service will once again be an effective method of serving the course of human progress.

This response astounded and angered many pacifists and they proceeded to denounce Einstein.

Einstein modified his attitude toward pacifism and military service only after long and grave reflection upon Hitler's rise to power. His name was at the top of Hitler's execution list, but he was just as horrified by Hitler's intention to reduce to servitude Slavs, blacks, and other groups regarded by the Nazis as racially inferior. Einstein's advocacy of resistance to Hitler must also be seen in the context of the military technology which was still in the prenuclear age. World War I demonstrated that the cost of war was almost as high for the victors as it was for the vanquished, yet war did not end civilization. Thus although Einstein scorned and opposed war all his life, it seemed preferable to an acceptance of Hitler's domination of Europe and possibly the world.

As the war in Europe approached, Einstein believed that German scientists were experimenting with new forms of energy capable of producing an atomic bomb. At the suggestion of fellow scientist Leo Szilard, he therefore wrote (on August 2, 1939, one month before war broke out in Europe) to President Roosevelt to inform him of the possibility that Hitler might acquire nuclear weapons and to urge allocation of funds for similar research. The letter was received on October 11 and was a decisive factor in Roosevelt's decision to establish the Manhattan Project.

After the war, Einstein wrote: "Had I known that Germany

would not succeed in developing an atom bomb, I would have done nothing." He deeply deplored the bombing of Hiroshima, believing that it was unnecessary because the war was almost over and Japan possessed no similar weapon. Einstein joined those who urged the American government not to kill defenseless women and children, and he felt to the end of his life a personal responsibility for the obliteration of Hiroshima and Nagasaki.

Einstein spent the last ten years of his life—from 1945 to 1955 —on two quite different tasks. One was scientific: an attempt to develop a unified field theory to reconcile the contradictions observable in particle physics. The second was humanitarian: the preservation of peace. He repeatedly warned of the destructive capacity of atomic war and was concerned that scientific progress might render a nuclear war unavoidable. He observed that "the worst aspect of this development lies in its apparently inexorable character. Each step appears as the inevitable consequence of the one that went before, and at the end, looming ever nearer, lies universal annihilation."

The perpetuation of old-fashioned, prenuclear international relations appeared to him to increase the likelihood of holocaust. The last words he wrote—found by his bedside in 1955—expressed this fear:

> In essence the conflict that exists today is no more than an old style struggle for power, once again presented to mankind in semi-religious trappings. The difference is that this time, the development of atomic weapons has imbued the struggle with a ghostly character, for both parties know and admit that, should the quarrel deteriorate into actual war, mankind is doomed. Despite this knowledge, statesmen in responsible positions on both sides continue to employ the well-known technique of seeking to intimidate and demoralize the opponent by marshalling superior military strength. They do so even though such a policy entails the risk of war and doom. Not one statesman in a position of responsibility has dared to pursue the only course that holds out a promise for peace, namely, the course of supra-national security and world government, since for any statesman to follow such a course would be tantamount to political suicide.

Despite his effort to create a climate of opinion conducive to peace, Einstein achieved little of a practical nature. He was helpless, being neither political by nature nor politically influential.

The last years of Einstein's life were sad and embittered. He was persecuted by the House Un-American Activities Committee. The Daughters of the American Revolution urged his deportation to Germany. The American right wing accused him of being a traitor. The depth of Einstein's pessimism about the state of the world is reflected in his reply to a letter from a youth asking what he should do with his life: "If I were a young man and had to decide on how to make a living, I would not choose to become a scientist or a scholar or a teacher. I would rather choose to be a plumber or a peddler in the hope of finding that modest degree of independence still available under present circumstances."

■

Before 1914 Freud, like Einstein, believed that war would never again occur. Freud's professional experience and twenty-five years of clinical work in psychoanalysis later led him to ruefully confess that he should have known better. World War I profoundly shocked him. His three sons were immediately conscripted and saw action on various Austrian fronts but fortunately they all survived. Freud himself never recovered from the traumatic experience and his disillusion and feeling of revulsion remained until his death.

In *Thoughts for the Times on War and Death,* Freud movingly revealed the depths of his agony. Well aware of his own pessimism, he wrote his publisher that "this is a work which gives me no enjoyment to write and will hardly please others." The war unmistakably revealed on a large scale what psychoanalysis deduced from human behavior. His study of the dreams of normal people and the symptoms of neurotics indicated that primitive impulses, hatred and aggression were not uprooted by civilization. They were only repressed into the unconscious, where they lay awaiting the opportunity to spring forth once more, endowed with primal energy.

The coming of the European war illustrated the inability of human reason to control powerful emotions—another truth emphasized by psychoanalysis. With few exceptions, intellectuals of all nations—including the United States in 1917—justified the outburst of hatred in the name of reason, and the masses committed themselves to war at the behest of their governments.

Freud argued, however, that disillusionment over barbarous human behavior in time of war was not really justified. The belief that mankind had become civilized was itself an illusion: "In reality our fellow citizens have not sunk so low as we have feared because they have never risen so high as we have believed."

The immense increase of power wielded by the state over the thoughts and lives of its citizens was another result of the war that disturbed Freud:

> The individual in any given nation has in this war a terrible opportunity to convince himself of what would only occasionally strike him in time of peace, namely, that the state has forbidden the individual the practice of wrong-doing, not because of desire to abolish it but because it desires to have a monopoly of it, like salt and tobacco selling. At the behest of the state, murder—in ordinary life the most heinous of crimes—is suddenly transformed into the noblest civic duty, the obligation to kill. Such murder authorized by the state is encouraged by the strongest incentives and rewarded by the highest decorations that society had at its disposal.

Perhaps Freud's most disturbing conclusion was that aggressiveness would probably never be eradicated from human nature since we are the product of an animal heritage spanning millions of years.

The human race is a species of animal which has survived through sheer inventiveness, cunning, and aggression. Some scientists—particularly social psychologists—contest the domination of instinct but biologists and geneticists generally confirm it. Behaviorists frequently argue that instincts can ultimately be eradicated or controlled and that aggression can be modified and sublimated. Freud himself believed that hate could be sublimated into love. The aggressive instinct in human beings, however, is not transformed but merely covered by a veneer of civilization and it will reassert itself given appropriate circumstances.

■

In 1932, Einstein, at the height of his fame as a scientist and pacifist, was asked by a committee of the League of Nations to discuss the problem of war with any contemporary. Einstein chose Freud. The results of this discussion by letter were published as a small book called *Why War?*

Einstein began by speculating on the reasons for war. Why did mankind attempt to abolish poverty, disease, and starvation, yet fail to make a serious effort to abolish war?

> Only one answer to the question is possible. It is that man has within him a lust for hatred and destruction. In normal times this passion exists in a latent state and emerges only in unusual circumstances, mob violence, lynch law, etc., but it is a comparatively easy task to call these instincts into play and to raise them to a power of a collective psychosis.

Later Einstein wrote:

> The tendencies to love and hatred, to create joyfully and cruelly destroy are intimately bound together in the soul of every man.... Only in congenital criminals do these dark aspects of human nature erupt, despite the counteracting influences of society. But in war they erupt among almost all men.

This was precisely the view of human nature Freud had elaborated for twenty years. Yet Einstein concluded that humanity might rid itself of war if it were confronted with the facts of its own nature and the ultimate horror of war. This inconsistency, that inherently aggressive men might yet renounce aggression, may have arisen from a conflict between Einstein's hopes and his observation of reality.

Freud yielded to no such hope. He doubted that men would ever reject war, however frightful. He believed that human nature was virtually unchanged for millions of years and that it was difficult to alter fundamentally—it could not be changed within a generation. Yet such a change was required to avoid renewed war in Europe.

The views expressed by Einstein and Freud represented basic approaches to the problem of war. Einstein's hope that mankind would banish war through self-knowledge and revulsion was ultimately a moral position. It was an emotional assertion of faith in humanity. Freud had serious doubts about the efficacy of that position: war could only be eradicated through a gradual transformation of the human psyche. Freud's position was analytical, concerned more with reality than with emotion.

■

Freud was proven correct in the short run. Hitler took over the following year and Europe was again at war within a decade. At the time of their discussion,there was little inclination in the nations at large to renounce war. Several Afghans appeared at the disarmament conference of 1931 and the other conferees were delighted that the prospect of disarmament had spread so widely. But when asked why they were there, the Afghans replied, "Well, if they are really going to disarm, perhaps we can pick up a few weapons cheaply." This is still the mood of the world. No member of the United Nations recognizes any law other than what it imposes upon itself. The jungle of 1914 persists and it is now infested with nuclear weapons.

# The American War Film

## Richard T. Jameson

The changes in popular American attitudes toward war have been reflected in war movies: from the spectacular romanticism of *Wings* (1927) to the reflective horror of *All Quiet on the Western Front* (1930), from the virtuous homefront celebration of *Mrs. Miniver* (1942) and the enthralling antifascist melodrama of *Casablanca* (1942) to the postwar realism and guarded hopefulness of *The Best Years of Our Lives* (1946), from the quasi-documentary reconstruction and covert nostalgia of *The Longest Day* (1962) to the judicious character study in *Patton* (1970). These films are only a few of the hundreds of war and war-related movies that are part of the American cultural heritage. Directly and indirectly, consciously and unconsciously, overtly and insidiously, this body of film has both reflected and influenced our perception of war.

The passage of time and the recurrence of war tends to create a notably regular rhythm of attitudes toward war. Indeed, cycles of war and antiwar movies may be roughly demarcated by decades. During World War I, patriotism, democracy, the sanctity of the home and of womankind came to the fore in motion pictures. D. W. Griffith brought these issues together in *Hearts of the World* (1918) by focusing on the attempt of professional Hun Erich von Stroheim to have his way with French villager Lillian Gish, whose proper lover, Robert Harron, was off defending their homeland. The blatancy of this overall structure characterizes the ideological and emotional thrust of most wartime fiction features, which of necessity became a medium of propaganda as well as (ideally) personal artistic expression.

■

With victory won and war presumably banished from human experience, battlefront entertainments during the twenties evolved into less propagandistic forms. *Wings* then portrayed a flier shooting his best friend out of the sky as the result of a tragic confusion. King Vidor's *Big Parade* (1925) and Raoul Walsh's *What Price Glory?* (1926) involved some magnificent screen warfare but also bitterly denounced the appalling engine of destruction that chewed up individual lives for abstract values.

An increasing bitterness about the war crept into American war films of the thirties. Lewis Milestone's version of Erich Maria Remarque's *All Quiet on the Western Front* recounts the experience of a handful of German schoolboys inspired by their teacher to fight for the Fatherland. All came to grief but nothing happened to the lecturer. Near the end of the film, the protagonist (Lew Ayres), home on his final leave, finds the professor giving the same patriotic harangue. When the veteran tried to describe the reality of life at the front, the new class hissed him down as a coward and a traitor.

*All Quiet* was a large-scale antiwar film but some of the most devastating attacks on war as a glorious enterprise in the name of one's country were delivered by movies outside the war genre. In William Wellman's *Heroes for Sale* (1933), one man is seriously wounded while successfully concluding a mission entrusted to another. The latter receives credit for the mission and returns home a hero, destined for automatic advancement in his chosen business. The real hero meanwhile becomes addicted to morphine. He is thus stigmatized and denied a secure and honorable place in the peacetime world. At the end of the film, he joins the army of jobless men walking the nation's roads.

*Heroes for Sale* typified the socially conscious motion pictures that flowed from the Warner Brothers–First National plant in the thirties. Other studios also produced their share of disenchanted films. RKO's *Lost Squadron* (directed by George Archainbaud, 1932), for example, followed the struggle of a group of heroic World War I aviators to make a living in the postwar world with skills no longer crucial to the national interest. In Hollywood, they found wealth and an ironic kind of fame as stunt pilots in spuriously romanticized reenactments of their wartime experiences.

War-connected movies in the forties drew upon the nostalgia of World War I, for inspirational stories of men redeemed in action (the James Cagney character in William Keighley's *Fighting 69th,* 1940). They also involved stories of men who learned to accept the grim moral imperatives of battle (Sgt. Alvin C. York, who, despite his pacifist faith, became an expert killer in order to *save* the lives of his comrades). America's entry into World War II introduced scores of feature films—high- and low-budget, showcase items, and program pictures—each year. The headlines vouchsafed new names, new battles, new atrocities, or new victories to validate scenarios that may or may not have been intrinsically worthy. These films are what most people recall when they think of "war movies."

Some of Hollywood's ablest filmmakers abandoned their soundstages and fiction films to produce documentaries. Frank Capra, the passionately patriotic director of *Mr. Smith Goes to Washington* (1939), created the brilliant *Why We Fight* series (1942–1945), and John Ford, John Huston, William Wyler, and George Stevens shot front-line action in various theaters of the global conflict. These same men shaped eloquently reflective postwar films when victory relieved them of propagandistic urgencies: Huston's *Let There Be Light* (1945), a documentary about shellshock victims, is still being suppressed by the Pentagon; Wyler's *Best Years of Our Lives* (1946), about veterans' difficulties reentering civilian life; and Ford's elegiac *They Were Expendable* (1945).

Citizens and movie audiences had enough of war by the time the conflict ended. The temper of American films in the late forties changed from a patriotic, even expansionist fervor toward skepticism about values that seemed sacred in wartime. Thrillers like *Dead Reckoning* (John Cromwell, 1947) and *Ride the Pink Horse* (Robert Montgomery, 1947) featured cynical heroes returning from years of personal sacrifice to find friends dead or defected, their businesses failed or stolen, and gangsters, rich from war-connected wheeling and dealing, in positions of social and governmental prominence.

War films reappeared only when the Korean "police action" became a fact of American life. The Korean War, like a later undeclared war, generated scarcely any movies about itself while it was in progress. Lewis Milestone, whose films about World War II— *North Star* (1943), *Edge of Darkness* (1943), *The Purple Heart* (1944) —were made during the war, staged a lavish World War II reenactment, *Halls of Montezuma* (1950).

David Lean's *Bridge on the River Kwai* (1957) enjoyed great popular success despite its ironic attitude toward warfare that obscured just what was happening at its conclusion. Stanley Kubrick's *Paths of Glory* (1957) was less elusive. Set in World War I, the film depicted a criminally stupid French assault on a virtually impregnable German position, followed by a cold-blooded court martial enacted by the aristocratic officers who want to make three infantrymen the scapegoats for their own incompetence. The attack on "the Anthill" was dynamically filmed, but the second half of the movie is a more scathing comment on military bureaucracy. The officers play with their victims' lives and their own political futures in an immaculate chateau miles from battle.

By the early sixties, World War II became fair game for nostalgia buffs. Darryl F. Zanuck's production of Cornelius Ryan's *Longest Day* (1962) was a divertingly detailed, on-location, all-star replay of the Normandy invasion. Sixties warfare inspired only two contemporaneous films. *A Yank in Vietnam* (written and directed by its star, Marshall Thompson) was made in 1964; it played the drive-in circuit and moved almost immediately to other-than-prime-time television. *The Green Berets* (1968), the only generally known American fiction feature about the Vietnam War, succeeded enormously at the box office while being roasted by every reviewer of consequence (for its political stance, it should be noted, rather than its execrable production values and staggering lack of narrative intelligence). There has been no companion piece and, significantly, before the American cease-fire and withdrawal were negotiated, films like Elia Kazan's *Visitors* (1972) explored—and sometimes exploited—the problem of war-hardened killers reintroduced to stateside society, with a horrific, melodramatic impact.

War movies changed as the American public's attitude toward war fluctuated between World War I and Vietnam. Whether helping to shape public opinion or bringing undercurrents in that opinion to the surface, motion pictures individually and collectively serve as invaluable time capsules for preserving an essential aspect of an era in the nation's history.

■

The sociohistorical approach is only one means of seeking to understand war films. Another method is to distinguish subtypes within the general category. In this way the continuities among war movies become evident, as structures and themes recur, albeit in ever-modified forms.

Distillations of war as a potent realm of human experience are not limited to official war movies. Griffith's Civil War epic *The Birth of a Nation* (1915) includes a definitive statement of the elemental issues of war. We observe a mother, framed by an iris shot, embracing several children; they appear to be cowering under a bush. The same take shows a valley below the bluff on which the family hides. A line of men marches up the center of the screen, passing near a country church in flames. That one shot thus encompassed the intimate, impotent circle of the family and the distant, impersonal, destructive force of war. The war ended before the film is half over but Griffith anticipated two generic prototypes: the persistence of warlike conditions imposed by a hostile force of occupation is established in the South; and the rise of a heroic underground (the Ku Klux Klan).

In contrast to *The Birth of a Nation*, which spanned a number of years, involved a large cast of characters, and generally made good its ambitious title, war films usually aspire to less. War films often focus on one incident, one group, or a specialized form of warfare (they can be called unit or mission movies). Films produced on the eve of World War II often stressed the training an outfit would undergo in preparation for battle and included melodramatic complications involving (often experimental) equipment that might break down. While in training, military units were depicted in competition for efficiency ratings and speed records; unduly individualistic enlisted men were shown to suffer humiliation to learn that life affords no greater glory than "playing for the team." When war started training episodes became a dramatic means of building toward *the* mission—*Gung Ho* (1943), *Thirty Seconds over Tokyo* (1944), *Sands of Iwo Jima* (1949).

Underground stories have a special narrative virtue in that audiences tend to accept the sometimes superhuman heroics of the characters. Conventional battle films are ethically and aesthetically dubious when they imply that two or three photogenic and highly salaried actors were strategically indispensable in months-long campaigns to drive their enemies off entire islands. The focus tends to be more restrictive in underground movies—the critical value of the individual is more apparent, and the dramatic issues are more personal. Some pictures in this category are the most enduringly valuable film works of the World War II era. Their durability is partly due to their life-size scale. They symbolize the clash of nationalistic ideologies. They also admit moral and psychological ambiguities that temper the "good guy–bad guy" dichotomy on an interpersonal level. Fritz Lang's *Hangmen Also Die* (1943) depicted some of the most iconographically memorable Nazi perverts ever loosed on the screen. But in Lang's (characteristic) development of a symmetrically formal and dramatic structure the historically virtuous Czech underground became as morally tarnished as its enemies. The balance is further—and subtly—adjusted in that Lang pictures the Nazis to be more weirdly sympathetic than the real life protagonists.

The mission and underground type of films were merged to produce the caper war film which became prevalent in the sixties. Within the paramilitary structure of films like *The Guns of Navarone* (J. Lee Thompson, 1961), the teams involved in the caper have many opportunities to thrash out higher moral issues: whether to condone an expedient sacrifice of a few in the interests of many; the abstract ethics of "the mission"; whether it is courageous to refuse an officer's commission because the whole ranking system is wrong or accept responsibility because "somebody has to." Such possibilities are not overlooked by humorless craftsmen like Thompson and Carl Foreman, who made *The Victors* (1962), one of the most hamfisted—

albeit sincere—denunciations of war in the cinema. On the other hand, a sardonic, vital, and intelligent moviemaker like Robert Aldrich indulges his wryness in caper movies without sacrificing seriousness in the least. He demonstrates this ability in *The Dirty Dozen* (1967), a caper film, an exemplary training film, mission film, and anti-Establishment satire. Unfortunately, the phenomenal commercial success of Aldrich's film precipitated several imitations (e.g., *Kelly's Heroes,* Brian G. Hutton, 1970) that adopted Aldrich's cynicism without matching his perverse moralism. Consequently most imitations were outright sick comedies.

Comedy can be a legitimate, aesthetically exciting, and morally informed approach to war in cinema. Stanley Kubrick's nightmare comedy, *Dr. Strangelove, or How I Learned to Stop Worrying and Love the Bomb* (1964) depicts SAC commander Jack D. Ripper (Sterling Hayden) initiating a nuclear holocaust because he knows the Commies are fluoridating his water. Robert Altman's *M*A*S*H* (1970) is the story of a team of army surgeons during the Korean War who preserve their sanity in a front-line mobile surgical unit by indulging in hip humor, feigned callousness, and rankless communal rapport. Both of these films received widespread critical and popular approval but other daring and original black-comedy endeavors fared less well. Richard Lester's *How I Won the War* (1967) involved manically comic types meeting grisly deaths during key battles of World War II, yet continuing to march and fight with their platoon —each a mute ghost, dyed in the color of the battle in which he fell (the battle scenes are in tinted black-and-white). Mike Nichols's multimillion-dollar adaptation of Joseph Heller's *Catch-22* (1970) affronted and bewildered most viewers and reviewers with its highly stylized surrealism—in places *Catch-22* moves like a wartime version of *Fellini Satyricon.* But Nichols's sense of classical visual form provides a more substantial framework for the film's errant metaphysics than has been generally acknowledged.

Comedy, even black comedy, as an approach to war in the cinema does not date from the sixties. A critic once opined that the Marx Brothers' *Duck Soup* (1933) was the most devastating antiwar film ever made. Charles Chaplin had already sent his Tramp into the trenches in *Shoulder Arms* (1918) and would again in the opening reels of *The Great Dictator* (1940). The film subsequently developed into a treatment of fascist oppression in which Chaplin alternately assumed the roles of an innocuous Jewish barber and of Adenoid Hynkel, leader of the Nutsy party. The speech at the end of the film, urging humanity to "Look up!," violates comic form, but nevertheless achieves moving eloquence by demonstrating the helplessness of even a world-renowned artist before the cosmic catastrophe of war. Ernst Lubitsch, famous for sparkling, deliciously risqué Continental farces, alienated many viewers with *To Be or Not to Be* (1942). Lubitsch instinctively apprehended that the obscene horrors of Naziism defied description (contemporaneously, at least) except in terms of the most grotesque seriocomedy. At the same time he reminded an overawed public that Hitler was "just a little man with a funny mustache."

Finally, the war experience influenced nonwar films. During World War II, even the heroes of program Westerns in vaguely contemporary settings were suddenly called upon to deal with fifth-columnists. Alfred Hitchcock and John Steinbeck devised an allegorical treatment of the war in *Lifeboat* (1944), giving a workable cross section of current attitudes toward the issues of the war. In his masterpiece *Shadow of a Doubt* (1943), Hitchcock unobtrusively and effectively incorporated the war into the evil that infiltrated the small town of Santa Rosa, California. His treatment failed to penetrate the complacent public consciousness. David O. Selznick's *Gone with the Wind* was a less (consciously) subversive portrait of home-front life during World War II; *Since You Went Away* (John Cromwell, 1944) was a laudably epic treatment of the same subject.

■

War films should not be perceived exclusively as phenomena of their era. They should also be considered in the context of the directors' careers, personal histories, and recurring thematic preoccupations.

The directorial bent is often as strong as that of John Huston, whose documentary *The Battle of San Pietro* (1944) led to a powerful thematic parallel traceable in his fiction-film, soundstage work. *San Pietro* was a tribute to the heroic, costly fight to liberate an Italian town in which the ultimate purpose of the operation is left in question. The climactic theme of Huston's *Red Badge of Courage* (1951) is the battle for a hill that, once taken, is immediately left by the troops. Most of Huston's films made before and after these two pictures involve an objective—a fabulous jeweled falcon, gold in the Sierra Madre, the assassination of a dictator, the destruction of a German battleship, etc.—which is almost achieved but always evaporates, proves worthless, or is resolved by freak accident. Theoretical inquiries into John Huston's position on war should consider this attitude.

Howard Hawks also deals with a recurring situation in virtually all of his adventure films and, more covertly, in his comedies. His films involve groups of men (sometimes a few women), comrades in a uniquely dangerous profession, who pit themselves against the elements or a human enemy and always against their own mortality. This scenario quite naturally fits the war film, as demonstrated by the director's numerous creations. Hawks is the undisputed master of aerial action onscreen. Yet, his *Dawn Patrol* (1930) subordinated action sequences to scenes at squadron headquarters which portray the effects of the apparently endless war on the men involved. Hawks's fliers are "gallant gentlemen" on the brink of extinction who adhere to a chivalric code of behavior because that is all they have. No token patriotic motivation is written into Hawks's films: "duty to one's country" is subordinated entirely to the imperative of doing the job. Friendship is a cardinal value in his films but friendships fall apart when former comrades are promoted to command and become responsible for assigning suicide missions ordered by general headquarters. This grim motif was repeated in *The Road to Glory* (1936), in which a succession of commanders, former comrades, are isolated behind a door marked "The Throne." Each emerges to make the same speech to a band of newly arrived replacements. Both films fade out on that image.

The notion of being killed by friends and allies runs throughout *The Road to Glory* and that is joined to another familiar Hawks theme in which two crippled men cooperate to do one able bodied man's job. A variation on this fatalistic theme provides one of the most devastating examples of individual impotence in war. In this picture a relief unit is told that enemy sappers are tunneling under their bunker to plant explosives. The troops listen to the digging for three days and nights until it stops, indicating that detonation is imminent. At this point the original unit returns to relieve them just in time to be blown up.

*The Dawn Patrol* and *The Road to Glory* were made when the United States was at peace. *Air Force* (1943), which Hawks termed his contribution to the war effort, plays down the existential absurdities so thematically strong in the other films. This masterpiece is a depiction of democratic cooperation in the level-by-level formation of a fighting force. It is framed by quotations from Lincoln's Gettysburg Address and Franklin Roosevelt's vow to carry the war to the enemy "on his homeground." The film is a lucid demonstration of how Hawks, the arch-celebrator of professionalism, would see the job get done. Finally, *Air Force,* filmed in the midst of the war, characteristically concentrates on its opening hours and throbs with determination to win.

*They Were Expendable* (1945), perhaps the finest, most poetically majestic film to come out of the war, is typical of John Ford. Most of Ford's work is permeated with a poignant intuition that something—a home or homeland, a long-ago war, a great love, a sense of tradition, of family or innate decency—has been lost. *They Were Expendable* opens on the eve of Pearl Harbor and recounts the early days of the war as experienced by a motor torpedo boat squadron in the Philippines. The squadron gradually breaks up—not through a loss of camaraderie, but rather because of the hopeless, time-buying holding action against a temporarily superior enemy.

It has been said that John Ford filmed the history of the United States—an imagined history of enormous poetic integrity and an apparent sense of ambiguity, even ambivalence. Ford's vision of war —and of the military, and military men, military regulations, military traditions—similarly extends beyond what we normally regard as war movies. One of his cavalry Westerns, *She Wore a Yellow Ribbon* (1949), exemplifies the director's ambivalence. An officer (John Wayne) protests an order to escort his commandant's wife and niece to a stage depot while conducting other army business. The commandant (George O'Brien) invites him to put his protest in writing. After correcting the captain's spelling, O'Brien compliments Wayne on his succinctness. Wayne inquires after the health of O'Brien's wife— there was never any question that he would carry out the mission but he wanted to satisfy the formalities.

This incident reveals a paradox. No filmmaker satisfies the formalities as well as Ford. Yet he is deeply anarchic. The horses under his riders never stand at respectful attention; the ceremonial splendor of a troop on review is counterpointed by a mongrel dog sprawled in the dust right in front of the commanding officer; the troopers tend to adapt their uniforms to their own notions of elegant haberdashery; pageantry and wild Irish comedy break in upon one another without warning. In Ford's vision tradition is good and officers must lead, yet tradition also becomes rockbound and unresponsive to reality. Officers who follow the book too closely at the expense of humanity are clearly dangerous.

Ford's penchant for visual grandeur never obscures the harshness of war. When John Wayne sees his PT boat explode in the surf in *They Were Expendable,* a momentary artificial rain thrown up by the blast falls around him. This brilliantly imaginative and emotionally expressive stroke is utterly consistent with the reality. In *Yellow Ribbon,* a wounded man is operated on in a bucking wagon while the troop continues to march through the desert during a thunderstorm. This unprecedented coup in on-location Technicolor camerawork grimly indexed the bleakness of the cavalry trooper's existence.

Lewis Milestone is best known for his war films, which are unfailingly impressive in their seriousness. They nevertheless seem more arty than artistic. *All Quiet on the Western Front* (1930) includes a superb device which eloquently communicates the pointlessness of combat. As one army charges the other's trenches the camera sweeps along the barbed wire, a machine gun is heard, and the attackers fall as they come into the frame. There is a terrible beauty about the scene; the camera in effect *becomes* the machine gun. The trenches

are overrun, the occupants driven out and then, as the soldiers coun-
terattack they are shot down in a similar camera movement. Milestone's ingenuity served him poorly in that sequence. The camera
tracks parallel to the trench as the attacking soldiers come spilling
into it; the camera catches each soldier as he leaps into the ditch.
There is *no internal photographic logic* to the scene and war thus
becomes a precisely choreographed but heinous ballet—a suggestion
contradictory to the intentions implicit in the rest of the film.

Along with Milestone, Samuel Fuller and Robert Aldrich are the
directors most consistently identified with the war genre. Fuller has
said that a movie is like a battlefield, and most of his movies become
battlefields whether they are war films or not. Fuller's screenplays
reference his personal experiences in Europe during World War II.
His dialogue and images are hard-hitting, but his orchestration of
simplistic effects creates an astonishing ambiguity. *The Steel Helmet*
(1950), one of the few contemporary Korean War films, makes do
with a few spindly trees in the fog and a pasteboard Buddhist temple
from the roof of which no landscape is visible. Yet the film's narrative
energy translates these limited means into forceful abstractions.
*China Gate* (1957) may appall post–Vietnam War viewers but it was
the only American movie for a long while which paid attention to
that "rice bowl of Asia" (from Fuller's commentary). It develops a
formal intensity beyond the reach of more conventional directors.

Robert Aldrich has made penetratingly revisionist films about
the U.S. wars against the Indian (*Apache,* 1954, and the richly complex *Ulzana's Raid,* 1972). Like Fuller, Aldrich conspicuously seeks
new visual and philosophical angles to view the generic terrain. The
imagery of *Attack!* (1956) focuses on the conflict of honesty and
cynicism in wartime and it is visually brutal. Uncosmeticized faces
are seen in cruel closeups; people are seen through gun-slits and
breached walls; a profound blackness frequently impinges on the
frame, slashing across parts of faces and bodies. During this period
Aldrich frequently slipped into artiness. *Attack!*'s title shot shows a
fallen helmet lying beside a lone flower on a battlefield—reminiscent
of the hand reaching for the butterfly at the end of *All Quiet.* Curi-
ously, his color films eschew such prettiness, consisting instead of
fully but unappealingly colored images that roll solidly after one
another like boxcars.

The caper at the heart of *The Dirty Dozen* (1967) was originally
cast in terms of the conventional World War II war-movie. But Aldrich and his personal screenwriter (Lukas Heller) took over, and the
film depends upon half-comic, entirely cynical, anti-Establishment
gestures for its momentum for two hours before an actual battlefield
is shown. As so often in Aldrich movies, the real tensions arise within
the hierarchical structures of the institution—in this case, the mili-

tary. Lee Marvin considers the idea for the mission "insane" but finally appreciates its possibilities for outraging and upstaging his straitlaced fellow officers. Marvin is forced to conclude: "I can't think of a *better* way to fight a war."

Aldrich was not the first filmmaker to suggest that antisocial types are useful in wartime. Donald Siegel's *Hell is for Heroes* (1962) culminates in the image of a mortally wounded, near-psychopathic loner (Steve McQueen) lurching into an enemy pillbox with an armload of explosives and immolating himself and the machine-gun crews inside. Denis Sanders's *War Hunt* (1962) also deals with a psychopathic killer (John Saxon) who slips through no-man's-land each night to cut the throats of a few enemy troops and performs a war dance around each corpse. Films like these have so restructured the genre and audience expectations that it is now virtually impossible to make a "straight" war movie. The seeds have, of course, always been there. In World War II pictures like *Flying Tigers* (1942) and *I Remember Pearl Harbor* (1942) the heroes could only redeem themselves for their un-American refusals to settle down and play for the team by diving their planes into the nearest Japanese target of opportunity. Neither McQueen in *Hell Is for Heroes* nor the *Dirty Dozen* want to redeem anything and that may be the ultimate meaning of these films—war redeems nothing.

# British Poetry
# of World War I

## Giovanni Costigan

When war broke out in 1914, governments and the press on both sides of the conflict were certain of victory and predicted a short war. The people were jubilant, and believed the war would be over by Christmas. In fear that they might arrive too late to participate in such a glorious enterprise, young men everywhere rushed to the colors. Among them were the young poets, many of whom would not survive.

Rupert Brooke expressed, in a poem written after his enlistment, a view of war probably shared by most of his contemporaries in 1914:

> Now, God be thanked who has matched us with His hour,
> And caught our youth, and wakened us from sleeping,
> With hand made sure, clear eye and sharpened power,
> To turn, as swimmers into cleanness leaping,
> Glad from a world grown old and cold and weary,
> Leave the sick hearts that honour could not move,
> And half-men, and their dirty songs and dreary,
> And all the little emptiness of love!

But in his most famous poem, Brooke, who died of disease at the Dardanelles before he even saw combat, strikes a different note.

> If I should die, think only this of me:
> That there's some corner of a foreign field
> That is forever England. . . .

■

247

Patrick Shaw-Stewart, a friend of Brooke's, was killed in the Dardanelles. He wrote there a poem steeped in allusions to Homer, for the site of ancient Troy was visible beyond two miles of sea.

> O hell of ships and cities,
> Hell of men like me,
> Fatal second Helen,
> Why must I follow thee?
> Was it so hard to die, Achilles,
> So very hard to die?
> Thou knowest and I know not—
> So much the happier I.
>   I will go back this morning
> From Imbros over the sea;
> Stand in the trench, Achilles,
> And shout, plume-capped, for me.

Another of England's young poets whose future was promising before war intervened was Julian Grenfell. In a poem he wrote not long before he died, one stanza illustrates a variant of the prevailing romantic view of war:

> The thundering line of battle stands,
>   And in the air death moans and sings;
> But Day shall clasp him with strong hands,
>   And Night shall fold him in soft wings.

In this instance, poetic sensibility is not enhancing war with the luster of glory, but rather turning away from its murderous reality. Grenfell was killed in May 1915.

The war continued past Christmas and intensified during 1915 without Victory and no end in sight. Public confidence and optimism were gradually undermined by doubt and a growing sense of the futility of so much human slaughter. One of the first poets to express concern for the future, lest the dead shall have died in vain, was John McCrae, a Canadian. He wrote "In Flanders Fields" during the Battle of Ypres (1915):

> In Flanders fields, the poppies grow
> Between the Crosses, row on row
> That mark our place; and in the sky
> The larks still bravely singing, fly
> Scarce heard amid the guns below.
>   We are the Dead. Short days ago
> We lived, felt dawn, saw sunset glow,
> Loved and were loved, and now we lie
>   In Flanders fields.
>   Take up our quarrel with the foe:
> To you from failing hands we throw
> The torch; be yours to hold it high.
> If ye break faith with us who die
> We shall not sleep, though poppies grow
>   In Flanders fields.

McCrae died of his wounds at a base hospital in 1918.

Each of the great battles of late 1915 through 1917, in which the British suffered heavy casualties, was brought home to the British people with ever-increasing impact. But the misery and horror of the conflict could be experienced only by those on the battlefield.

The first mass slaughter involving British troops took place in the Battle of Loos during November 1915, fought under frightful conditions of mud, fog, rain, and cold. During the Battle of Verdun, one million men—half French, half German—were casualties between February 21, 1916, when the German Crown Prince's assault troops lost their way in the snow, and July, when the attack petered out.

The Battle of the Somme began on July 1, 1916. Britain pinned its hopes on this single decisive blow which would end the war. When the battle ended in November, having claimed 400,000 casualties, the British were led to believe it was a victory. The next year the ritual was repeated in the Battle of Passchendaele, when Haig launched his offensive on July 31, 1917. The battle lasted into November; 400,000 more young Englishmen were maimed, mutilated or killed for a small gain in territory.

The terrible experiences of these battles were reflected in the poets' mood of deepening horror and despair. One of these poets was Charles Sorley, killed at nineteen in the Battle of Loos on October 13, 1915. In what little remains of his verse, he shows an awareness of the war's reality, quite different in spirit from Brooke, Grenfell, and McCrae:

> When you see millions of the mouthless dead
> Across your dreams in pale battalion go,
> Say not soft things as other men have said,
> That you'll remember. For you need not so.
> Give them not praise. For, deaf, how should they know
> It is not curses heaped on each gashed head?
> Nor tears. Their blind eyes see not your tears flow.
> Nor honour. It is easy to be dead.

Within a week of Sorley's death, another nineteen-year-old, Leslie Coulson, died. He too was beginning to question the insanity of war and issued this challenge:

> Who made the Law that men should die in meadows?
> Who spake the word that blood should splash in lanes?
> Who gave it forth that gardens should be boneyards?
> Who spread the hills with flesh, and blood, and brains?
> Who made the Law?

Perhaps the most moving and memorable poem of all was Wilfrid Owen's "Anthem for Doomed Youth." Owen was the most promising of all contemporary poets. After spending three years in the trenches, he was killed during the last week of the war.

What passing-bells for these who die as cattle?
    Only the monstrous anger of the guns.
    Only the stuttering rifles' rapid rattle
Can patter out their hasty orisons.
No mockeries for them from prayers or bells,
    Nor any voice of mourning save the choirs,—
The shrill demented choirs of wailing shells;
    And bugles calling for them from sad shires.

What candles may be held to speed them all?
    Not in the hands of boys, but in their eyes
Shall shine the holy glimmers of good-byes.
    The pallor of girls' brows shall be their pall;
Their flowers the tenderness of silent minds,
And each slow dusk a drawing-down of blinds.

And in another poem, Owen summed up the disenchantment and disillusionment of many soldiers:

My friend, you would not tell with such high zest
To children ardent for some desperate glory,
The old Lie: Dulce et decorum est
Pro patria mori.

After the war, there was a great tendency to tell "the old Lie." Perhaps this was unavoidable. Those who survived felt a need to believe that those who died had not died in vain—a need that became a compulsion as evidence to the contrary mounted.

One of the best-known statements of this patriotic sentiment is that of Lawrence Binyon, now inscribed in gold at the entrance to the British Museum.

They shall not grow old
As we that are left grow old.
Age shall not wither them
Or the years condemn.
At the going down of the sun
And in the evening, we will remember them.

Countless monuments were built all over Europe to commemorate the dead. One, a triumphal arch in Flanders, the Menin Gate, honored those dead who had no individual graves in the 175 British cemeteries—in addition to Canadian and German cemeteries—in a small area around Ypres. The arch was dignified, peaceful, even beautiful—all that war was not. Siegfried Sassoon, who survived the war, wrote a powerful sonnet in protest (1927):

Who will remember, passing through this gate,
The unheroic Dead who fed the Guns?
Who shall absolve the foulness of their fate
Those doomed, conscripted, unvictorious ones?
    Crudely renewed, the Salient holds its own.
Paid are its dim defenders by its Pomp;

Paid, with a pile of peace-complacent stone,
The armies who endured that sullen swamp.
  Here was the world's worst wound. And here with pride
'Their name liveth forever,' the Gateway claims.
Was ever immolation so belied
As these intolerably nameless names?
  Well might the Dead who struggled in the slime
Rise and deride this sepulchre of crime.

World War I took the lives of many young poets. Their poetry only suggests what they might have written had they lived. It reminds us that civilizations traditionally send their best young men to die in war, thereby paying with their greatest treasure.

# Reflections on War

## L. L. Farrar, jr.

It would be both unrealistic and unjust to summarize in a few pages thirty essays which contain unique views and must ultimately be judged on their own merits. Nonetheless, it may prove useful to consider the volume as a whole. Several themes recur and constitute the major aspects of war, namely, its definition, causation, socialization, specialization, evaluation, and prevention.

The varied views on these issues cannot be integrated into a harmonious and unified theory. All the essayists do not deal with all these issues and those who raise the same questions arrive at different, occasionally contradictory answers. They do, however, provide a basis for some tentative conclusions.

■

Comprehension of a complex phenomenon such as war depends upon a definition of the problem. Definitions can be either dichotomous or polychotomous, that is, can separate phenomena into two or more groups. Thus dichotomous definitions distinguish wars from nonwars; a polychotomous definition conceives of a series of events from most to least warlike. The former runs the risk of oversimplification, while the latter is more realistic but more complex. It provides for the distribution of violent events on a scale according to a number of characteristics, i.e., homogeneity, violence, duration, pervasiveness, organization, geography, power, participants, evaluation, and

■

metamorphosis. Events which exhibit these characteristics to a high degree are generally considered wars.

Like most other important concepts, war as a general phenomenon is homogeneous—despite great diversity in form and disagreement on details. The notion is fairly well established.

Events involving violence can be arranged according to size. Those at the upper end of the scale are usually regarded as wars, those at the lower end are not. Size is not, however, an absolute criterion.

Duration involves similar variations. Events lasting only days and those spanning centuries are traditionally subsumed under the heading of war. Certain distinctions must be made here as well.

War, despite considerable formal variety, has apparently been a characteristic of human society throughout history and perhaps prehistory. It has been a prominent feature of so-called civilizations, i.e., highly structured societies.

The existence of political, social, and economic groups which come into conflict and form various intergroup systems suggests the notion of war as "organized violence." Implicit here is some degree of purpose—gain, disagreement, security, prestige. These impulses are infrequently differentiated, operate at different levels of society, and vary among individuals.

Geography involves the subordinate concepts of locus, proximity, and extent. Wars require a location which allows contact between the opponents. Proximity and conflict are directly related: contiguous groups tend to fight and fighting groups tend to be contiguous. Thus, as in personal relations, familiarity seems to breed contempt. Wars vary in extent from local to global.

The nature of power varies. Historically it has been a mix of population, organization, natural resources, and military technology but industrialism has augmented the importance of material factors. The relativity of power is a determinant, since opponents are generally of comparable power.

War can be defined in terms of participants, who are overwhelmingly male and young. Thus, in at least a general sense, war is conditioned by men but masculinity is also determined in part by warlike attitudes.

Evaluation is an essential element of war, since conflict would not occur unless the activity is somehow perceived as desirable. Evaluative standards include morality (good-bad), utility (useful-harmful), and functionality (functional-dysfunctional).

Wars can also be perceived as processes with beginnings, middles, and ends. Actually, many wars pass through specific stages including background (long-term causes), crisis (short-term causes), a declaration of hostilities, a struggle for initiative, a test of endurance, efforts to break a stalemate, a final campaign, truce or surrender, and peace arrangements.

Typologies of war can be based, for instance, on geographic extent (from local to global), method of fighting (from formal/traditional to informal/nontraditional), degree of mobilization (from limited to total), etc. The wars of the last two centuries can be categorized for the most part as local, formal, and limited, with a few exceptions which were global, formal, and total. Since World War II the general pattern of wars involving superpowers and other previously existing states has been limited, informal, and local, whereas newly established states have fought total, informal, and local conflicts.

■

The difficulty of establishing the causes of war is due in part to the complexity of war itself. There are, however, several problems in defining causality, and these should at least be acknowledged. First, a theory of causation should be neither overly broad by including insignificant events or explaining war in terms of humanity or history; nor should it be overly narrow by excluding important elements or by explaining only one aspect or type of war. Second, the evaluative basis for a theory should be carefully examined. A moral view of war risks bias, whereas amoral views (utility and functionality) involve the danger of determinism. Third, a distinction must be made between causality and chronology, between causes and events which precede and resemble but are not related to war. Fourth, the isolation of causes and consequences is a complex dialectical process. There is no formula for resolving these problems but students of war may at least have the consolation of company in their misery, since all social phenomena involve comparable difficulties.

Theories of causation can be categorized by levels of analysis. The first focuses on all creatures including human beings (biological-psychological), the second on relations between individual humans and the group (psychological-sociological), and the third on the group (sociological-political-economic-geographic).

In terms of biological-psychological theories man is perceived as an animal governed by a struggle for survival in which aggression is functional. Biologists, however, distinguish between individual and group aggression—the latter presupposes the cooperation of individuals. The contest for survival is consequently shifted from inside to outside the group. War, one manifestation of the general phenomenon of violence, is best understood in the context of evolution. The psychological explanation focuses less on physical than psychic survival. The basic model provided by Freud suggests that individual emotional drives, thwarted by society, build up and periodically explode in individual, subgroup, or group violence, i.e., war. Thus war is a consequence of individual tension.

Biological and psychological theories provide simple and universal explanations in which conflict is the essential mechanism of life and violence a logical, indeed necessary, consequence. Biological explanations, however, perceive individual and group violence as mutually exclusive, whereas psychological explanations see group violence as an extension of individual violence.

In terms of psychological-sociological theories individual violence is attributed to psychological responses to circumstantial, i.e., social, impulses—above all, fear, frustration, and social demands. Such emotions are generally lacking in soldiers, who sometimes feel a kind of comradeship with their opponents, so individual participation in war must be explained in other terms. The focus here is on man as a social animal. Groups are formed for both practical and psychological reasons and encourage identification (patriotism), conformity, and obedience. Such theories generally regard the relationship between individual and group as a complex nexus rather than as a simple cause-effect relationship, but they nonetheless tend to emphasize the group.

The group theory is considerably more heterogeneous and it can be subdivided into intragroup, intra/intergroup, and intergroup explanations. Intragroup, i.e., internal, conflict is caused by subgroups within a society that are in competition for power, wealth, and status. The most notable example is Marx's model of class conflict, a point of departure for most explanations of peasant revolts, revolutions, and civil wars.

Intra/intergroup wars are caused either by internal conflicts which overlap external affairs or by external conflicts which impinge on domestic relations. The first type is exemplified by Lenin's assertion that capitalism develops into imperialism, which requires international war, and by leaders who use wars to consolidate domestic power. The second type includes intervention by one group in the domestic affairs of another. A corollary is that war facilitates internal order and authority, which in turn facilitate war.

Intergroup wars are caused by economic impulses (acquisition of booty, territory, markets, and resources), geographic factors (proximity), and political considerations (the search for power, prestige, and security). These models are based on the assumption that relations between groups are a form of struggle for survival which necessitates and therefore justifies violence. The result is a pattern of relations among groups which become systematized and which determine the behavior of member groups.

A satisfactory macrotheory of war must consider these tentative explanations. The biologist's notion of struggle is compelling as a basic model of violence. Individuals and groups frequently respond violently to fear and frustration and both must learn restraint to avoid reprisal. Yet, the psychological explanation is less persuasive, since individual participation in war is motivated less by fear and frustration than by loyalty and obedience. The primary impulse for war thus apparently originates with groups and a macrotheory of war should take that into account.

Group explanations start from the assumption that survival is the basic precondition and overriding concern of any society. The choice between violent and nonviolent means of assuring survival must be determined by perceptions of utility. Such decisions generally find popular support, since populations and governments usually share their preconceptions. A consensus is essential to internal stability and it is also a precondition for intergroup conflict: internal order allows external conflict, which reinforces the need for internal order. Moreover, relationships between groups constitute a system which in turn affects group behavior. Thus there is evidence to support the macro theory that war is caused by the existence of groups and group systems.

Microtheories deal with how specific decisions for war are made, and must clarify relationships between decision-makers and the circumstances they confront. Western historians generally exaggerate the importance of leaders and minimize the constraints upon them, i.e., the requirements of role, influence of advisors, inertia of the bureaucracy and military institutions, the demands of public opinion, and the limitations of existing forces and institutions. Thus micro- and macrotheories are useful in accounting for how general systemic considerations determine the details of particular wars. The causes of war can be found in the nature of groups and group relations. War is not an isolated or aberrant phenomenon but an integral part of society.

■

Most societies are militarized to some degree, and war is a socialized process. The prevalence of war is a significant measure of how war and society are integrated. Societies of all organizational types and at all levels of economic development experience war, with a few exceptions—e.g., prehistoric tribes and contemporary isolated gathering peoples. The social organization of a society affects the impact of war in terms of casualties, duration, and objectives, and in the centralization of authority.

Intergroup conflicts frequently precipitate wars and war, no matter how resolved, often creates new conflicts. Divisive social issues are often associated with violence and violence is itself a social problem. Serious problems involving a society's organization and survival increase the likelihood of violence.

War is also associated with social change and a broad distinction can be made between changes which cause war and wars which cause change. Both kinds of change are most notable in the political realm, but violence also results from economic change or from psychological changes, e.g., changes in group attitudes. Conversely, the involvement in war alters internal and external political relations and institutions, economic and social structures, and social and psychological attitudes. The relationship here is also proportional, large changes being more likely to result in violence.

Social groups are essential to the psychic and physical well-being of most human beings. Group cohesiveness is fostered by internal cooperation but it also requires external competition and even conflict. The existence of several groups apparently provides individual groups limits and thus identity, a sense of inclusive as well as exclusive membership, and external threats which provide a rationale for group survival.

War becomes integrated into society through ritualization. Rituals range from traditional taboos to the most sophisticated efforts to develop international law. In each case the objective is to establish responses which direct violence into acceptable channels. Within groups, war is discouraged by prohibition, mediation, sanctification, compensation, or diversion; outside of groups, it is encouraged in the form of revenge, punishment, prestige, and deterrence.

Wars are used to explain the so-called turning points so fascinating to historians. Some wars, however, dramatically appeal to the narrative tradition in historical writing. Others are cited out of convenience because they have relatively clear beginnings and endings or because they seemingly prove certain historiographical qualities. Wars are also used to explain certain cultural myths (origins, heroes, and heroic events) or to rationalize successful and just wars. The causes of war are difficult to explain, partly because war itself is used to explain otherwise inexplicable events. War is a cohesive impulse that tends to drive together the members of society. This effect is not constant and it often fosters the establishment of sub-groups with special roles and interests.

■

Leadership has been closely linked to war from the beginning of history. The leaders of early social groups were warriors, kingship evolved from warrior chieftains, and presidents of modern democracies retain near-absolute powers in formulating war policies. The form of leadership and degree of centralized authority in a given society partly depends upon past experience. The constant and compelling mythology associated with war leaders had religious overtones in ancient societies and it appears in the charismatic appeal of mass leaders in modern times during war crises. The superhuman power attributed to charismatic leaders reflects a mass faith in the leader's ability to control events. War leaders invariably have constitutional responsibility, and they are expected to produce victory. This expectation has great emotional appeal during war time and it is of primary interest to historians. But appeal and interest do not validate the myth. Responsibility assumes that leaders have a free choice among options that will produce known results; yet wartime leaders have often been confronted with forced choices, ineffective options, and unpredictable results. Wartime leaders are not gods, they are totems created to serve the needs of desperate subjects.

Most societies maintain subgroups specifically oriented toward war or preparation for war—a warrior class, mercenary force, professional establishment, or conscripted army. These subgroups are assumed to be inherently different from the rest of society, thought to be governed by "military mentalities," and inclined to resort to violence. Military subgroups can be classified in terms of numbers, or their degree of professionalization, control, status, and role, but they are not monolithic and their characteristics vary as much as their parent societies. Actually the distinction between civil-military functionaries differs in contemporary societies. Modernized societies, democratic and totalitarian, both maintain clearly defined military professionals with little independent political power or status. The military professionals in developing societies frequently play an active, even dominant, political role. The presumably bellicose "military mentality" and pacific "civilian mentality" are well-established popular assumptions, but recent history nonetheless reveals that civilians have been mainly responsible for making war decisions. Certainly both military professionals and civilians may have bellicose or nonbellicose mentalities. The political influence of the military varies widely—it is typically low in modernized states and high in developing nations.

■

The relationship between the availability of arms and violence is also not as clear as sometimes assumed. The greatest arms buildup in history (between the USA and the USSR) has not culminated in war, and the most post-1945 violence (in modernizing, ex-colonial states) has usually involved little arms buildup. In general, arms buildups are a symptom rather than a cause of tension conducive to violence. Thus many of the assumptions about arms races are questionable and infrequently applicable.

Military technology (i.e., organization, tactics, weaponry, etc.) affects the nature of war, both as a force for change (all the great breakthroughs of manpower, missiles, and movement caused revolutions in warfare) and a force for continuity (military technology changes slowly). When controlled by the ruling classes, technology tends to reinforce the status quo; when controlled by revolutionary groups, it tends to alter the social structure. Military technology is limited by the social organization and technical developments. Societies tend to get the kind of military technology they deserve.

A third military subgroup is comprised of "the people." There are several models of popular involvement in war: governments dominate the people (e.g., the "nation of sheep"): people dominate their governments (e.g., their acts result in nationalist wars or mob violence): government-people partnerships. Generally, the people in modern societies exert little direct influence in making war decisions or in formulating war policies. Mass support for war policies, however, is crucial. Consequently, the government-people partnership appears to be the best model for analyzing modernized societies.

■

The effect of war is generally evaluated in terms of moral, utilitarian or functional standards. Moral standards deal with the "good-bad" aspects of individual behavior and are the concern of humanists. Utilitarian standards are used to calculate the advantage-disadvantage of war with regard to group behavior and are mainly of concern to decisionmakers and historians. Functional standards involve the necessity of war in broad social systems and they are the concern of social scientists.

Religions have traditionally treated war in a positive sense. Their myths explain the beginning in terms of war and apocalypse; most establish gods of war tested in battle, and most have some notion of a just war. Only a few religious groups have condemned war and opposition to war by established churches has usually focused on attempts to restrict violence within their own societies and among co-religions. The moral ambiguity inherent in most religions toward war is striking.

The conduct of war has been praised as a therapeutic release from tension, as an escape from boredom or from personal problems and from life itself. It has also been viewed as a stimulus to the finest human virtues—courage, selflessness, and comradeship. It has a storied place as the ultimate adventure and excitement, a rite of passage. War is as frequently condemned for bringing out the worst human characteristics, bestiality, selfishness, cowardice, hate, and greed. It has also been widely deplored as a source of psychic terror and physical wounds and for an incalculable waste of human and material resources. It has been excoriated for dehumanizing men, for destroying morality, and for justifying immorality, for fostering hypocrisy jeopardizing the fabric of society. It is also considered to be the ultimate human absurdity.

The general thrust of law is antithetical to war and violence, but in practice laws tend to limit rather than proscribe war. Law is thus indicative of the general tendency of societies to ritualize and thereby control violence. Its main concern is to distinguish between acceptable and unacceptable wars and to codify acceptable wartime behavior. The law condemns aggressive wars and war crimes and condones defensive wars and the punishment of aggressive wars and war crimes. These legalistic distinctions are difficult to legislate and enforce, so they are employed to legitimize rather than to limit violence. As a result the laws of war are largely ambiguous and ineffective.

The utility of war is determined on the basis of whether it is desirable in terms of costs and benefits or useful in terms of self-interest. The establishment of utilitarian standards is often openly cynical and opportunistic and sometimes hypocritically idealistic and beneficent. The determination should be a rational calculation, but it commonly involves considerable emotion. Politicians tend to present war decisions to their constituents rationally in order to win popular support. Decision-makers are aware that peace and war each involve costs and benefits so decisions involving either alternative are often treated as though they were predetermined by the opponents or circumstances. The ultimate decision is, of course, determined by a sense of self-preservation. The utility of war is fundamentally related to survival but it is often calculated on the basis of subordinate grounds. The real purpose of war is concealed behind commendable motives, but gain is probably the most obvious. Traditionally war is fought to gain such booty as women, livestock, resources, territory, power and prestige. Wars are also fought to "punish" the enemy for his "moral" derelictions or to maintain intergroup order. More likely such wars are fought to maintain a desirable status quo—i.e., group or "national" security. These motivations are related to the notion of deterrence, which assumes that the "enemy" can be restrained by war or the threat of war.

Wars are sometimes fought ostensibly to preserve a way of life, often dignified by abstract goals, e.g., "a world safe for democracy," "four freedoms," "a new order," "Asian co-prosperity." War is considered to be a means of resolving conflicts involving specific disagreements or general issues. For example, World War I supposedly was "the war to end war." Finally, the utility of war is sometimes evaluated in terms of internal objectives, to either appease or reject public opinion in the name of national unity against external threats.

A third standard for rationalizing war is functionality, or the role of war in society. Behavioralists note that wars recur frequently in association with social problems involving change, group interests, and power. They therefore assume that war is an essential part of social processes and thus is functional. Idealists judge societies on the basis of efficiency and rational order and since peace is conducive to order they view it as functional. The idealist standard considers the elements conducive to war such as change, group interests, and power to be dysfunctional and anachronistic—a measure of how far society falls short of optimal efficiency.

War is therefore variously good or bad, useful or harmful, functional or dysfunctional and these standards are applied in myriad combinations.

■

The prevention of war suggests the need to understand its causes, the effects of socialization and specialization, and better modes of evaluation.

To prevent war we need to first understand and then remove its causes. If war is a biological-psychological imperative and if mankind is not comprised of social and cooperative beings, the cause of war can only be removed through the process of evolution—not a very likely prospect in the near future. Alternatively, we need to develop programs to divert and control individual aggressions. The psychological-sociological causes of war may lead to the conclusion that individuals are aggressive or that it is necessary to restrict governmental authority, alter social mores and myths, and increase self-reliance at the expense of depending on the group. The sociological-political-geographic-economic causes of war may be resolved by applying other theories or by reducing the centralized authority of the group and increasing the importance of individuals and their humanistic impulses.

War is a socialized process and societies are militarized by war and its frequency reinforces its importance. The cessation or prevention of war would reduce its importance and thus demilitarize society. The continued attempt to resolve important social problems through war suggests that war could be avoided by finding other means of resolving those problems—or avoiding them entirely. Certainly the prevention of war will both require and cause fundamental changes in society.

The prevention of war requires a fundamental adjustment in selecting leaders. They would have to be chosen for an ability to conduct peace rather than war and be honored for their passivity rather than their bellicosity. The prevention of war requires that military institutions be converted to organizations devoted to peace.

Such a change would doubtless cause military technology to disappear. The prevention of war would require a change in relationships between governments and the governed and the myths and mores associated with war.

The prevention of war requires that it be evaluated as bad, harmful, and dysfunctional. The religious acceptance of war as occasionally just must be replaced with the thought that it is *always* unjust. The suggestion that war is exciting, glorious, and virtuous must be sacrificed and replaced by a view of war that will either discourage war or find ways to extol nonviolence. All wars must be declared illegal. People must be educated to dispel the belief that war is useful—and they must be conditioned to recognize that the cost of war always exceeds its benefits. War is socially dysfunctional and social elements that rely on war need to be altered so that peace is functional. These changes are probably impossible to achieve, and some of them are incompatible—it is impossible to simultaneously rely on pacifism and deterrence as a means of preventing war. Yet war must somehow be universally condemned if it is to be prevented.

One possible approach may be to assume that all inter-social or international problems are resolvable and that the opponents are willing to negotiate resolutions. Another may be to find ways of diverting hostility by remunerating the parties in conflict. It may be possible to impose peace on potentially hostile parties by invoking superior outside forces. The threat of retaliation against aggressors remains only a threat of war so the ultimate solution is a complete renunciation of war. None of these approaches will be simple to implement yet they summarize the only recourses available. They must be made to work if war is to be prevented.

■

The phenomenon of war may be incomprehensible and it may not be preventable. Even if war can be avoided some segments of humanity may not consider prevention desirable. Unbiased and objective predictions are difficult to make yet it is clear that war will continue to both fascinate and repel human beings—this ambivalence is particularly relevant in the twentieth century. By focusing attention on this problem we may yet attract the financial, political, and intellectual resources needed to isolate likely conflicts in order to avoid them.

The prevention of war depends upon whether war is comprehensible, controllable, and undesirable. If these conditions are lacking we will continue to experience war. War is best understood and more controllable by the superpowers. The smaller nations seemingly desire war the most. It follows that the superpowers are least likely and the small states most likely to go to war. This has been the pattern of wars since 1945.

If this prediction is evaluated in terms of specific considerations there remains considerable ground for pessimism. The superpowers are not likely to engage in nuclear war and that prospect has been widely mooted. Yet, the prospect for war is real if those who regard conflict to be inherent in human nature are correct. If wars are determined by cyclical patterns of history, or if they are a probable result of modernization, colonialism, and totalitarianism there is little hope. The inadequacies of the means we use to prevent war—collective security, disarmament, arms control, international law, adjudication, and international government—reinforce this pessimism. Since no serious effort has been made to establish an effective international government as insurance against war, it is all too likely that war will continue to be part of world politics.

There are a few reasons for optimism nonetheless. An increased allocation of resources devoted to the study of conflict will deepen our understanding. The means employed to avoid conflict at the small group level may prove applicable to larger groups. Successful efforts to limit preparations for war and the limited utility of traditional armies result in a reduction of military budgets. The "unthinkability" of nuclear war is becoming all too apparent and the slowly emerging Russo-American detente suggests that the superpowers, at least, may avoid war. The limitation of lesser conflicts hopefully suggests that we may yet find ways to perfect and expand war prevention techniques.

In summary, there is more reason to be pessimistic than optimistic. Yet the human and material costs of conflict, especially nuclear war, are so high that it is difficult not to hope that wars can be limited and possibly avoided. In the end we may be faced with an impossible dilemma: war may be inevitable and necessary, yet peace may be the only way humanity can survive.

# Contributors

# Contributors

JOHN ALCOCK is associate professor in the department of zoology, Arizona State University. He is the author of *Animal Behavior: An Evolutionary Approach,* and forty scientific papers on bird and insect behavior.

ALDON D. BELL is associate professor in the department of history, University of Washington. He is the author of *London in the Age of Dickens* (University of Oklahoma Press, Norman, 1967) and several articles on Victorian England.

JON M. BRIDGMAN is associate professor in the department of history, University of Washington, where he teaches courses on German and modern European history.

FRANK F. CONLON is associate professor in the department of history, University of Washington. He is the author of *A Caste in a Changing World: The Chitrapur Saraswat Brahmans, 1700–1935* (University of California, Berkeley, 1977).

GIOVANNI COSTIGAN is professor emeritus in the department of history, University of Washington. He is the author of *Sir Robert Wilson: A Soldier of Fortune in the Napoleonic Wars* (1932); *Sigmund Freud: A Short Biography* (Macmillan, New York, 1965); *Makers of Modern England* (Macmillan, New York, 1967); *History of Modern Ireland* (Pegasus, Indianapolis, 1969).

L. L. FARRAR, JR. is lecturer in the department of history, Trinity College (Hartford, Connecticut). He is the author of *The Short-War Illusion: A Study of German Policy, Strategy and Domestic Affairs,*

■

*August-December, 1914* (ABC-Clio, Santa Barbara, 1973) and *Divide and Conquer: German Efforts to Conclude a Separate Peace, 1914–1918* (East European Quarterly Press, Boulder, Colorado, distributed by Columbia University Press, forthcoming). He translated and wrote the introduction to Fritz Fischer's *World Power or Decline* (Norton, New York, 1974). He has published articles in *The Canadian Journal of History, The East European Quarterly, The Journal of Conflict Resolution, World Affairs, Militärgeschichtliche Mitteilungen,* and reviews for *The American Historical Review, History, The Canadian Journal of History* and *The Annals of the American Academy of Political and Social Science.*

MARJORIE M. FARRAR is assistant professor in the department of history, Boston College. She is the author of *Conflict and Compromise: The Strategy, Politics and Diplomacy of the French Blockade, 1914–1918* (Nijhoff, The Hague, 1974). She has published articles in *The Economic History Review, Revue d'Histoire économique et sociale, Revue d'Histoire diplomatique, Revue d'Histoire moderne et contemporaine,* and reviews for *The Annals of the American Academy of Political and Social Science.*

LYNNE B. IGLITZIN is assistant director of undergraduate studies and lecturer in the department of political science, University of Washington. She is author of *Violent Conflict in American Society* (1972) and co-editor of *Women in the World: A Comparative Study* (ABC-Clio, Santa Barbara, 1976) and author of numerous articles on feminist political theory issues.

RICHARD T. JAMESON is lecturer in cinema studies, University of Washington. He is editor of *Movietone News* and has published articles and reviews in *Film Comment, Film Quarterly, The Velvet Light Trap* and *Focus on Orson Welles.*

LYMAN H. LEGTERS is professor of Russian and East European studies and chairman in social theory, University of Washington. He is author of *Research in the Social Sciences and Humanities* (ABC-Clio, Santa Barbara, 1967) and *Higher Education in the German Democratic Republic* (Columbia University Press, New York, 1977). He is editor of *Essays in Russian History and Literature* (Brill, Leiden, 1971). He has published articles in *Forschungen zur osteuropäischen Geschichte, Russian Review, Journal of the American Academy of Religion, Saturday Review, Intellect* and numerous reviews.

PETER H. MERKL is professor of political science, University of California, Santa Barbara. Author of *Origin of the West German Republic* (Oxford University Press, 1963); *Die Entstehung der Bundesrepublik Deutschland* (Kohlhammer Verlag, 1965); *Germany: Yesterday, Today and Tomorrow* (Oxford University Press, 1965); *Rassenfrage und Rechtsradikalismus in den USA* (with

Otey M. Scruggs) (Colloquim Verlag, 1966); *Political Continuity and Change* (Harper & Row, New York, 1967); *Modern Comparative Politics* (Holt, Rinehart & Winston, New York, 1970); *German Foreign Policies: East and West* (ABC-Clio, 1974) and numerous articles in scholarly periodicals. Professor Merkl is the editor of the series of Studies in Comparative Politics published by ABC-Clio, Inc.

GEORGE MODELSKI is professor in the department of political science, University of Washington. He is author of *A Theory of Foreign Policy* (1962) and *Principles of World Politics* (Free Press, New York, 1972) and numerous articles.

ARVAL A. MORRIS is professor of constitutional law and legal philosophy in the school of law, University of Washington. He is author of *The Constitution and American Education* (1974) and numerous articles.

SIMON OTTENBERG is professor in the department of anthropology and adjunct professor in the department of political science, University of Washington. He is co-editor of *Cultures and Societies of Africa* (Random House, New York, 1960), *Double Descent in an African Society* (University of Washington, Seattle, 1968), *Leadership and Authority in an African Society* (University of Washington, Seattle, 1971), and *Masked Rituals of Afikpo: The Context of an African Art* (University of Washington, Seattle, 1975). He is author of numerous articles on Ibo kinship, politics, religion and art.

OTIS A. PEASE is professor in the department of history, University of Washington. He is author of *Parkman's History* (Archon, Hamden, Conn., 1968), *The Responsibilities of American Advertising* (Yale University Press, New Haven, 1960), editor of *The Progressive Years* (Braziller, New York, 1972), and has published several articles.

THOMAS J. PRESSLY is professor in the department of history, University of Washington. He is author of *Americans Interpret Their Civil War* (Princeton University Press, Princeton, 1954) and co-editor of *Farm Real Estate Values* (University of Washington, Seattle, 1965) and *American Political Behavior: Historical Essays and Readings* (Harper and Row, New York, 1974).

ROY L. PROSTERMAN is professor of law and chairman of the graduate school committee on conflict studies, University of Washington. He is author and editor of *Surviving to 3000: An Introduction to the Study of Lethal Conflict* (Duxbury Press, North Scituate, Mass., 1972).

CARL E. SOLBERG is associate professor in the department of history, University of Washington. He is the author of *Immigration and Nationalism: Argentina and Chile, 1890–1914* (University of

Texas Press, Austin, 1970) and "Rural Unrest and Agrarian Policy in Argentina, 1912–1930," published in the *Journal of Inter-American Studies and World Affairs.*

EDWARD A. STERN is professor in the department of physics, University of Washington, and specializes in solid state physics.

EZRA STOTLAND is professor in the department of psychology and director of the society and justice program, University of Washington. He is author or co-author of *Psychology of Hope* (Jossey-Bass, San Francisco, 1969); *Life and Death of a Mental Hospital* (University of Washington Press, Seattle, 1965); *Social Psychology* (Saunders, Philadelphia, 1972); *Empathy and Birth Order* (University of Nebraska Press, Lincoln, 1971); *The End of Hope* (Free Press, New York, 1964); and numerous articles.

PETER F. SUGAR is professor of history, University of Washington and associate director, Russian and East European studies program, Institute for Comparative and Foreign Area Studies. Editor and co-author of *Native Fascism in the Successor States* (ABC-Clio, Santa Barbara, 1971); and numerous articles in scholarly periodicals.

CAROL G. THOMAS is associate professor in the department of history and adjunct associate professor in the department of classics, University of Washington. She is editor of *Homer's History: Mycenaean or Dark Age?* (Holt, Rinehart and Winston, New York, 1970) and author of articles in *Historia, Antichthon,* and *Classical World.*

JUDITH A. THORNTON is professor in the department of economics, University of Washington. She is author of articles in *The Journal of Economic History, The American Economic Review, The Slavic Review, The Journal of Political Economy, The Western Economic Journal, The ASTE Bulletin, The Soviet Cybernetics Review, Economics of Planning* and of chapters in *Planning in the Soviet-type Economy* (Cambridge University Press, Cambridge, England, 1977), and reviews for numerous journals.

JAMES R. TOWNSEND is professor in the department of political science, University of Washington. He is author of *Political Participation in Communist China* (University of California Press, Los Angeles and Berkeley, 1967); *The Revolutionization of Chinese Youth* (University of California Press, Los Angeles and Berkeley, 1967); *Politics in China* (Little, Brown, Boston, 1974); and chapters in Barnett (ed.), *Chinese Communist Politics in Action* (University of Washington Press, Seattle, 1969); Jacobs (ed.), *The New Communisms* (Harper and Row, New York, 1969); Huntington and Moore (eds.), *Authoritarian Politics in Modern Society* (Basic, New York, 1970).

DONALD W. TREADGOLD is professor in and chairman of the department of history, University of Washington. He is the author of

*Lenin and His Rivals* (Praeger, New York, 1955); *The Great Siberian Migration* (Princeton University Press, Princeton, 1957); *Twentieth Century Russia* (Rand-McNally, Chicago, 1976); *The West in Russia and China* (Cambridge University Press, Cambridge, England, 1973), and editor of *The Development of the USSR* (University of Washington Press, Seattle, 1964); *Soviet and Chinese Communism* (University of Washington Press, Seattle, 1967); and of *The Slavic Review.* He has published articles and reviews in numerous journals.

PIERRE L. VAN DEN BERGHE is professor in the department of sociology, University of Washington. He has published a dozen books and many articles dealing mostly with social stratification and ethnic and race relations in Africa and Latin America.

# Index

# Index

■

# Y

# Z

*War: A Historical, Political, and Social Study*
was compiled and edited by Lancelot L. Farrar, Jr.;
copy editing by Barbara Phillips,
proofing by Jean Holzinger and Gail Marceaux,
index compiled by Marianne Morgan,
cover design by Nielsen/Alexander/Baron,
text design by Shelly Lowenkopf.
Composition in Caledonia Text and display was
done on a Videocomp 830 by
Datagraphics, Phoenix, Ariz.
Printing and binding by Braun-Brumfield, Inc.,
Ann Arbor, Mich.,
using a 60# Warren's 66 text stock
and Kivar 6 cover

SALVE REGINA COLLEGE LIBRARY.
OCHRE POINT AVENUE
NEWPORT, RHODE ISLAND 02840